THE ROAD
TO HOLOCAUST

Books by Hal Lindsey

The Late Great Planet Earth
Satan Is Alive and Well on Planet Earth
There's a New World Coming
The Liberation of Planet Earth
The Terminal Generation
The 1980s: Countdown to Armageddon
The Promise
The Rapture: Truth or Consequences
Combat Faith
A Prophetical Walk
Through the Holy Land
The Road to Holocaust

THE ROAD
TO HOLOCAUST

Hal Lindsey

BANTAM BOOKS
NEW YORK • TORONTO • LONDON • SYDNEY • AUCKLAND

THE ROAD TO HOLOCAUST

A Bantam Book / July 1989

Library of Congress Cataloging-in-Publication Data

Lindsey, Hal.
    The road to holocaust / Hal Lindsey.
      p.   cm.
    Bibliography: p.
    ISBN 0-553-05724-3
    1. Holocaust (Christian theology)   2. Christianity and
antisemitism.   3. Judaism (Christian theology)   4. Dominion
theology—Controversial literature.   I. Title.
BT93.L55   1989
231.7'6—dc20   89-31429
                                                   CIP

To my spiritual father, Col. Robert B. Thieme, Jr., whose systematic teaching of God's word and personal encouragement changed the entire direction of my life. If I have any crowns in heaven, it will be because of him. Thanks, Dad.

CONTENTS

CHAPTER ONE

The Roots
of Holocaust

You will be uprooted from the land you are entering to possess. Then the LORD will scatter you among the nations, from the one end of the earth to the other. . . . Among those nations you will find no repose, no resting place for the sole of your foot. . . . You will live in suspense, filled with dread both night and day, never sure of your life. . . . When all these blessings and curses I have set before you come upon you and you take them to heart wherever the LORD your God disperses you among the nations . . . then the LORD your God will restore your fortunes and have compassion on you and gather you again from all the nations where he scattered you . . . and the LORD your God will put all these curses on your enemies who hate and persecute you.

The Prophet Moses
Deuteronomy 28:63–66; 30:1, 7

THE ROOTS OF HOLOCAUST

"Hence today I believe that I am acting in acordance with the Almighty Creator: by defending myself against the JEW, I am fighting for the work of the Lord."[1] This fateful justification of a murderous purpose was penned by Adolph Hitler in his personal manifesto, *Mein Kampf*, as he point by point built the case for annihilating the Jewish race. Hitler and his henchmen clearly planned from the beginning of the Nazi Party to execute a plan they called by the code name "The Final Solution of the Jewish Problem."

A Premillennialist in Hitler's Germany

In an unusual turn of providence, I learned first hand what some of the early plans of the Nazi leaders were from one who was an eyewitness. A Christian friend, who was born in Germany, related to me some of the secret negotiations conducted by Adolph Hitler and his top party leaders before they assumed control of Germany.

My friend's father was the head of the German army officer's union, which in English is called *The Steel Helmet*. Hitler, Hess, Goering, Dr. Goebbels, and many other top Nazi leaders came to my friend's Bavarian home to negotiate with his father. Hitler desperately needed the support of the German army officer's union to grasp control of the government.

My friend remembers many long and heated discussions around the fireplace between his father and the future leaders of the Third Reich. His father actually agreed with Hitler about many of the reforms that he wanted to bring to Germany. But when he began to grasp Hitler's "Final Solution" plan for the Jews, he flatly disagreed. He was an evangelical Christian, a Plymouth Brethren who believed in a literal interpretation of prophecy and the covenants God made with the Israelites. In other words, he was a true *Premillennialist* (this will be defined in detail in chapter two) in his beliefs concerning Bible prophecy.

One of the fundamental elements of a Premillennialist's faith is that God has bound Himself by unconditional covenants to the Jews and that even though they are currently under His discipline He will punish anyone who mistreats them. As God swore to Abraham and reconfirmed to his successors, **"I will bless those** who bless you, and whoever curses you I will curse. . . ." (Genesis 12:3)

At considerable personal risk and financial loss, he packed up the family, sneaked out what money he could, and came to the U.S.A. He left Hitler's Germany for one fundamental reason—he believed God's Word when it said concerning Israel, **"For thus says the LORD of hosts, 'After glory He has sent me against the nations which plunder you** [Israel], **for he who touches you, touches the apple of His eye.'"** (Zechariah 2:8 NASB)

What you are about to read may startle you. But I strongly believe that unless we learn from past history, we are doomed to repeat it. The purpose of this book is to warn about a rapidly expanding new movement in the Church that is subtly introducing the same old errors that eventually but inevitably led to centuries of atrocities against the Jews and culminated with the Holocaust of the Third Reich. I do not believe that the leaders of this new movement are consciously anti-Semitic—their historical predecessors were not either. But just as their historical counterparts did, they are setting up a philosophical system that will result in anti-Semitism.

How Did A Hitler Happen?

How did Hitler come to have such a fanatical hatred of the Jews? From whom or from what source did he get the insane idea that he was "doing the work of the LORD" by exterminating the Jews? And even more disturbing, how did he rally so many educated, cultured, and religious people to follow him in his scheme? On rereading *Mein Kampf*, I find it difficult to understand the oft-repeated disclaimer of many German people of that era who say, "We had no idea that Hitler was really going to do those terrible things." He clearly spelled out what he intended to do. In his speeches to great mass rallies, he blatantly spewed out his hatred of the Jews and his intentions to get rid of them. Hitler actually predicted the extermination of European Jewry before the whole Reichstag (the German Parliament) on January 31, 1939.[2]

In another public speech given the day before, Hitler elaborated on this prediction: "In my life I have often been a prophet, and most of the time I have been laughed at. During the period of my struggle for power, it was the Jewish people that received with laughter my prophecies that some day I would take over the leadership of the state and thereby of the whole people, and that

3

I would among other things also solve the Jewish problem. Today I want to be a prophet once more: If international-finance Jewry inside and outside of Europe should succeed once more in plunging nations into another world war, the consequence will not be the Bolshevization of the earth and thereby the victory of Jewry, but THE ANNIHILATION OF THE JEWISH RACE IN EUROPE."[3] (Emphasis added.)

The utter audacity of Hitler's capacity to lie and deceive is revealed in this speech. At the very moment that Hitler warned the Jews of what he would do if they started a world war, he had already planned to start the war himself. My friend's father had clearly grasped Hitler's intentions toward the Jews long before this speech, and left his beloved Fatherland to avoid being a part of it.

It is perplexing to note that the Nazi movement was initiated in Munich, in the southern state of Bavaria. Almost entirely Catholic, Bavaria has for centuries been the most overtly religious region of Germany. Beautiful baroque churches are everywhere, even in the smallest villages. The countryside is dotted with little roadside prayer stations containing images of Christ, many over a hundred years old. To this day, the customary greeting in Bavaria and Austria is, literally translated, "Greet God."

The paradox of Hitler's rise to power, particularly in this region, is reflected in Konrad Heiden's introduction to the English translation of *Mein Kampf:*

> For years *Mein Kampf* stood as proof of the blindness and complacency of the world. For in its pages Hitler announced—long before he came to power—a program of blood and terror in a self-revelation of such overwhelming frankness that few among its readers had the courage to believe it. Once again it was demonstrated that there was no more effective method of concealment than the broadest publicity. . . . That such a man could go so far toward realizing his ambitions, and—above all—could find millions of willing tools and helpers; that is a phenomenon the world will ponder for centuries to come.

The Supernatural Origins of Anti-Semitism

An objective study of anti-Semitism's history soon brings one face-to-face with a phenomenon that goes far beyond other cases

4

of prejudice toward a race, minority group, or displaced nationality. I have found that even among otherwise good and decent people, the slightest rumor about a "Jewish conspiracy to control world events," a nation's economics, or the media, usually meets with an all-too-willing acceptance.

Anti-Semitism is like a virulent disease that is always lurking just under the surface of civilization, ready to seize the slightest opportunity to spring into life and spread like wildfire. And as we shall see, Christians are not immune to this disease. The Apostle John gave a panoramic view of historical anti-Semitism, with its origin and supernatural cause, in Revelation chapter twelve.[4] **The Woman** (Israel) is hated and persecuted by **the Dragon** (Satan 12:9) because she gives birth to **a Son** (the Messiah) **who is to rule all the nations.** (12:1–6) Satan hates Israel with an undying passion because she is the instrument through which the Messiah, His conqueror, was born. Satan also hates Israel because God's reality and veracity are proven by the way He has kept the many prophecies and promises He made to Israel, even though she hasn't deserved it. These amazing fulfillments are recorded in history for all honest inquirers to see.[5]

Anti-Semitism—The Core of Nazism

Dr. Barry Leventhal, a popular theologian and teacher in Washington, D.C., noted in his doctoral thesis for Dallas Theological Seminary one of the sad reasons for the general acceptance of Nazism: "One of the major sources to the rise of Nazism in Germany *came from within the Church.* It was the growing interest in the evolutionary and destructive higher criticism of the Bible in Germany that fueled the anti-semitic Nazi war machine. [And also the fact that] Germany had a long history of 'Christian' anti-Semitism, not only from within the Roman Catholic Church, but even from within the Protestant Church. It was Martin Luther, who in his latter years turned upon the Jews with a religious fury, thus paving the way for Adolph Hitler to consummate the Reformer's great desire for the elimination of the Jewish people. Is it any wonder that Hitler cited Martin Luther in *Mein Kampf* as one of the great heroes of the German people."[6]

Holocaust historian Raul Hilberg makes a similarly shocking observation when he relates how the infamous anti-Semite and

Nazi war criminal Julius Streicher quoted Luther in his own defense at the Nuremburg trials.[7]

One of the world's leading scholars on Nazi Germany is William L. Shirer, a news correspondent in Germany during almost the entire Nazi era. He wrote concerning this one sad aspect of Martin Luther's theology: "The time has come for those who study Luther and admire him to acknowledge, more unequivocally and less pugnaciously than they have, that on this issue [i.e., Luther's anti-Semitism] Luther's thought and language are simply beyond defense."[8]

Raul Hilberg makes some observations about this issue that all should weigh carefully. Hilberg maintains that the Holocaust did not happen in a theological vacuum, but rather was the inevitable result of three consecutive anti-Jewish policies that occurred throughout Western history. Hilberg says:

> Anti-Jewish policies and anti-Jewish actions did not have their beginning in 1933. For many centuries, and in many countries, the Jews have been victims of destructive action.
>
> What was the object of these activities? What were the aims of those who persisted in anti-Jewish deeds? Throughout Western history, three consecutive policies have been applied against Jewry in its dispersion.
>
> To summarize: Since the fourth century after Christ, there have been three anti-Jewish policies: *conversion, expulsion,* and *annihilation.* The second [*expulsion*] appeared as an alternative to the first, and the third [*annihilation*] as an alternative to the second.
>
> The Nazi destruction process did not come out of a void; it was the culmination of a cyclical trend. We have observed the trend in three successive goals of anti-Jewish administrators. (1) The missionaries of Christianity had said in effect: YOU HAVE NO RIGHT TO LIVE AMONG US AS JEWS. (2) The secular rulers who followed had proclaimed: YOU HAVE NO RIGHT TO LIVE AMONG US. (3) The German Nazis at last decreed: YOU HAVE NO RIGHT TO LIVE.
>
> These progressively more drastic goals brought in their wake a slow and steady growth of anti-Jewish actions and anti-Jewish thinking. The process began with the attempt to drive the Jews into Christianity. The

development was continued in order to force the victims into exile. It was finished when the Jews were driven to their deaths.

The German Nazis, then, did not discard the past; they built upon it. They did not begin the development; they completed it.[9] (Emphases mine.)

A MAJOR ROOT OF ANTI-SEMITISM

I must confess that I believe that what these men have observed is woefully true. But the most important factor in this chain of the development of anti-Semitism has been overlooked by almost everyone. Hilberg astutely observes above that the anti-Jewish policies can be traced to the attitudes of the Church that began in the fourth century. This was the very time when the teachings of an influential early Church Father named Origen of Alexandria (A.D. 185–254) began to take effect in the Church.

A Change in Prophetic Belief With Enormous Consequences

Christians today need to pay close attention to the following historical record of how good Christian leaders with erroneous prophetic views laid the theological groundwork for evil men, often masquerading as Christians, to justify the extermination of the Jewish race. And sadly, it also influenced many true Christians to join in with the prevailing anti-Semitism.

The man most responsible for changing the way the Church interpreted prophecy was Origen. He was a leading teacher of theology and philosophy at the influential catechetical school of Alexandria, Egypt, at the beginning of the third century.

Church historian A. H. Newman reports, "Origen was the first to reduce the allegorical method of interpretation to a system. . . . His method of Scripture interpretation was soon adopted throughout the church, and prevailed throughout the Middle Ages. In this particular Origen's influence was bad, and only bad."[10]

It must be noted that Origen was not an evil man. In fact, he was a scholarly Christian philospher with a courageous faith who lived a humble and ascetic life. But because of his desire to harmonize the New Testament with the philosophy of Plato, he powerfully introduced, taught, and spread the allegorical method of interpreting the Scriptures, particularly in the area of prophecy.

7

From this seemingly harmless fact of Church history evolved a system of prophetic interpretation that created the atmosphere in which "Christian" anti-Semitism took root and spread.

Using this method of prophetic interpretation, Church theologians began to develop the idea that the Israelites had permanently forfeited all their covenants by rejecting Jesus as the Messiah. This view taught that these covenants now belong to the Church, and that *it* is the only *true Israel* now and forever. The view also taught that the Jews will never again have a future as a Divinely chosen people, and that the Messiah will never establish His Messianic Kingdom on earth that was promised to them.

The consequences of this doctrine were subtle at first. The most serious consequence was that the protections provided by the clear Scriptural warnings of God against those who would harm His covenant people were snatched away. A feeling of contempt naturally followed, since, in the eyes of those who held this view, the Jews were clinging to a hope that now belonged only to the Church. From these attitudes evolved the idea that they were blind impostors under the curse of God, and unrepentant Christ-killers. Their tenacious efforts to remain a separate and distinct race with the hope of the Messiah's future coming to establish a promised Kingdom of God were viewed as a special arrogance. The Church leaders saw no justification for the Jews to remain a distinct people, since in their view, their hopes belonged exclusively to the Church forever.

Many of these factors were correctly observed by the Encyclopedia Judaica, though it is in error in some of its analyses of the causes:

> The reasons for the extraordinary and tragic tension between Christianity and Judaism are not to be sought merely in the differences in religious beliefs and dogmas, which exist also in relation to all other religions. . . . The tension is due essentially to the ambivalent position in which the Church found itself vis-a-vis with Israel. By explicitly claiming not to be a new religion, and by conceiving itself the FULFILLMENT OF THE PROMISES IN THE BIBLE [the Old Testament] as expressed in THE COVENANT WITH THE PATRIARCHS and in the message of the prophets, the Church placed itself squarely on a Jewish foundation: IT was the consummation of the

biblical promise. . . . THE CHURCH WAS THE "TRUE ISRAEL" OF GOD. . . .

The image implied that theologically Judaism was an inferior religion, historically the Jewish people had played out its positive role, and morally the Jews were examples of stubborn blindness and obduracy. Even at best, i.e., in its biblical phase, Israel had been rebellious and had persecuted its prophets, and its Law—albeit divine—was but a preparatory discipline. . . . The CHURCH BEING GOD'S "TRUE ISRAEL" ACCORDING TO THE SPIRIT, THE JEWISH PEOPLE NO LONGER HAD ANY VOCATION OR *REASON TO EXIST* except as a witness to the misery and degradation that would befall a people originally chosen by God, but unfaithful to its election by rejecting the Messiah and bringing about his death.[11] (Emphases added.)

This quote brings out correctly that when the Church began to see itself as God's true Israel, the inheritor of the covenant promises made to Israel, then in the eyes of the Church, the Israelites ceased to have any legitimate purpose or right to exist as a people. Again, it is important to note that the only way the Church could arrive at this view was by interpreting prophecy allegorically. From this error in eschatology (the doctrine of last things or prophecy) to outright anti-Semitism was only a matter of time.

Augustine's Legacy

By the time of Augustine (A.D.354—425), the famous Bishop of Hippo, Origen's system of interpretation dominated the Christian scene. But it was Augustine who systematized the allegorically based teachings into a cohesive theology that would dominate the Church for over a thousand years. Even the Reformers continued to hold most of his views, including his allegorically based, unrefined eschatology. The Roman Catholic Church, using Origen's system of interpretation and Augustine's theology, soon applied and instituted the teaching that they were the inheritors of Israel's promises—that they were the inheritors of the Kingdom promised to Israel and therefore must take ultimate authority over the political powers of this world. At one point during the Middle Ages, the Church held authority over virtually all the rulers of

Europe. History witnesses that this was one of the most oppressive periods of Christianity, both toward the Christians and those outside of the Church.

THE APOSTOLIC FATHERS' VIEWS

These prophetic views were a complete departure from the original teachings of the Apostolic Fathers of the Church, whose period extended from A.D. 33 to shortly after A.D. 100. Lutheran historian J. L. Neve traces the intense interest in prophecy that permeated the church during this period:

> The time of the Apostolic Fathers was thoroughly eschatological in tendency, as was that of primitive Christianity. Men had the consciousness that they were living in the last times. The immediate return of Jesus was anticipated. It was this expectation that held the congregations together.
>
> Men considered it their imperative task to keep an eye on the approaching end and to work for their moral betterment, so as not to be surprised by its appearance. In looking for the consummation, men learned to observe the signs of the times and to watch for definite indications which would precede Christ's coming.
>
> The precursors were to take the form of false prophets and seducers, increase of wickedness and persecutions, AntiChrist, signs and wonders, the resurrection of the dead. CHILIASM was defended by Papias in a gross and materialistic form. According to Barnabas, THE RETURN OF CHRIST WOULD BE FOLLOWED BY HIS TEMPORAL REIGN FOR A THOUSAND YEARS.[12] (Emphases mine.)

Note carefully the following crucial facts from this quote:

First, the Apostolic Fathers were either Apostles and disciples who had been taught by the LORD Himself, or first generation disciples of this group.

Second, although the early Church rightly believed that the Jew must believe in Jesus as the Messiah to be saved in this age, they firmly believed that Israel was yet to be redeemed as a Nation and given her unconditionally promised Messianic Kingdom. They believed that this theocratic kingdom would be set up on earth by Christ at His Second Coming, and that it would last for a thousand years. This teaching was called the doctrine of Chiliasm. (*Chilias* [χιλιας] is the Greek word for one thousand. The term *chiliasm* meant the belief in a literal one thousand year Messianic Kingdom on earth.)

Third, they believed that the Lord Jesus could come at any moment, thus confirming that one of the major factors in the doctrine of the Rapture, though undefined, was present in the early Church's faith.

Fourth, they believed that a literal time of great distress for the whole world, which is commonly called the Tribulation by Premillennial theologians today, would precede the Lord Jesus' Second Coming.

Fifth, they believed that a personal Antichrist would come during the Tribulation period and work signs and wonders.

Sixth, the Church Fathers, who succeeded the Apostolic Fathers, continued to hold these views long after the destruction of Jerusalem in A.D. 70, and on into the fourth century. This fact will be developed later, because it disproves a basic teaching of a dangerous new movement called variously Reconstructionism, Dominionism, or Kingdom Now, which holds that almost all of the prophetic sections of the New Testament, including the Book of Revelation, were fulfilled in A.D. 70.

These six prophetic views caused the early Christians to recognize the Jews as a chosen people with whom God will yet fulfill His promises. These views also promoted a compassion for the Jews because the Christians saw them as a demonstration of God's faithfulness to His Word. And most important, the early believers held that God would judge anyone who unjustly harmed a Jew in accordance with His promise of protection to him in the Abrahamic Covenant. **"I will bless those who bless you, and the one who curses you I will curse."** (Genesis 12:3)

The Trail from Origen to Auschwitz

In addition to the foundational factors mentioned before, another very important event took place that helped implement the Church's growing anti-Jewish policy. Emperor Constantine was "converted" to Christianity and made it the official State religion in A.D. 313. History reveals that whenever Church and State marry, it strangely results in many errors and evils. Jewish historian H. H.

Ben-Sasson comments on some of the consequences of this development:

> [In the fourth century] a new force was rising on the political horizon: the Church Militant, whose beginnings may be said to date from the recognition of the Christian religion by Constantine (A.D. 313). This new factor was to have a decisive effect on the status of Palestine and of the Jews in the Roman Diaspora and indirectly also on the Jews in the Persian Empire.
>
> With Christianity's rise to power and (within a relatively short time after 313) to the status of the official religion of the empire, a basic change took place in the relations between the Jews and their environment. Christianity was to prove much more intolerant than Judaism, for it claimed a double inheritance from "SPIRITUAL ISRAEL" and from the PAGAN WORLD, endowing it with both the spiritual and political right to rule.
>
> The standard-bearers of the hatred [for the Jews] were the Church Fathers [i.e., Church leaders from the fourth century onward] and the monks, and its practical reflection may be found in the insulting language of imperial anti-Jewish legislation, in the decrees of rulers and administrators at all levels and in the attacks by fanatics against the Jews and their institutions. The case of the monk Barsauma of Nisibis, who roamed over Palestine with a band of followers in the years 419–422 and razed synagogues, was only one instance that had many parallels in the Diaspora.
>
> In respect to the Land of Israel, the attitude of the Church was compounded by two additional elements. First, Christianity claimed ownership of what it regarded as its Holy Land by virtue of the Jewish past, OF WHICH IT CLAIMED TO BE THE HEIR. . . . Second, the Christian message based itself on the premise that, with the destruction of Jerusalem and the rejection of the Jewish people by the LORD, the ENTIRE COVENANT, INCLUDING THE PROMISE OF THE LAND OF ISRAEL, BECAME VESTED IN CHRISTENDOM.[13] (Emphases mine.)

This passage underscores the fact that by the early fifth century, the Church believed that it was the sole possessor of

Israel's covenant promises, including the ownership of the promised land. Acting from this false premise, the Church began to use its new political power to create and enforce anti-Jewish legislation—a practice that became usual in the Middle Ages. In many cases throughout the Middle Ages, the institutional Church either forced Jews to convert by political oppression and terror, or put them to the sword.

Once again, it was the false prophetic premises of the Church that were the basis of the Church's anti-Jewish attitudes and actions. The Church began to act in a way that was in diametric contradiction to the teachings of the Lord Jesus Christ. He never taught that we should convert a person by force, or harm and persecute people simply because they disagreed with His message.

The Church's anti-Jewish attitude continued to ferment and fester within Christendom throughout the Middle Ages. Concerning the Jews, Augustine had taught two important things which were to become widely quoted and applied during the Middle Ages. First, he taught that the Jews should be allowed to live among the Christian communities because their wretched circumstances were an evidence of the truthfulness of the Old Testament prophecies that predicted their rejection and dispersion. Second, he taught, on the basis of his allegorical interpretation of Psalm 59:12, that the Jews should nevertheless be restricted in their privileges and continually humiliated.[14]

Persecution followed the Jews wherever they went in the centuries that followed Emperor Constantine. He enacted many laws that started the practice of restricting the Jew's freedoms. Only two years after Constantine made Christianity the official religion of the empire, he initiated a series of repressive edicts, including those forbidding Jews to seek converts or to intermarry with Christians. His reason for their exclusion from the rest of society was that they were "a nefarious and perverse sect." The impact of teaching like this was enormous. Prejudice against the Jews was guaranteed.

Historian Ausubel reports another important milestone along the infamous road of anti-Semitism: "Two centuries later [i.e., after Constantine's reign], the Emperor Justinian (A.D. 527–565) issued his celebrated code which laid the legal groundwork for anti-Semitism as a PERMANENT CHRISTIAN STATE POLICY. One clause provided: 'They (the Jews) shall enjoy no honors.

Their status shall reflect the baseness which in their souls they have elected and desired.'"[15] (Emphasis added.)

THE CRUSADES AND ANTI-SEMITISM

Though the Jews were degraded, forced to wear special clothes and "hats of humiliations," forced to live in ghettos, and sporadically massacred in various places in the centuries that followed Augustine, their plight greatly worsened beginning with the First Crusade of A.D. 1096.

The Crusades were military expeditions conducted by European Christendom in the eleventh, twelfth, and thirteenth centuries for the purpose of retaking the Land of Israel from the Muslims. Certain dispatches arrived from Jerusalem Christians who told of the maltreatment of Christian pilgrims and the obstruction of access to the Holy Places. The Crusades were allegedly begun to right these wrongs.

In many of these reports, the malevolence of the Jews was also stressed, so that from the beginning the ground was prepared for including the Jews along with the Muslims in the freshly stimulated animosity against "the enemies of Christianity."

The First Crusade: The Terror Begins

Pope Urban II whipped up popular support for the First Crusade with sermons first delivered at Clermont-Ferrand on November 27, 1095. I'm sure that he and the following Popes were not oblivious to the fact that these great "religious" enterprises helped them to establish more authority over the secular princes.

Even the Pope, however, was unprepared for the great numbers and diversity of cultures that responded to the challenge to go fight the unbelieving usurpers of the Christian Holy Places.

Thousands of nobles, knights, and common people began to assemble in France under the overall leadership of Godfrey of Bouillon. The swelling throng of Crusaders, which surpassed all expectations, and the religious frenzy preceding the departure of the army, soon induced an ominous change of mood toward the Jews. The centuries of misguided sermons about the whole Jewish race being exclusively guilty for the crucifixion of the Lord Jesus, the long history of an official Church policy of humiliating and persecuting them, and the clergy-cultivated image of the Jews as being obstinate impostors with no future as a people in God's plan, all began to bear their murderous fruit among the lower class of the Crusaders.

Soon there were cries for the blood of the "Christ-killer" before going to Palestine to deal with the Muslims. There is nothing more dangerous or uncontrollable than a mob which has been deluded into thinking it is doing a religious deed by eliminating an enemy of God. In spite of the efforts of many of the local bishops, politicians, and even the high nobles in the army, the lower-class Crusaders, spurred on by anti-Jewish slogans and propaganda, began to storm one city after another in search for Jews.

Terrible massacres took place in Rouen and Lorraine in France; in Mainz, Cologne, Speyer, Worms, Neuss, Mehr, Kerpen, Geldern, and Ellen in Germany. At Regensburg, Metz, Prague, and throughout Bohemia, one massacre followed another.

When the Crusaders, led by Godfrey, captured Jerusalem on July 15, 1099, they first entered the city through the Jewish quarter. A terrible slaughter took place. The surviving Jews were sold as slaves. The Jewish community of Jerusalem was obliterated. In all, tens of thousands of Jews were massacred in the name of Christianity as a consequence of the first Crusade.

The Second Crusade

The Church's hold on the Holy Land was threatened when the Muslims took Edessa from the Crusaders in 1144. Pope Eugene III began to preach another Crusade to save the Christian Kingdom in Palestine.

The Encyclopedia Judaica reports concerning that time:

> As soon as the Second Crusade was announced, the storm clouds began to gather once more over the Jews of Europe. As early as the summer of 1146, a Cistercian monk, Radulph, while preaching the Crusade, violently attacked the Jewish communities of the Rhineland, exhorting the Crusaders to avenge themselves on "those who had crucified Jesus" before setting out to fight the Muslims.
>
> Because the Jews and their local political rulers had learned of the dangers posed by the crusaders, they took

precautions. As a result, relatively few, a few hundred, were massacred.[16]

The Third Crusade: Terror Comes to England

The successful Holy Land campaigns of the great Muslim warrior Saladin and his capture of Jerusalem in 1187 occasioned the Third Crusade in the twelfth century. The Jews of Continental Europe had learned their lessons from the first two Crusades and took every precaution possible to protect themselves. But the Jews of England, who had heretofore been spared, caught the most savage repercussions of this Crusade.

When Richard the Lionhearted decided to personally take part in the Third Crusade, England, little interested in the previous Crusades, became intensely zealous. Every knight and noble seemed to "get religion."

Soon after the new Crusaders began to assemble, all the old anti-Semitic tales and slogans circulated among the knights and soldiers who were spoiling for action. Once again the cry of "kill the 'Christ-killers'" was sounded.

The Encyclopedia Judaica traces the slaughter: "The first massacre occurred at the port of Lynn, where most of the Jewish community was ruthlessly murdered. The same fate befell the Jewish communities of Norwich and Stamford. The worst outrage took place in York, where a number of local nobles, in heavy debt to the Jews, seized the opportunity to rid themselves of their burden. When attacked, the Jews took refuge in the Castle Keep, which the guard had opened for them; those who remained in the town were slaughtered."[17]

The Tragic Crusade

Perhaps the most tragic of all the Crusades was the one known as the Pastoureaux (French for "shepherd") of A.D. 1320. Forty thousand of these "shepherds," averaging sixteen years of age, without any designated leader, marched from the north of France to the south. They left a trail of death and destruction upon all the Jewish communities they encountered. Pope John XXII excommunicated all those who set forth on this unauthorized Crusade, but it did not stop them before they had slaughtered Jews throughout France. The lethal effect of home-taught anti-Jewish prejudice can clearly be seen here.

THE ROOTS OF HOLOCAUST

The Impact of the Crusade Period on the Jews

There is no question but that the long era of the Crusades marked a turning point in the history of Jews in western Europe. Many Jews began to move eastward in Europe. In A.D. 1211, three hundred rabbis emigrated to the Holy Land from western Europe.

Even the Church was forced to reassess her long-standing policies toward the Jews in the light of the savage attacks and massacres that took place in the name of Christianity during this period. A number of Popes did seek to prevent the more flagrant acts of anti-Semitism. Pope Calixtus II (1194–1224) issued a Bull (an edict issued by the Pope that is viewed as having Divine authority) which was renewed after the Second and Third Crusades between 1199 and 1250. It stipulated that although no new privileges should be granted to the Jews, they should not be deprived of a single one of the rights that had been secured to them.

But sadly, the Church did not change its interpretation of Scripture, which was the real fountainhead of the problem. This period should serve as a warning to us today during this current controversy. The Crusaders were taught that they were fighting to establish the "Kingdom of God on earth." They firmly believed they were "the New Israel," and that they had a Divine commission to drive both the Muslims and the Jews from the Holy Land. The Conquistadores of Spain and Portugal conquered the New World in the name of the Catholic Church and planted its flag in the New Land. Those who did not embrace the Catholic religion were often killed or branded on the cheek. This false form of the Church emerged through wrong theology initiated by men who were not themselves evil. These early Church Fathers, like Origen and Augustine, had no idea of the far-reaching implications of their errors, especially in the area of prophecy.

THE BLOOD-LIBEL HOAX

One of the most dangerous developments of anti-Semitism during the twelfth century was the first known libel charge against the Jews. They were accused of plotting against the Christian world.

Because of the intense spreading of malicious lies against the Jews during the Crusade period, the Christian attitude became solidified against them as an implacable enemy of their faith. It was in this atmosphere that one of the worst hoaxes of all was fabricated that would produce Jewish massacres from then until modern times.

Blood-libel is defined as "the allegation that Jews murder non-Jews, especially Christians, in order to obtain blood for the Passover or other rituals; a complex of deliberate lies, trumped-up accusations, and popular beliefs about the murder-lust of the Jews and their bloodthirstiness, based on the conception that Jews hate Christianity and mankind in general. It is combined with the delusion that Jews are in some way not human and must have recourse to special remedies and subterfuges in order to appear, at least outwardly, like other men."[18]

During the Crusade period many basic elements of the blood-libel story had evolved concerning the alleged "inhumanity and sadism of the Jews." Popular thinking concerning the Jews had reached a point where people would believe them guilty of any crime, no matter how bizarre or bestial.

The Origin of the Blood-Libel Hoax

The first known specific case of blood-libel occurred in Norwich, England, in A.D. 1144. It involved a boy named William who had disappeared at Easter time and was later found dead. The vicious rumor-mill started and soon it was alleged that the Jews had bought a Christian child, the "Boy-Martyr" William, before Easter and tortured him with all the tortures that had been inflicted upon the Lord Jesus, and on Good Friday hanged him on a cross in hatred of the LORD. The body of the boy William showed no evidence of foul play to support these monstrous lies, but no one seemed to care about the facts. It was the legend that counted. The Jews were later expelled from England as a result of this and other allegations of blood-libel.

These terrible trumped-up charges were leveled against the Jews, "with sordid and colorful embellishments," throughout the twelfth century. Specific cases were recorded in Gloucester, England (1168); Blois, France (1171); Saragossa, Spain (1182), to mention a few.

The number of blood-libel cases greatly increased in the thirteenth century, particularly in Germany. Munich alone had six cases alleging this horrible lie during this period. In the fourteenth, fifteenth, and sixteenth centuries, the blood-libel charges were an established practice, not only in western Europe, but eastward through Europe and Russia as well.

Though various secular princes and popes investigated and disproved the libel charges, they persisted in the minds of the people. Even artwork, music, and writings from these centuries vividly depict the Jews sacrificing Christian children at Passover.

The Nazis, therefore, found a rich heritage of lies from which to draw their murderous propaganda campaign of hate against the Jews. Julius Streicher's Nazi newspaper, *Der Stuermer*, revived the old charge of blood-libel with a front page article and cartoon depicting it in the most despicable way on May 1, 1934.[19]

Just in case you are tempted to think that Nazi Germany was simply a freak of history, never to be repeated again, the following eulogy was given in a recent article entitled "Patriots From The Past," published by the *Christian Defense League Report:*

> On the morning of October 16, 1946, in a vicious act of Talmudic "justice," Julius Streicher was hanged at Nuremburg (although some accounts indicate he was strangled). What was his "crime"? He dared to speak the truth about the Jews and for doing so he too was crucified.
>
> From 1923 until the final collapse of the Third Reich in 1945, Streicher published and edited "Der Sturmer" [sic] newspaper. From the beginning, Streicher wrote that "Der Sturmer" [sic] was to be "a paper in the struggle for truth." It was for this reason that Streicher was murdered by the Jews.[20]

Whoever the people are that publish the *CDL Report*, they certainly do not follow the teachings of Jesus. The entire issue was filled with lies and distortions of history. They illustrate the point that a false theological climate can breed anti-Semitism like a plague. Even good people are not immune to these kinds of lies, because the master deceiver, that father of lies, Satan himself, is behind it. This is why the Church must not allow this kind of climate to develop again.

Much blame for these tragic past crimes against the Jews must once again be laid at the doorstep of the Church. It was the atmosphere created by official Church policies against the Jews that made these things believable to the general public. Popular preachers engraved the libel in the minds of the common people.

It became embedded in their minds through various claims of miracles associated with the "martyrdom" of the Christian children. Several of the children who were allegedly "sacrificed" were canonized as martyrs of the Church, and their shrines within the Churches perpetuated the heinous hoax.

The Desecration of the Host Hoax

Another almost unbelievable hoax that resulted in more Jewish massacres for centuries was made possible by another misinterpretation of the Scriptures. At the Fourth Lateran Council (A.D. 1215), the Doctrine of Transubstantiation was officially endorsed and adopted by the Roman Church. The doctrine teaches that when the bread wafers (called the Host) and wine are consecrated by a priest, they actually become the body and blood of the Lord Jesus Christ. Here is another tragic illustration of the harm that can come when the Church interprets something intended to be figurative in a literal sense.

Legends and myths were soon put into circulation about the miraculous powers of the Host when it was rejected by disbelief or desecrated. It was reported that on certain occasions the Host would even speak.

It wasn't long before the virulent and widespread anti-Semitism was brought into the scenario of the miraculous powers of the Host. It is reported, "At the same time, it was imagined in some Christian circles that the Jews, believing paradoxically [which they obviously could not and remain Jews] that the consecrated wafer was in fact the very body of Jesus, desired to renew upon it and him the agonies of the Passion, by stabbing, tormenting, or burning it. Such was the intensity of their paradoxical hatred that they would not abandon their Jewish Perfidy even if the sacred wafer manifested its indignation and its miraculous essence by shedding blood, emitting voices, or even taking to flight. . . . The charge of desecrating the Host was leveled against Jews all over the Roman Catholic world, frequently bringing in its train persecution and massacre."[21]

The first reported case of this alleged desecration of the Host was at Belitz near Berlin in 1243. As a result, a number of Jews, both men and women, were burned at the stake.

This vicious libel continued to be leveled against the Jews even into the eighteenth century, especially in Germany. The charge was made in Deggendorf, Bavaria, in 1337–1338 and sparked off a series of massacres affecting scores of places in the region. The charge was made in 1370 in Brussels and resulted in the extermination of Belgian Jewry.

The list of savagery resulting from this hoax is too long to include in this work, but suffice it to say that no evidence or rational logic was ever produced to prove even one case. The evidence is that, based on the deliberate spreading of lies and superstitions by "Christians," thousands more Jews were horribly tortured and massacred for centuries.

Is it any wonder that the LORD warned us through James, **"And the tongue is a fire, the very world of iniquity; the tongue is set among our members as that which defiles the entire body, and sets on fire the course of our life, and is set on fire by hell."** (James 3:6 NASB)

Scapegoats of the Black Death

The Black Death was a plague of almost unimaginable proportions that ravaged Europe. Between the years of 1347 and 1351, it took a greater toll of life than any other known epidemic or war.

It is estimated that between one-third to one-half of the total population of greater Europe perished because of this terrible plague. In the heavily crowded larger cities, much higher percentages of the population died.

The terrified Europeans had various responses to the tragedy. Some turned to God, sought forgiveness and deliverance from Him. Others turned to all-out lawlessness and savagery.

But soon, the old anti-Semitic prejudices began to surface and find a way to make the ever-hated Jews the scapegoats for this catastrophe. It is highly probable that Jews did not contract the plague in as great a number as the Gentiles because of the Mosaic laws of cleansing the hands and of hygienic food handling. This would naturally have drawn suspicion. The Encyclopedia Judaica reports:

> Soon, however, the feeling of helplessness to stem the plague, and the fierce urge to react against the death and destruction it caused, concentrated the force of the populace on the age-old target of popular Christian hostility, the Jews. Anti-Jewish violence was particularly rabid in Germany, where it had been preceded by a dark half-century of anti-Jewish persecution in conjunction

with a succession of blood-libels and accusations of Host desecration. This had added to the sinister traits already attributed to the hateful image of the Jew. . . .

The first occasion on which Jews were tortured to confess complicity in spreading the Black Death took place in September 1348, in the Castle of Chillon on Lake Geneva. The "confessions" thus extracted indicate that their accusers wished to prove that the Jews had set out to poison the wells and food "so as to kill and destroy the whole of Christianity."

The disease was allegedly spread by a Jew of Savoy on the instructions of a rabbi. . . . As the case dragged on, details were extracted telling of further consultations held among the Jews, about messengers from Toledo, and other wild allegations. On October 3, 1348, during the summing up, an allegation providing a motive for the total destruction of Jewry was made; it was asserted that "before their end they said on their Law that it is true that all Jews, from the age of seven, cannot excuse themselves of this [crime], since all of them in their totality were cognizant and are guilty of the above actions."

These "confessions" were sent to various cities in Germany. The accusation that the Jews had poisoned the wells spread like wildfire, fanned by the general atmosphere of terror. . . .

In various cities, Jews were tortured to confess their part in the conspiracy. The defamation, killings, and expulsions spread through the kingdoms of Christian Spain, France, Germany, and to Poland-Lithuania, affecting about 300 Jewish communities.

On September 26, 1348, Pope Clement VI issued a bull in Avignon denouncing this allegation, stating that "certain Christians, seduced by that liar, the devil, are imputing the pestilence to poisoning by Jews." This imputation and the massacre of Jews in consequence were defined by the pope as "a horrible thing."[22]

The catastrophe of the Black Death persecutions and massacres of 1348–49 was both the culmination of the suspicion and distrust of the Jew which made it conceivable to see him as the natural perpetrator of the crime of well-poisoning, and in Germany, the culmination of over 50 years of almost uninterrupted anti-Jewish attacks. . . . [23]

Martin Luther Succumbs

It is tragic that even the great reformer Martin Luther was finally seduced by all the anti-Jewish propaganda of his times. Although in his earlier ministry Luther wrote a most sympathetic tract acknowledging the shameful way that the Church had treated the Jews and urged kind treatment of them, in later life he wrote another tract that was the complete opposite. Here in part is Luther's tract written in A.D. 1543:

> What then shall we Christians do with this damned, rejected race of Jews? Since they live among us and we know about their lying and blasphemy and cursing, we cannot tolerate them if we do not wish to share in their lies, curses, and blasphemy. . . . We must prayerfully and reverentially practice a merciful severity. . . . Let me give you my honest advice:
> First, to set fire to their synagogues or schools and to bury and cover with dirt whatever will not burn, so that no man will ever again see a stone or cinder of them. This is to be done in honor of our LORD and of Christendom . . .
> Second, I advise that their houses also be razed and destroyed
> Third, I advise that all their prayer books and Talmudic writings, in which such idolatry, lies, cursing, and blasphemy are taught, be taken from them.
> Fourth, I advise that their rabbis be forbidden to teach henceforth on pain of loss of life and limb . . .
> Fifth, I advise that safe-conduct on the highways be abolished completely for the Jews. For they have no business in the country-side, since they are not lords, officials, tradesmen, or the like. Let them stay at home . . . [We might well ask "What home?", since they were all presumably burned in point two!]
> Sixth, I advise that usury be prohibited to them, and that all cash and treasure of silver and gold be taken from them, and put aside for safe keeping . . .
> Seventh, I recommend putting a flail, an ax, a hoe, a

spade, a distaff, or a spindle into the hand of young, strong Jews and Jewesses and letting them earn their bread in the sweat of their brow.[24]

The Encyclopedia Judaica rightly comments about Luther's tract: "Short of the Auschwitz oven and extermination, the whole Nazi Holocaust is pre-outlined here."[25] Is it any wonder that Hitler and Julius Streicher quoted Martin Luther as justification for their murderous "Final Solution for the Jews?"

The fact that such a great man of faith and the Scriptures as Luther could be seduced by Satan to write such a monstrous thing proves two things:

First, the anti-Jewish propaganda within the Church and society in general was virulently latent and thoroughly embedded in the culture.

Second, the original false interpretation of prophecy, which Luther retained from Augustine, was a powerful blinding force that kept even the great reformer, who was an otherwise brilliant and literal interpreter of the Scriptures, from grasping what God's Word literally and unconditionally taught: that the Jews are still His elect people with a definite future in His plan. It also kept him from seeing an oft repeated Biblical lesson: that even though God Himself disciplines Israel, woe to the man or nation who mistreats them. History is strewn with the wreckage of former great leaders and nations who treated the Israelites unjustly.

An Imperative Lesson for Our Times

As we have briefly reviewed, the fact that many of the Church Fathers interpreted Biblical prophecies concerning Israel and its future allegorically, resulted in incredible suffering for the Israelites. The Church has some wretched and shameful periods of history for which to seek God's forgiveness.

A notable exception to this shameful history has been a Premillennial interpretation of the prophetic Scriptures. My German friend's father, the Plymouth Brethren, demonstrated how a faith in the literal interpretation of prophecy translated into courageous and sacrificial action. The vast majority of the other Christians in Germany were swept along by the propaganda of the Third Reich. Many other Premillennialists, like Corrie Ten Boom of Holland, suffered greatly in concentration camps for seeking to protect and hide Jews from the Nazis.

One of the main reasons I write this book is to seek to prevent Christians from once again contributing to this same kind of tragedy (even though it may be through ignorance). I believe we are witnessing a growing revival of the same false interpretation of prophecy that in the past led to such tragedy for so many centuries by a movement that calls itself either Reconstructionism, Dominionism and/or Kingdom Now. Who its believers are and what they are teaching is the theme of this book.

An example of the attitude engendered against the Jews and Israel by the Dominionist interpretation of Bible prophecy is reflected in one of Reconstructionist David Chilton's recent messages: "The Kingdom has been taken over from Israel, and it has been possessed by the New Covenant People. Israel has become demon possessed. It has become a nation of false prophets. A nation in the image of a Pagan Roman state. Jerusalem has become a harlot. And is going to be excommunicated. And the covenant promises are inherited by the faithful, witnessing, ruling Church of royal priests. That's what [the book of] Revelation is all about."[26] This is the same sort of rhetoric that in the past formed the basis of contempt for the Jews that later developed into outright anti-Semitism.

I urge you to carefully consider the imperative issues that are set forth in this book. Let Christians not sit idly by while a system of prophetic interpretation that historically furnished the philosophical basis for anti-Semitism infects the Church again.

CHAPTER TWO

Is History
Repeating Itself?

History teaches us that man learns nothing from history.

Hegel

I have quoted philosopher Hegel's maxim many times. Though I don't agree with Hegel on most things, I do agree with this statement.

In the last chapter I related how an erroneous interpretation of prophecy by mostly well-meaning Christian leaders led to a system of thought which resulted in centuries of tragic anti-Semitism. The modern champions of this method of interpreting the Scriptures call themselves Christian Reconstructionists. They believe that they have a mandate from God to *reconstruct society* by strictly instituting the civil code of the Law of Moses over the governments of the world, beginning with the United States. They believe that this is the way the Church will establish the Kingdom of God on earth *before* the personal return of the Lord Jesus Christ.

It is not the purpose of this book to deal with all the many doctrinal ramifications of the Christian Reconstructionist Movement (CRM). I have chosen to focus mainly on their prophetic views and the dangers they pose to the Church in general and the Jewish people in particular. If you wish to study the movement in more detail, I recommend Dr. H. Wayne House and Thomas Ice's excellent book, *Dominion Theology: Blessing or Curse?*,[1] which thoroughly analyzes the movement.

The heart of the Reconstructionist Movement's teaching is a system of prophetic interpretation called Postmillennialism. In order to understand this central concept of their view, it is necessary to have a working definition of the three main systems of prophetic interpretation: Amillennialism, Postmillennialism, and Premillennialism.

Amillennialism literally means *no millennium*. "Millennium" comes from two Latin words *mille* (thousand) and *annus* (year). As the name suggests, the Amillennialist does not believe that Christ will *personally* reign on earth for a literal thousand years.

Amillennialist Floyd E. Hamilton reveals their allegorical interpretation of the millennium by defining it as "Christ's millennial kingdom extending from His Resurrection from the tomb to the time of His Second Coming on the clouds at the end of this age."[2] Since this period of time has already extended over almost two thousand years, they see the word *millennium* merely in a symbolic sense.

Here are some of the central teachings of the Amillennialists:

- There will be no future reign of Christ on the earth from Jerusalem, as is literally predicted in numerous Bible passages.
- The Second Coming of Christ will occur at the end of history.
- There will be one general resurrection of both believers and unbelievers from throughout history.
- At this same time the Last Judgment of all mankind will take place. The believers will be given eternal life and the unbelievers will be condemned to eternal judgment.

Amillennialism was the predominant view of Christendom from around the fourth century until the eighteenth century when the literal method of interpreting Scripture, which was revived with the Reformation, was applied to the field of prophecy.

Postmillennialism literally means *after the millennium*. This theory states that Christ will come only after the Spirit-empowered Church has established God's Kingdom on the earth by progressively subduing the world and taking dominion over it.

The Postmillennialists, like the Amillennialists, believe that the present age is the Kingdom of God and understand the word *millennium* only in a symbolic sense. The major difference between them is that Postmillennialists believe the Kingdom of God is not just a spiritual reign of Christ in thc hearts of believers, but *an actual reign of the Church over all society in this age.* They believe that this will usher in an extended period of global righteousness and prosperity in which the Church will become purified, holy, and without blemish. Postmillennialists believe this must happen *before* Christ can return.

In a nutshell, they have transferred to the Church all of Israel's covenants and promises concerning a global Theocratic Kingdom, and shifted the time of their fulfillment to *before* Christ's Second Advent rather than *after* it.

Postmillennialist Norman Shepherd explains:

> [Postmillennialists] expect a future period when re-vealed truth will be diffused throughout the world and accepted by the vast majority. The millennial era will therefore be a time of peace, material prosperity, and spiritual glory.
>
> The millennium will be of extended duration though not necessarily a precise 1,000 years. Because it is estab-lished through means presently operative, its beginning is imperceptible. Some postmillennialists provide for gradual establishment of the millennium; others for a more abrupt beginning. Most, but not all, allow for a brief apostasy or resurgence of evil just prior to the advent and in preparation for the judgment. Even during the millen-nium, the world will not be entirely without sin, and not every person will be converted.[3]

One of the principle spokesmen for the Reconstructionists, David Chilton, made a clever observation about the close relation-ship between these two systems, "Amillennialism and Postmillen-nialism are the same thing. The only fundamental difference is that 'Postmils' believe the world will be converted, and 'Amils' don't."[4] This definition allows the modern Postmillennialists to claim that their system originated in the earliest days of Church history. I believe that Chilton's distinction between the two views is correct, as far as it goes, but that his frequent claim of an extremely early origin for Postmillennialism is false. There is no evidence of the distinctive teachings of Postmillennialism earlier than the seventeenth century.

However, from the standpoint of anti-Semitism, both Post-mils and Amils are equally guilty of creating a climate of thought wherein the Jew is viewed as an obstinate and rebellious pretender to the covenants and promises that are now exclusively owned by the Church. Since in this view the Jew has no more special purpose in God's plan as a national people, they see no reason for them to exist as a distinct people or as a modern state. And since they believe the covenants have been forfeited by the Jews, the special protection afforded the Jews by the warning of Divine judgment upon all those who would mistreat them as a people is removed. Historically, these factors created the kind of soil in which anti-Semitism easily took root and sprang to life.

In summary, the most important doctrines the Amils and Postmils hold in common are: (1) that the Church has been given all the covenants and promises made to Israel; (2) that the Church has forever taken Israel's place in God's plan, and therefore Israel has no future as a believing Nation; (3) that Christ's coming for the Church is *not* an any-moment possibility or expectancy, but something that can only occur after the Church has purified herself and established the Kingdom of God.

The Predominant View of the Nineteenth and Twentieth Centuries

There is a third view of prophecy called **Premillennialism**. Premillennialists believe that Christ will return to the earth with a cataclysmic judgment of the whole world. He will then separate the surviving unbelievers from the believers, casting the unbelievers off the earth directly into judgment (Matthew 25:31–46).

Premillennialists believe that the Lord Jesus will at that time remove the curse from nature and restore the earth to its original pre-sin condition during the one-thousand-year Messianic Kingdom (Isaiah 65:17–25; Romans 8:18–25, etc.).

The believers who survive the seven-year Tribulation period will be taken as mortals into a global Theocratic Kingdom over which Jesus the Messiah will reign for a thousand years. He will reign on the Davidic throne from Jerusalem.

At this time, the believing survivors from the physical descendants of Abraham, Isaac, and Jacob will receive all the things promised to them in the Abrahamic, Palestinian, Davidic, and New Covenants. (These will be defined in chapters four and five.)

Premillennialists also believe in a distinct, sudden snatching out of believers to meet the LORD in the air. In this event, believers will be instantaneously transformed from mortality to immortality without experiencing physical death (1 Corinthians 15:50–53; 1 Thessalonians 4:13–18, etc.). This is commonly called "the Rapture." The Church will return to the earth with Christ at His Second Advent in immortal form to reign with him as priests during the millennium.

There is a disagreement among Premillennialists as to whether the Rapture will occur before, in the middle, or at the end of the seven year Tribulation that ends with Christ's return to earth. But all agree that there will be a Rapture and that it will be before the beginning of the one-thousand-year Messianic Kingdom.

In contrast to this, some of the recent converts to the Reconstructionist Movement from the Pentecostal churches believe that the Rapture will *not* remove the believer, *but the unbeliever*. They teach that this will be God's judgment which will establish the Church's dominion over the earth and begin its Kingdom rule. They call this "the Harvest" as per the Wheat and Tares parable of Matthew 13:24–30 and 36–43. They also base this interpretation on Matthew 24:40–44, where it teaches that one will be taken, and the other left. The one taken, in their view, is the unbeliever.

Reconstructionism, the Child of Postmillennialism

The early American settlers known as Puritans were among the first known Postmillennialists in history. As a consequence of this view they were dedicated to establishing a Christian Society in America. Wayne House and Thomas Ice trace the movement:

> The Puritans wanted a government that would adhere rigidly to the civil code of the Old Testament, thereby creating a model of the kingdom of God on earth for all the world to see.
>
> They failed in their attempt. The reasons for the Puritans' failure are not relevant here, but their effort to build a Christian society is. It is being imitated today by a small and increasingly influential group of persons who believe that only through the establishment and enforcement of Old Testament civil law can America—and the world—be saved from destruction. Calling themselves *Christian Reconstructionists,* they propose to institute a theocractic government in America, and they are gaining

31

support in some elements of the evangelical community.[5] (Emphasis added.)

The Leaders of the Movement

The man most responsible for forging Postmillennialism into the modern Reconstructionist Movement is **Dr. Rousas J. Rushdoony**. He was born of Armenian immigrants in New York City in 1916. Rushdoony is a famous name in Armenian history. Rousas Rushdoony's own family tree includes an unbroken chain of priests in the Armenian Church back to the fourth century. After receiving his B.S. and M.A. from the University of California, and his Ph.D. from the Pacific School of Religion and the Valley Christian University, he worked for a time as a missionary among the Chinese youth of San Francisco, and then among the Paiute and Shoshone Indians. He has pastored several Presbyterian Churches. He is the author of thirty books beginning with his first book, *By What Standard?*, in 1959.

Rushdoony founded the Chalcedon Foundation in 1965 in Vallecito, California. It is from this foundation that he has systematically spread Reconstructionism through the newsletter *Chalcedon Report*, the more scholarly *Journal of Christian Reconstruction*, his many books, and frequent seminars and lectures.

Rushdoony's most significant work has been his two volume set entitled *Institutes of Biblical Law*. It is a treatise on the relationship of the Ten Commandments and modern society. From the publication of the first volume of this set in 1973, the Reconstructionist Movement began to break outside of the small group around Rushdoony and spread to some of the scholars of the evangelical community who were impressed with some of his insights into the relationship of the Bible to government.

Mr. Rushdoony is frequently called as an expert witness in Church-State educational trials. He is unquestionably a brilliant, original thinker who deserves respect whether one agrees with him or not.

Another key leader in the spread of Reconstructionism is **Gary North**. He is both a convert to Reconstructionism and the son-in-law of Dr. Rushdoony. Though North is even more prolific as a writer than Rushdoony, he is most known for his Rambo-like literary style. He obviously enjoys "doctrinal dueling" as much or more than he enjoys the doctrine. If North were as tough with his fists as he is with his words, Mike Tyson would be in real trouble.

Nevertheless, Gary North has been very successful at spreading the message of Reconstructionism.

Gary North earned his doctor's degree in economics from the University of California-Riverside. He worked for several years with Rushdoony as editor of *The Journal of Christian Reconstruction* until a personal dispute over a point of doctrine separated them in 1981.

Dr. North afterward founded the Institute for Christian Economics in Tyler, Texas, where he works closely with a group known as the Geneva Ministries. He has not only written many books, articles, and monthly publications, but has also trained and encouraged many young converts to do the same. It was North who cracked into the Charismatic churches and won many converts to the Christian Reconstructionist Movement. (A Charismatic is one who believes in the supernatural gifts of the Holy Spirit, particularly the gift of speaking in an ecstatic language.)

Another leader in the spread of the CRM is **Greg Bahnsen**. It is rumored that he read Dr. Rushdoony's works as a boy. He was the first student at Westminister Seminary to earn both the Master of Divinity and Master of Theology degrees at the same time. After receiving his Ph.D. from the University of Southern California, he went on to teach at the Reformed Seminary in Jackson, Mississippi.

His controversial book, *Theonomy in Christian Ethics*, caused an uproar among many of the evangelical scholars. The thesis of the book is that all of God's Law, as codified in the Law of Moses, should be applied directly to American life. Bahnsen contends that "every jot and tittle of the Law of Moses, with the exception of the ceremonial code, is binding upon mankind today." His book also teaches that all the Mosaic penal code should be applied directly to American civil law. Such criticism and controversy resulted that Bahnsen lost his teaching position. Bahnsen's teaching on Theonomy is accepted by most in Christian Reconstructionism.

Bahnsen is currently the pastor of an Orthodox Presbyterian church in Southern California. He is a brilliant and keen thinker, and even though few people outside Reconstructionism agree with his book, it is nevertheless widely studied.

The man most responsible for popularizing the Reconstructionist prophetic view is **David Chilton**. He was associated with Gary North for several years. His books *Paradise Restored* and *Days of Vengeance* have been the most influential in spreading the Reconstructionist interpretation of prophetic Scripture to the new converts to the movement. He is regarded by the movement as the leading spokesman for the Reconstructionist view of prophecy.

Chilton is now a pastor in Placerville, California, and continues to travel and lecture.

Other men who have played a role in developing and spreading the CRM message are:

- **Joseph C. Morecraft III**, the pastor of the Chalcedon Presbyterian Church in Atlanta.
- **Joseph Kickasola**, a professor of international affairs at the CBN University who teaches along the lines of Bahnsen's Theonomy.
- **Gary DeMar**, the head of the Institute of Christian Government in Atlanta. He has become more prominent as a spokesman since the publishing of his book, *The Reduction of Christianity*.
- **James Jordan**, the pastor of the Reconstructionist Church in Tyler, Texas. He is recognized as a scholar and influential thinker in the movement. He too is a prolific writer and frequently works with Gary North.
- **Ray Sutton**, the pastor of the Good Shepherd Episcopal Church in Tyler. He is a Dallas Theological Seminary graduate who was seduced by the CRM message. His book, *That You May Prosper*, is considered by the other Reconstructionists to be the standard for understanding their view of the Biblical covenants.

The Appeal of Reconstructionism

The CRM was a small movement until the last few years. But some of the new converts proved to be better communicators than the old guard. Their prolific writings, particularly on conservative political concerns, began to attract the interest of some influential people.

The movement has been aided by several current world conditions. House and Ice wrote:

> Disillusionment with big government, concern over America's moral decay, and the failure of the Great Society programs combined to activate the conservative movement in America in the 70s and 80s. Conservative evangelicals have been increasingly active in voicing their

concerns about the social crises plaguing the United States. The Reconstructionists not only share these concerns, but offer what to some are convincing solutions for them. According to one observer, Reconstructionism "provides an immediate alternative 'for religious and political conservatives' who aren't going to take it anymore."[6]

A Strange Wedding

One of the most significant factors in the Reconstructionist expansion occurred when some of them were invited to speak to a large group of "Positive Confession," Charismatic ministers. This was like inviting the fox into the chicken coop. "Positive Confession" is a label that has been given to those who believe that if you "think positively" and "keep confessing what you desire," the words themselves have power. Conversely, they believe that a "negative confession" also has the power to produce a negative result. Critics have called them the "name it and claim it" people.

Although there is some truth in this teaching, I believe that its basic assumption is in error. The fundamental thesis of the Positive Confession teaching is that God always wants his people to be healthy, wealthy, and without problems. The main problem with this thesis is that very little emphasis is placed on finding out what God's specific will is before storming God's throne with positive thinking techniques. There is more emphasis on the faith technique than on God, the object of true faith. The Bible teaches that the power is not in our faith, but in the object of our faith—God Himself.

When I confronted some of the leaders of this movement with the Apostle Paul's testimony of numerous trials and sufferings in the performance of God's will, they answered that "we follow Jesus, not Paul." But then Jesus didn't have wealth or freedom from suffering and trouble either.

The natural attraction of the Positive Confessors to the Reconstructionist message revolves around their belief that they can conquer any and all obstacles by "taking authority over them" in the name of Jesus. So when many were introduced to the Reconstructionist emphasis—that the Church has a mandate from God to take authority over the world and establish His dominion over it—most saw it as the ultimate, logical challenge for their kind of faith. Another factor that has drawn many Positive Confessors to the CRM message is that they believe they have the advantage of the miracle gifts of the Holy Spirit. They reasoned that since they have these two unique advantages (i.e., positive confession faith and the miracle gifts), it is impossible that the Church should fall into apostasy and the Antichrist take over the world.

This caused many to cast away the traditional Premillennial position on prophecy that the Pentecostals have always believed, and to embrace the Reconstructionists' Postmillennial interpretation. But the real issue is this: What does the Bible teach? If something is not God's will or plan, no matter how much we positively confess, it will not happen. The Premillennialist takes literally the many passages that predict the world will progressively harden its heart against the Gospel and plunge itself into destruction.

When the Foxes Entered the Chicken Coop

Gary North boasts about how the Reconstructionists made a major breakthrough into Charismatic churches: "It began when Robert Tilton's wife read Gary DeMar's book *God and Government* in late 1983, and then persuaded her husband to invite a group of Reconstructionists to speak before 1,000 'positive confession' pastors and their wives at a January 1984 rally sponsored by Rev. Tilton's Church. The all-day panel was very well received. DeMar subsequently taught a course on the Christian basis of civil government on Rev. Tilton's satellite network. It too was well received."[7]

To everyone's amazement (including the Reconstructionists'), they have become the "intellectual shepherds" of the Charismatic leaders. This is truly an amazing turn of events for the Reconstructionists, especially since they used to view Charismatics as a bunch of theologically naive emotionalists. In fact, David Chilton reflects what a number of the more conservative Reconstructionists still feel about the Charismatics when he refers to them as "Gary's flaky friends."[8] But when Gary North and the Reconstructionists won some converts among the Charismatics, they saw a new dynamic and articulate force for spreading their doctrine— one that already possessed a vast means of mass-media communication. Yet, as we will see, the Charismatics and the Reconstructionists are strange bedfellows indeed.

Those Charismatics who converted over to the Reconstructionist message began to call themselves by two titles—*Kingdom Now* and *Dominionists*.

The title **"Dominion"** grows out of Postmillennial emphasis that the Church is *to take dominion over the earth, its environment and inhabitants,* as per the command of God to Adam in Genesis 1:28. Some vary as to just how much dominion must be established over the earth before Christ can return, but the basic idea is common to all.

Likewise, the title **"Kingdom Now"** resulted from their belief that the *Kingdom of God in its literal earthly form is being established by the Church NOW, before the Second Advent of Christ.* Many believe that the Kingdom age actually began in A.D. 70 with the destruction of the Nation of Israel.

These are the two names used primarily by the Charismatic converts to the new movement. For the sake of simplicity, I will primarily use the title *Dominionist* to refer to the whole movement.

The Difficulty of Identifying

It is extremely difficult to identify what the various Dominionists actually believe. Sometimes it's like trying to nail the proverbial custard pie to the wall. There are about as many variations to the system as there are ministers who profess to believe it. I found that especially among the Charismatic converts hardly any two of them teach the same thing. Each one seems to add his own particular twist to the original Reconstructionist system. Trying to keep up with the movement's latest "revelations" is like trying to give speeding tickets at the Indy 500.

This was a predictable development for several reasons. First, the allegorical method of interpretation, which is an indispensable factor in establishing the system, virtually guaranteed a wide divergence of views. There is simply no solid check over the biases, traditional backgrounds, and imaginations of the interpreters. They can easily read into the Biblical text their particular mind-sets.

A second reason is because of the extremely different theological and denominational traditions from which the converts come.

A third reason is that some Charismatics have justified "new interpretations" by claiming they are direct "Divine revelations from God." This has been brought fully to bear in the development of their version of Dominion Theology. To me, this presents one of the greatest dangers. When a person gets a "Divine revelation" about how a certain passage should be interpreted, he almost always ceases to be objective. But the interpreter should be especially careful when the "revelation" is in contradiction to the normal clear sense of a given passage of Scripture, and out of harmony with other parallel passages. Too often, the "Divine revelation" becomes the judge of what the Scriptures mean, rather than the Scriptures judging whether the revelation is in fact "Divine." In fairness, I must say that most Reconstructionists are equally appalled at this kind of practice.

The New Testament not only does not teach this kind of personal infallibility, but warns the individual Christians to beware of leaders who make such claims. Local churches are commanded to have elders who pass judgment on what the prophets say. (1 Corinthians 14:29) The Lord Jesus commended the Ephesian Church for testing men who claimed great authority: **". . . and you put to the test those who call themselves apostles, and they are not, and you found them to be false. . . ."** (Revelation 2:2 NASB)

Paul praised the Bereans for testing what he preached to them: **"Now these were more nobleminded than those in Thessalonica, for they received the word with great eagerness, EXAMINING the Scriptures daily, TO SEE WHETHER THESE THINGS WERE SO."** (Acts 17:11 NASB)

Each Christian is commanded to search the Scriptures and to test what he is taught. (1 John 2:26–27) An old Biblically based axiom certainly applies to preachers as well as everyone else, "Power corrupts, and absolute power corrupts absolutely." If you don't believe this, look at the carnage caused by unchecked clergy down through history. Jonestown demonstrates what can happen when a pastor carries personal authority to the extreme.

Optimism in Spite of Truth

As mentioned above, the churches which have previously embraced the doctrines of "positive thinking," "positive confession," and "motivational science" have been the most susceptible to the Reconstructionists' doctrine. The reason is obvious. Those who preach Dominion doctrine continually talk about it being "the only optimistic and positive view of future history." In order to teach what I call this "new Gospel of optimism," they have had to redefine what victory for the Church must be in terms of human standards.

Is this "new doctrine of optimism," which teaches that the Church is going to perfect itself and conquer the world before Christ returns, really based on God's Word? To me, this is the only question that counts. If "optimism" is not based on God's truth, it is a cruel hoax. I believe that whatever God truly predicts will always be a ground of hope and optimism that never disappoints. God's plan and purpose can never be understood in terms of the human viewpoint.

Jeremiah and the Positive-confessing Optimists of His Day

There are many parallels between the situation today and the one in Jeremiah's time. Jeremiah was commanded to give an extremely negative message if judged by the human viewpoint. He was sent to a rebellious people who had rejected God's Word and refused to repent. Even though God continued to offer Israel forgiveness if they repented, He predicted to Jeremiah that they would *not* repent, and that they were surely going to be destroyed by the Babylonians. Here is an example of one of Jeremiah's more "nonpositive" prophecies:

> **Furthermore, tell the people, "This is what the LORD says: See, I am setting before you the way of life and the way of death. Whoever stays in this city will die by the sword, famine, or plague. But whoever goes out and surrenders to the Babylonians who are besieging you will live; he will escape with his life. I have determined to do this city harm and not good, declares the LORD. It will be given into the hands of the king of Babylon, and he will destroy it with fire." (Jeremiah 21:8–10)**

Now, you can just imagine how popular this prophecy was. Jeremiah was telling the Judeans to surrender to the Babylonian enemy. From the human viewpoint, this was considered defeatism at best and treason at worst. The LORD would never counsel His people to surrender to their enemies, they reasoned. So prophets rose up and predicted things that were more "positive" and "inspiring" to the peoples' ears. But this is what the LORD said to them:

"Do not listen to what the prophets are prophesying to you; they fill you with FALSE HOPES. They speak visions from THEIR OWN MINDS, not from the mouth of the LORD. They keep saying to those who despise me, 'The LORD says: You will have peace.' And to all who follow the stubbornness of their hearts they say, 'No harm will come to you.' But which of them has stood in the council of the LORD to see or to hear his word? Who has listened and heard his word?"

"I have heard what the prophets say who prophesy lies in my name, They say, 'I had a dream! I had a dream!' How long will this continue in the hearts of these lying prophets, who prophesy the delusions of their own minds?" (Jeremiah 23:16–18, 25, 26 NASB)

The "macho" prophets of optimism of that day discounted Jeremiah's message and branded him a pessimist and a traitor. They even labeled him a false prophet, beat him, and locked him in prison stocks. But no matter how pessimistic, negative, and defeatist Jeremiah's message sounded to those who were seeking to operate by human reason instead of God's revelation—WHAT GOD SAID HAPPENED!

The lesson is this: God's Word does not always line up with the changing popular fads of human reasoning. From the human viewpoint, it was "humanly unreasonable" for God to destroy a nation and a land that He Himself had created and preserved. An order to surrender to the enemy was totally contrary to normal human passions of patriotism and manly courage. Yet those who believed God's Word and surrendered were spared, and those who didn't were horribly slaughtered.

More to the point at hand, the idea that things are going to get worse and worse as the time for Christ's return draws near may not fit in with the popular teachings of the Positive Confession/ Dominion movement, but as will be shown, that is what God has clearly predicted. The only way that anyone can come up with something different than this is to give many prophetic passages an allegorical meaning and say that "special Divine revelation" is the source of their "new insight." It is always dangerous to reinterpret the Bible so that it fits the bias of a newly acquired system of thought. It should be noted carefully, GOD'S PROPH-ETS WERE SELDOM CONSIDERED TO HAVE A "POSITIVE

MESSAGE" BY THE RECIPIENTS OF THEIR PROPHECIES OF
JUDGMENT.

But as then, so now! We have many claiming to be prophets
who speak in the name of the LORD. They bring messages that
"tickle the ears" of those who have swallowed an erroneous
concept of what success for the Church really is.

A Proper Definition of Success

One of the main errors of the Dominion movement is their
definition of what success is for the Church, and just what its goal
and destiny is. From their point of view, success is the Church's
gradually taking dominion over the entire world-system, and
substantially establishing the Kingdom of God before Christ
personally returns to the earth.

David Chilton states the Dominion view clearly: "The Bible
gives us an eschatology of dominion, an eschatology of victory.
This is not some blind, 'everything-will-work-out-somehow' kind
of optimism. It is a solid, confident, Bible-based assurance that,
before the Second Coming of Christ, the gospel will be victorious
throughout the entire world."[9]

Gary North clarifies their view concerning those who look for
a tribulation and the return of Christ to establish God's Kingdom:
"They (Premillennialists) begin with the presupposition that God
has not given His church the vision, program and first principles
to defeat God's enemies, even with Christ's victory over Satan at
Calvary as the foundation of the Church's ministry."[10]

But what the Dominionists fail to consider is that Satan's
defeat at the cross did not eliminate man's freedom of choice. Nor
has Satan been bound from operating on earth during this age.
The Apostle John makes it clear that the world-system is still
under Satan's control: ". . . the WHOLE WORLD [system] is
under the control of the evil one." (1 John 5:19b) The Scriptures do
not say that Satan will be bound until the personal, cataclysmic
intervention of the Lord Jesus at His Second Advent. (Revelation
19:11–20:11)

North continues his attack against the Premillennialists: "The
traditional pessimillennialists [his term for Premils] have issued a
clarion call: 'Come join us; we're historical losers.' They have built
their institutions by attracting people who are content to remain
historical (pre-second coming) losers.

And earlier in the publisher's preface to *Days of Vengeance,*

41

North writes, "If their [meaning the Premils] followers ever sit down and read *Days Of Vengeance*, Christian Reconstructionism will pick off the best and the brightest of them. Why? BECAUSE EARTHLY HOPE IS EASIER TO SELL THAN EARTHLY DEFEAT, at least to people who are not happy to accept their condition as historical losers."[11] (Emphasis mine.)

There is one thing that is very true about North's statement, *earthly hope is indeed easier to sell than earthly defeat to those who are looking at the world from the human viewpoint and don't understand what the true Biblical hope is.* But the Bible says that our hope is not in this world: **"If only for this life we have hope in Christ, we are to be pitied more than all men."** (1 Corinthians 15:19) And again, **"For our Citizenship is in heaven, from which also we EAGERLY WAIT for a Savior, the Lord Jesus Christ."** (Philippians 3:20 NASB) These Scriptures, and many more like them, do not reflect an earthly focused hope, but a heavenly one. This does not mean that we sit around doing nothing, but it does mean that our ultimate hope is not in an earthly theocracy that God hasn't promised for this age.

A big factor the Dominionists forget is that Satan's judgment at the cross has not yet been executed to the point of him being bound. Satan is clearly portrayed in the Bible as being active right up to the return of Christ.

As will be shown, God does not view the snatching of Christ's bride out of the world as defeat. This is one of the most pernicious deceptions of Dominion teaching. They define from the human viewpoint what they think is victory, and then make that the criterion by which the Bible must be interpreted. What an editor for the *London Economist* once wrote about a different subject aptly applies to them, "They proceed from an unwarranted assumption to a foregone conclusion."

What is Victory for the Gospel?

The Bible simply *does not* teach the basic premises upon which much of Dominion theology is built. Jesus commanded us to preach the Gospel to all the world. But victory in evangelism was never promised to result in the conversion of all who heard, or even a majority who heard. The LORD warned, **"Enter through the narrow gate. For wide is the gate and broad is the road that leads to destruction, and MANY enter through it. But small is the gate and narrow the road that leads to life, and only a FEW find** it." (Matthew 6:13–14) And in another place He said, **"For many are called, but few are chosen."** (Matthew 22:14 NASB)

Humorously, the Reconstructionists become more dispensational in their approach to interpreting these verses than C. I. Scofield himself. They contend that the above verses only applied to Israel, not to the general reception of the Gospel among the Gentiles. But they can't have it both ways. If it is wrong, as they teach, for the Dispensationalists to recognize progressive revelation in distinguishable Divine economies, then it's also wrong for them to do so.

The Freedom-to-choose Factor

God made a sovereign decision to give man the freedom to make a choice concerning the Gospel. Peter explained that the LORD withholds judgment because He is not willing that any should perish, but that all should come to repentance. (2 Peter 3:8–9) But in order for mankind to have the freedom to accept the Gospel, he must also have the freedom to reject it. The reason why there is such evil in the world today is because God has allowed man the freedom to choose to do evil so that he can also have the freedom to choose to believe the Gospel. God could stop evil immediately. But to do so, He would have to annihilate the whole human race.

This is why the Lord Jesus delays His coming. When He returns, it will be to judge the world and set up His Kingdom. The Bible teaches us that the world will become increasingly hardened to the message of grace as the time for Christ's return approaches. This will *not* happen because of some flaw in the Gospel, nor because of a lack of spiritual power in the witnesses, but rather because of the hardness of the human heart. The LORD intends to allow the human heart to fully demonstrate its hardness in history. This is why there are distinguishable periods of history in which God has tested man's response to progressive revelations of His Will.

This is also why victory in this age is measured in terms of causing the whole world to HEAR the Gospel presented in the power of the Holy Spirit, and discipling those who believe it. Nowhere does the Bible teach that preaching the Gospel will convert so many people that the world-system will be brought under subjection to God during this age. That is always presented as the exclusive work of the King-Messiah at His coming in power and glory. It is only then that the LORD will judge the Christ-rejecters. (Matthew 25:31–46)

PARABLES ABOUT COUNTERFEIT BELIEVERS

The broad course of history between Christ's ascension to the Father and His Second Advent to the earth is clearly revealed in the Lord Jesus' parable of the Sower and the parable of the Wheat and Tares. In all these parables of Matthew chapter 13, the Lord Jesus is only dealing with the broad characteristics and trends that would develop between His First and Second Comings. He is not giving a detailed outline of all the events of prophecy that would take place in this period. At this point, Jesus was still dealing primarily with prophetic events as they applied to and affected Israel. I say this because the Reconstructionists teach that since there is no mention of a worldwide Tribulation or a Rapture of the Church in this parable, there cannot be one. Those intervening events are taught later in the Olivet Discourse (Matthew 24 and 25), the Epistles, and Revelation.

In the parable of the Sower, Jesus taught that receiving **the word** about the kingdom (the seed) did *not* depend upon the way it was sown, *nor* upon the quality of the seed, *but rather* upon the condition of the soil. Jesus described four different kinds of soil, but declared only one of the four as being good soil. It is only in the good soil that the seed takes firm root and produces lasting fruit. (See Matthew 13:3–9, 18–23.)

The parable of the tares is even more revealing about the course of this period. *Tare* is actually *darnel*, which is a weed that so closely resembles wheat that it is almost impossible to distinguish until fruit-bearing time. Only true wheat produces fruit, the darnel does not. The Bible emphasizes that the main point of the parable is to teach about the *tares* phenomenon (verse 36). The Lord Jesus interprets the parable for us:

> **And His disciples came to Him, saying, "Explain to us the parable of the TARES of the field."**
> **And He answered and said, "The ONE WHO SOWS the good seed is the Son of Man, and the FIELD is the world; and as for the GOOD SEED, these are the sons of the kingdom; and the TARES [darnel] are the sons of the evil one; and the ENEMY who sowed them is the devil,**

and the HARVEST is the end of the age [Israel's age was in view]; **and the REAPERS are angels.**

"The Son of Man will send forth His angels, and they will gather out of His kingdom all stumbling blocks, and those who commit lawlessness, and will cast them into the furnace of fire; in that place there will be gnashing of teeth. Then the righteous will shine forth as the sun in THE KINGDOM of their Father. He who has ears to hear, let him hear." (Matthew 13:36–43 NASB. Compare this with 25:31–46.)

Between Christ's Ascension and the Second Advent, the devil is continuing to infiltrate believers with his counterfeit ministers and disciples. The Apostle Paul graphically revealed what the tares symbolize:

For such men are false apostles, deceitful workmen, masquerading as apostles of Christ. And no wonder, for Satan himself masquerades as an angel of light. It is not surprising, then, if his servants [ministers] **masquerade as servants** [ministers] **of righteousness. Their end will be what their actions deserve.** (2 Corinthians 11:13–15)

Just as darnel looks almost exactly like wheat, the counterfeit believers closely resemble the real ones. This kind of deception and infiltration of God's people is said *to continue and increase* right up until the LORD's return to the earth.

This parable predicts exactly the same Judgment as the one prophesied by Jesus in Matthew 25:31–46. The LORD will gather all the Gentile survivors of the Tribulation, and will separate the believers from unbelievers. The unbelievers will be cast directly off the earth into judgment.

Only one-third of Israel will survive but all who do will be believers, according to Zechariah 13:1, 8–9. However, there will be a judgment of evaluation for the surviving remnant, according to Ezekiel 20:33–37.

Here is another Scripture that predicts exactly the same continuous increase of evil until the Second Advent of Christ as the parable of the wheat and tares:

For the secret power of lawlessness is already at work; but the one who now holds it back [the Holy

Spirit] **will continue to do so TILL he is taken out of the way** [the Rapture]. **And THEN the LAWLESS ONE** [the Antichrist] **will be revealed, whom the Lord Jesus will overthrow with the breath of his mouth and DESTROY BY THE SPLENDOR OF HIS COMING. The coming of THE LAWLESS ONE will be in accordance with the work of Satan displayed in all kinds of counterfeit miracles, signs and wonders, and in every sort of evil that deceives those who are perishing. They perished because they refused to love the truth** [the Bible] **and so be saved. For this reason God sends them a powerful delusion so that they will believe THE LIE and so that all will be condemned who have not believed the truth but have delighted in wickedness.** (2 Thessalonians 2:7–12)

Many errors in the Dominion teaching are pointed out by this passage.

The First Error

Most Dominionists teach that the Church will have bound the activity of Satan and established dominion over the world-system at the time of the Lord Jesus' return. In fact an essential part of their eschatology teaches that Jesus will not return until this has been accomplished.

This passage teaches the very opposite. Far from being bound, Satan will reach the pinnacle of his deceptive powers, and will deceive most of the world by the time of the Second Coming. In fact, this passage explicitly teaches that *it is the personal return of the Lord Jesus Christ in power and glory that directly brings about the destruction of Satan and his masterpiece, the Man of Lawlessness who is the Antichrist.* (2 Thessalonians 2:1–12)

The Second Error

This points to another doctrine of the Dominionists that is corrected by this passage. They teach that there will not be a personal Antichrist, only a spirit of antichrist. David Chilton wrote, "Antichrist is a term used by John to describe the widespread apostasy of the Christian Church prior to the fall of Jerusalem. In general, any apostate teacher or system can be called 'antichrist'; but the word does not refer to some 'future führer.' "[12]

In contradistinction to Chilton's statement, this passage teaches that although **"the power of lawlessness was already at work"** in Paul's day, there will nevertheless be at the time of Christ's return a person known as **"the Lawless One"** who will be possessed by Satan himself and given all his power and authority. This is the same one that is described in Revelation 13:1–10. The apostasy that the Lawless One will bring with him is described in Second Thessalonians 2:7–12 as the awful climax of the process of the continuing development of **"the mystery of lawlessness"** that was already at work in Paul's day. Once again, this mystery of lawlessness could not have been destroyed in A.D. 70 as Chilton claims, since this passage clearly predicts that it is the LORD's personal return that destroys it. So whether we call the Lawless One the Antichrist or whatever, he is Satan's masterpiece who will take over the whole world for three and a half years just prior to the Lord Jesus Christ's personal return.

Again, the Scriptures are very clear about the conditions of this age, **"We know that we are children of God, and that THE WHOLE WORLD [system] is under the control of the EVIL ONE."** (1 John 5:19) The parable of the tares teaches the same thing as Second Thessalonians, that it is the sons of the Evil One that will increase until the Second Coming of the Lord Jesus Christ.

A Parable About Evil's Explosive Power to Spread

Jesus' parable of leaven makes this point even more clearly, **"The kingdom of heaven is like leaven, which a woman took, and hid in three pecks of meal, until it was all leavened."** (Matthew 13:33 NASB) The Dominionist interpreters constantly emphasize the Bible's elaborate system of symbols. This is the foundation of their whole method of interpretation. But they depart from their own principle when it doesn't serve their purpose. They try to make the symbol of **leaven** in this parable refer to the Kingdom of God and how it will spread to take dominion over the earth. However, there's one big problem with that interpretation—**leaven** in the Bible *is always used as a symbol of evil's explosive power to spread*. It is never used as a symbol of good.

This was the whole point of the Feast of Unleavened Bread. This is why the Israelites were commanded to purge all leaven from their homes before the Passover feast. It was also the symbolic reason why they ate unleavened bread during the feast season. (See Exodus 12.)

Leaven is used as a symbol of the corrupting power of sin and evil in both Galatians 5:9 and First Corinthians 5:6. Paul interprets leaven as symbolic of evil in both passages.

Therefore, Jesus is teaching in this parable that Satan would permeate the world with deception and evil before His return. Jesus again confirms this point while teaching about His elect crying out for justice and relief from persecution just before He returns: **"However, when the Son of Man comes, will He find faith upon the earth?"** (Luke 18:8) In the original Greek, this question assumes a negative answer. The original text has a definite article before **faith**, which in context means **"this kind of faith."** The idea is that there will not be this kind of strong faith when He returns to earth.

The Third Error

The Dominionists also teach that the prophecies of Matthew 24 and 25, and Revelation 6–18, which teach about an unprecedented time of catastrophe just before Christ's Second Advent, were fulfilled in the Roman destruction of Jerusalem and Israel in A.D. 70. They teach that there is not going to be a period commonly known as "the Tribulation" that precedes the Second Advent. As we have seen, Second Thessalonians chapter two certainly presents another picture. (More will be said on this later.)

THE GREAT COMMISSION

The number who believe the Gospel is always left in the hands of God. Jesus commissioned us as follows:

> **Thus it is written, that the Christ should suffer and rise again from the dead the third day; and that repentance for forgiveness of sins should be proclaimed in His name to all the nations, beginning from Jerusalem. You are witness of these things.** (Luke 24:46–48 NASB)
> **But you shall receive power when the Holy Spirit has come upon you; and you shall be My witnesses both in Jerusalem, and in all Judea and Samaria, and even to the remotest part of the earth.** (Acts 1:8 NASB)
> **And Jesus came up and spoke to them, saying, "All**

authority has been given to Me in heaven and on earth. Go therefore and make disciples of [Greek=*out of*] **all the nations** [τα εθνη in Greek=*the Gentiles*]**, baptizing them in the name of the Father and the Son and the Holy Spirit, teaching them to observe all that I commanded you; and lo, I am with you always, even to the end of the age."** (Matthew 28:18–20 NASB)

Nothing in these great commission passages implies that we will convert the world and take dominion over it. We are commanded to go out in the power of the Holy Spirit and to proclaim the Gospel. We are told to make disciples from out of all the Gentiles. You don't disciple nations, you disciple individuals, so the Greek word translated *nations* should be understood in its most frequently used sense—*Gentiles*.

As previously noted, the nature of world evangelism is portrayed in the parable of the Sower. The reception of the Gospel message is *not* shown to depend so much upon the power with which it is presented, but more upon the receptivity of the human heart, which was illustrated in the parable by the four different kinds of soils. This is why the great evangelist and apostle Paul said:

> **But thanks be to God, who always leads us in His triumph in Christ, and manifests through us the sweet aroma of the knowledge of Him in every place. For we are a fragrance of Christ to God among those who are being saved and among those who are perishing, to the one an aroma from death to death, to the other an aroma from life to life. And who is adequate for these things?** (2 Corinthians 2:14–16 NASB)

You see, triumph is not presented as everyone accepting the knowledge of Christ, but rather giving everyone a chance to hear about it. We continue to be a sweet aroma to God whether our witness is accepted or rejected.

Now, it is on this very point that the Dominionists greatly err. Their definition of victory is to bring the whole world under the Dominion of God. David Chilton puts it even stronger: "The Gospel will convert the world." He means by this that virtually the whole world population will be converted. I wish that this were possible, but God Himself says that it is not. And it is not because the Church fails, but because the heart of man becomes progressively more hardened to the Gospel.

It is easy to see why the Dominionists make this error. They misapply to the Church passages that clearly refer to the Kingdom that Christ Himself will set up at His Second Coming. Since all the Scriptures that refer to the Messiah's Kingdom speak of virtually everyone in the world being believers, they assume that they will have been converted by the Church. But the Scriptures clearly show the reason for this future situation—the world will be purged of unbelievers by Christ at His coming, so that only believers remain. (See Matthew 25:31–46.)

The Apostle Peter makes a very appropriate prediction concerning this issue. He speaks of mockers within the Church in the last days who say, **"Where is the promise of His coming? For ever since the fathers fell asleep, all continues just as it was from the beginning of creation."** (2 Peter 3:4) Most Dominionists say that Christ won't come for some time and that it's not God's Will for us to be looking for signs of His return. I believe that the LORD gave us a very specific pattern of world events that would function as prophetic signs to tell us when Christ's coming is near. If we are actually in the generation that will see them all fulfilled, then it is of utmost importance not to be seduced by a false optimism. The generation who saw the First Coming of Christ was rebuked for not recognizing the prophetic signs of the time (Matthew 16:1–14). One of the main reasons for that generation of Israelites' failure to recognize and believe in Jesus as the Messiah was their refusal to interpret prophecy concerning His First Coming literally and accept it at face value.

There are many more prophecies concerning Christ's Second Coming than His First. And they are illuminated by the example of Israel's failure in the First Coming.

Take care that you are not led astray by a teaching that says we are going to conquer the world and that Christ's coming is a long ways off. No matter how good and positive that sounds, it is not the truth. Over and over again in the New Testament we are commanded to be **"looking for the blessed hope and the appearing of the glory of our great God and Savior, Christ Jesus. . . ."** (Titus 2:13) We are even told that there is a special crown for those who love and long for Christ's appearing. (2 Timothy 4:8)

Contend Earnestly for the Faith

The LORD through Jude commands us **"to contend earnestly for the faith which was once for all delivered to the saints."** (Jude 3 NASB) It is in this spirit and under this constraint that I have written this book.

If—just if—this is indeed the time for Christ's return, then this new view will ill prepare us for the events that may be very close at hand.

CHAPTER THREE

Controlling
the Imagination

About the time of the End, a body of men will be raised up who will turn their attention to the prophecies, and insist on their literal interpretation in the midst of much clamor and opposition.

Sir Isaac Newton (A.D. 1643–1727)

There are two basic ways of interpreting Scripture. One is to draw the meaning *from* the text itself. The other is to read a meaning *into* the text that is foreign to the normal sense of the words, grammar, and context.

The first method is commonly called *exegesis*. It is formed from two Greek words: *ek* (ἐκ), out of; and *egeomai* (ἡγεομαι), to lead. The literal meaning is "to lead out." The goal of this method is to allow the normal meaning of the words, grammar, and context to speak for itself.

The second method might best be described as *eisegesis*, which means to read into the text an allegorical or mythical meaning that is different from the natural meaning of the passage. This would best describe the Dominionist method of interpretation.

Gary North made an unconscious admission when he wrote in the publisher's preface to David Chilton's *Days of Vengeance,* "For over two decades, critics chided the Christian Reconstructionists with this refrain: 'You people just haven't produced any Biblical exegesis to prove your case for eschatological optimism.'"[1]

The fact is that for over two decades the Reconstructionists did have a huge superstructure of philosophically based eschatology with no exegetical foundation. Chilton was given the assignment of finding some Biblical passages on which the system might be based. Speaking from any point of view, that was not the best atmosphere in which to promote objectivity.

Chilton's books, far from establishing Dominion theology on a Biblical foundation, rather illustrate that they have no objective literal base of interpretation to justify their system. I found several attacks against Premillennialists, but unfortunately no definitive responses to the exegetical base of our doctrine. As I will demonstrate later, Chilton used the same technique as his colleagues before him. He built his system more upon attacking the Premillennialists than positively establishing his own system.

A further weakness in the Dominionist system was revealed by North when he admitted that "the final major work lacking for Reconstructionism is a book on hermeneutics." Hermeneutics, which means the science of interpretation, should be a foundational study, not the final capstone effort.

One of the greatest criticisms by Dominionists of Premillennialists is the fact that many seek to apply certain Second Advent prophecies to current events (and they have a precedent from the Apostolic Fathers for doing so). But at least Premillennialists start from a solid base of interpretation that is consistent with the whole counsel of Biblical prophecy. This is a unique time in history in which all of the predicated signs that were to precede the Second Coming of Christ are coming into focus within the same generation. So it should come as no surprise that there has been such a renewed interest in prophecy, or that there has been such a tremendous response to books about it.

A Cardinal Maxim

It gets back to one of the cardinal maxims of interpretation: every passage has one basic meaning, but many applications. You must first find the meaning of a passage before applying it, not start with your conclusion and find a Biblical illustration to support it.

The most common criticism leveled against me by the Dominionists is that I see "cobra helicopters" as possibly being described in Revelation 9:5–10. This was presented as an opinion in my book *There's a New World Coming*,[2] in which I gave a detailed explanation for it. Whatever this passage means, it is a composite description from many different things that is obviously intended to be symbolic. There is no insect, beast, or man in nature that fits what is described. Ample evidence can be found within the Book of Revelation to establish that John wrote about things he *saw* and *heard* while projected into the future in a Divine vision. I believe John actually saw and heard things by direct Divine revelation that were centuries future to his own time and still future to us. He was then commanded to write about what he had seen. He therefore had to describe very advanced scientific creations of a much later time in terms of his first-century knowledge and experience. This is my opinion, and I believe it makes good sense. If you don't buy that, it's okay with me; show me something better.

How to Avoid Error

The most important single principle in determining the true meaning of any doctrine of our faith is that we start with the clear statements of the Scriptures that specifically apply to it, and use those to interpret the parables, allegories, and obscure passages. This allows Scripture to interpret Scripture. The Dominionists frequently reverse this order, seeking to interpret the clear passages using obscure passages, parables, and allegories.

The second most important principle is to consistently interpret by the literal, grammatical, historical method. This means the following: (1) Each word should be interpreted in the light of its normal, ordinary usage that was accepted in the times in which it was written. (2) Each sentence should be interpreted according to the rules of grammar and syntax normally accepted when the document was written. (3) Each passage should also be interpreted in the light of its historical and cultural environment.

Most false doctrine and heresy of Church history can be traced to a failure to adhere to these principles. Church history is filled with examples of disasters and wrecked lives wrought by men failing to base their doctrine, faith, and practice upon these two principles.

The Reformation, more than anything else, was caused by an embracing of the literal, grammatical, and historical method of interpretation, and a discarding of the allegorical method. The allegorical system had veiled the Church's understanding of many vital truths for nearly a thousand years.

Alexandria, the Beginning of Darkness

As briefly mentioned previously, darkness began to envelop the Church from the time the Theological school of Alexandria began to rise to prominence. Dr. J. Dwight Pentecost, in his book *Things to Come*, which is a classic in scholarly interpretation of prophecy, quotes F. W. Farrar concerning the impact of the Alexandrian school:

> It was in the great catechetical school of Alexandria, founded, as tradition says, by St. Mark, that there sprang up the chief school of Christian Exegesis. Its object, like that of Philo [a Jewish allegorist who loved Greek philosophy], was to unite philosophy with revelation, and thus to use the borrowed "jewels of Egypt" to adorn the sanctuary of God. Hence, CLEMENT of Alexandria and ORIGEN furnished the direct antithesis of TER-TULLIAN and IRENAEUS.
>
> The first teacher of the school who rose to fame was the venerable Pantaenus, a converted Stoic, of whose writings only a few fragments remain. He was succeeded by Clement of Alexandria, who, believing in the divine origin of Greek philosophy, openly propounded the principle that all Scripture must be allegorically understood.[3]

One of the main reasons, then, for the initial rise of the allegorical method of interpretation within the Church was to facilitate the integration of Greek philosophy with the inspired Scriptures.

Premier Church historian Philip Schaff, who was not a Premillennialist, gave an unbiased assessment of Origen's method of interpretation that was passed on to the Church at large.

> Origen was the first to lay down, in connection with the allegorical method of the Jewish Platonist, Philo, a formal theory of interpretation, which he carried out in a long series of exegetical works remarkable for industry and ingenuity, but meager in solid results. He considered the Bible a living organism, consisting of three elements which answer to the body, soul, and spirit of man, after

the Platonic psychology. Accordingly he attributed to the Scriptures a threefold sense: (1) a somatic [body], literal, or historical sense, furnished immediately by the meaning of the words, but only serving as a veil for a higher idea; (2) a psyche [soul] or moral sense, animating the first, and serving for general edification; (3) a pneumatic [spirit] or mystic and ideal sense, for those who stand on the high ground of philosophical knowledge. In the application of this theory he shows the same tendency as Philo, to spiritualize away the letter of Scripture . . . and instead of simply bringing out the sense of the Bible, HE PUTS INTO IT ALL SORTS OF FOREIGN IDEAS AND IRRELEVANT FANCIES.[4] (Emphasis mine.)

The Blessing and Curse of Augustine

Pentecost accurately points out the reason for the rapid adoption by the Church of Origen's views: "It was the rise of ecclesiasticism and the recognition of the authority of the church in all doctrinal matters that gave great impetus to the adoption of the allegorical method. Augustine, according to Farrar, was one of the first to make Scripture conform to the interpretation of the church."[5] Pentecost then quotes Farrar:

> The exegesis of St. Augustine is marked by the most glaring defects. . . . He laid down the rule that the Bible must be interpreted with reference to Church Orthodoxy, and that no Scriptural expression can be out of accordance with any other. . . .
> Snatching up the old Philonian and Rabinic rule which had been repeated for so many generations, that everything in Scripture which appeared to be unorthodox or immoral must be interpreted mystically, he introduced confusion into his dogma of supernatural inspiration by admitting that there are many passages "written by the Holy Ghost," which are objectionable when taken in their obvious sense. He also opened the door to arbitrary fancy. . . .
> When once the principle of allegory is admitted, when once we start with the rule that whole passages and books of the Scripture say one thing when they mean

another, the reader is delivered bound hand and foot to the caprice of the interpreter. He can be sure of absolutely nothing except what is dictated to him by the Church, and in all ages the authority of the Church has been falsely claimed for the presumptuous tyranny of false prevalent opinions.[6]

The record of Church history shows that *the Alexandrian school's system of allegorical interpretation of the Bible did not arise out of a pursuit of a better understanding of God's message, but rather out of the desire to integrate Greek philosophy with the Scriptures. It grew out of the erroneous assumption that these philosophies were equal in Divine inspiration with the Word of God.*

Augustine not only accepted this cursed allegorical method, but added another equally dangerous principle—that the Church has authority superior to the Scriptures. The Roman Popes later grabbed hold of this error and developed two even greater errors—Papal infallibility, and the exclusive authority of the Priests to interpret the Bible. This resulted in the Bible being removed from the common man's hands.

Augustine was both a blessing and a curse. He was a blessing in that he used a more literal method of interpretation in establishing the doctrine of justification by faith, which was orthodox.

He was a curse in that he so powerfully injected the allegorical method of interpretation into the bloodstream of the Church that it prevailed for over one thousand years. Virtually all Bible prophecy was viewed as allegory. Ironically, the Church later used his teachings concerning its superior authority over the Scriptures and the allegorical method of interpretation to explain away Augustine's orthodox view of justification by faith alone.

David Chilton helped me to understand where he got his method of interpretation when he said, as he was teaching a series on the Book of Revelation, "Believe me, this is not brainy David Chilton coming up with a bunch of new ideas. You know what I did? I went back to the Church Fathers and I read Saint Athenasius. I read Saint AUGUSTINE and saw what he had to say about the mark of the beast. He says some very profound things. I saw what the Church Fathers said about this stuff, and the kind of EXEGESIS they did. . . ."[7]

Chilton got his system of interpretation from studying the Church Fathers who had all swallowed Origen's allegorical system. In essence, he ignored the example of the Apostolic Fathers (who were virtually all literalists), leaped-frogged right over the lessons of the post-Reformation, and plunged head-long into the allegorical method of interpretation that gave us the Dark Ages.

The Impact of the Reformation on Interpretation

The courageous Bible scholar William Tyndale (1494–1536) was one of the important spiritual lamps who showed the way to the Reformation. He said concerning Biblical interpretation, "Thou shalt understand, therefore, that the Scripture hath but one sense, which is the literal sense. And that literal sense is the root and ground of all, and the anchor that never faileth, whereunto if thou cleave, thou canst never err or go out of the way. And if thou leave the literal sense, thou canst not but go out of the way."[8] He was tried and convicted of heresy by the Catholic Church for the terrible crime of translating the Bible into the common language of the people. For this "heinous act," he was burned at the stake. But thank God his work was not in vain. His martyrdom ignited the flames of reformation that spread to the Continent and Martin Luther. His translation work later became the basis for the King James Bible.

When Luther turned to the literal, grammatical, historical method of interpretation, the Reformation was born. Luther said, "Every word should be allowed to stand in its natural meaning and that should not be abandoned unless faith forces us to it. . . ."[9] Unfortunately, he applied this method to all Scriptures except to the interpretation of prophecy. There he continued in the tradition of Augustine.

Luther, nevertheless, was used in an extraordinary way to recover the doctrines of salvation. To stand on the edge of a theological precipice staring back into a thousand years of institutionalized spiritual darkness, and then, in spite of all of the consequences, to choose to stand on the literal, naked statements of the Word of God, was a remarkable demonstration of faith.

John Calvin was one of the first of the reformers to truly systematize and apply the literal grammatical method of interpretation. But there was one major problem. The reformers were not concerned with prophecy per se. They were primarily concerned with the doctrines of salvation.

The Forerunners of Serious Prophetic Studies

In the seventeenth century, a few scholars began to apply the light of the reformers' interpretive methods to the study of prophecy. The great scientist Sir Isaac Newton (A.D. 1643–1727) was one of those men who began to study prophecy as something other than just a collection of allegories, symbols, poems, and meaningless metaphors that had already been fulfilled in past history. After a lifetime of studying Bible prophecy, Newton acted as an unwitting prophet when he predicted the following: "About the time of the End a body of men will be raised up who will turn their attention to the prophecies, and insist upon their literal intepretation in the midst of much clamor and opposition."[10]

The Bible scholar Bishop Richard Hooker (1553–1600) was also a trailblazer for the literal interpretation of prophecy. He said the following about those who had followed in the tradition of Origen and Augustine: "I hold it for a most infallible rule, that where a literal construction will stand, the farthest from the letter is commonly the worst. Nothing is more dangerous than this licentious deluding art which changes the meaning of words as Alchemy does, or would do, the substance of metals, makes of anything what it lists, and brings in the end all truth to nothing."[11]

LITERAL, GRAMMATICAL, AND HISTORICAL INTERPRETATION DEFINED

To interpret literally does not mean that there is no recognition of allegories, parables, or figures of speech in the Scriptures. Once again, it means to take each word and passage in its plain, common, normal, literal sense unless the context clearly demands otherwise. Dr. David L. Cooper, Hebrew scholar and missionary to Israel, gave the golden rule of Biblical interpretation: "When the plain sense of Scripture makes common sense, seek no other sense; therefore, take every word at its primary, ordinary, usual literal meaning unless the facts of the immediate context, studied in the light of related passages and axiomatic and fundamental truths, indicate clearly otherwise."[12]

Cooper succinctly states the whole issue. This rule should be followed by all interpreters. When the Bible uses an allegory or figure of speech, it is usually obvious. But when an interpreter arbitrarily takes a passage that is obviously intended to be a literal statement of fact, and treats it as allegory, he is twisting the Word of God and knowingly perverting its meaning.

The following are some examples of how the Lord Jesus, the ultimate exegete, interpreted the Old Testament.

Example #1, Jesus Interpreted Literally

The Lord Jesus left us some supreme examples of how to interpret the Word of God. Jesus *literally* interpreted a prophecy about Himself in a debate with the Pharisees concerning what kind of person the Messiah would truly be.

Late in the LORD's ministry, the Pharisees engaged Him in a debate in order to trap Him in a statement they could use to convict Him of blasphemy. After a few questions, the Lord Jesus fired one question that immediately silenced them for the rest of His ministry. Here is the question that left them on the horns of a dilemma:

> **Now while the Pharisees were gathered together, Jesus asked them a question, saying, "What do you think about the Messiah, whose son is He?"**
>
> **They said to Him, "The son of David." He said to them, "Then why does David in the Spirit call Him 'LORD,' saying, 'The LORD said to MY LORD, "Sit at My right hand, until I put Thine enemies beneath Thy feet"'? If David then calls Him 'LORD,' how is He his son?"**
>
> **And no one was able to answer Him a word, nor did anyone dare from that day on to ask Him another question.** (Matthew 22:41–46 NASB)

The Lord Jesus baited a logical trap for the Pharisees. He knew that they would answer that the Messiah was to be the son of David. He then quoted from Psalm 110:1, reminding them that it was given by David under the inspiration of the Spirit of God, which He knew they also professed to believe. The LORD then forced them to see the logical inconsistency of their interpretation of this prophecy which He knew they all believed to refer to the Messiah. Jesus pointed out that David himself called his future descendant "Lord," a title reserved for Deity. He drove home the fact that there were two persons called **LORD** in this prophecy, and that the second party, whom David called, **"My LORD,"** was the Messiah, David's greater son.

The dilemma was this, how could David's own son also be his Lord?

If the Messiah was only to be the physical descendant of David, then why did David, under the inspiration of the Holy Spirit, call Him by a title of Deity?

The only answer was that the Messiah would not only be a true man, but also God. No wonder the Pharisees kept quiet. They either had to completely change their theology and admit that the Messiah was to be a God-Man, which Jesus had taught from the beginning, or say that the Scriptures were in error. They couldn't admit either one of these to be true, so they kept quiet. A short time later they crucified Jesus for claiming to be God's own unique Son.

Now, this whole argument revolved around taking the clause **"The LORD said to my LORD"** literally. The Pharisees refused to do so because it didn't fit their preconceived theology. They held it impossible for God to become a man.

I believe that in the field of prophetic interpretation, Dominionists are making the same sort of errors today. As previously mentioned, Chilton teaches that there will be no personal Antichrist. Yet Second Thessalonians 2:1–12 clearly predicts such a person. But the Reconstructionists' doctrine of "optimism" hinders him from being objective with the passage. He cannot accept the clear teaching of this passage which says that the Man of Lawlessness will not only declare himself to be God, but personally oppose the Lord Jesus Christ at His Second Coming. The reason is because the Reconstructionists would have to admit that this present age will end in a great cataclysm and not with the Church conquering the world and establishing the Kingdom of God.

Example #2, Jesus Interpreted Grammatically

On another occasion, Jesus debated the Sadducees concerning the resurrection of the dead (which they didn't believe). His whole argument turned upon the Hebrew grammatical construction which described God as *perpetually being* the God of Abraham, Isaac, and Jacob. Jesus taught, **"But regarding the resurrection of the dead, have you not read that which was spoken to you by God, saying, 'I AM the God of Abraham, and the God of Isaac, and the God of Jacob'? He is not the God of the dead but of the living."** (Matthew 22:31–32 NASB)

Jesus quoted this from Exodus 3:6 and took it at literal face value. He testified that this is what God had said, and to Him it was the ultimate authority. His argument was based on a minute point of grammar. If the Scripture had said, "**I WAS the God of Abraham, Isaac, and Jacob**," then God would have indeed been the God of the dead. But since God used a grammatical construction in Hebrew that means continuous being, it revealed that Abraham, Isaac, and Jacob were alive before Him, and would continue to be alive, which necessitated a resurrection.

Example #3, Jesus Recognized Double Reference in Prophecy

One of the most instructive examples of the Lord Jesus' interpretations of prophecy is recorded in Luke 4:14–21:

> **Jesus returned to Galilee IN THE POWER OF THE SPIRIT, and news about him spread through the whole countryside. He taught in their synagogues and everyone praised him.**
>
> **He went to Nazareth, where he had been brought up, and on the Sabbath day he went into the synagogue, as was his custom. And He stood up to read. The scroll of the Prophet Isaiah was handed to him. Unrolling it, he found the place where it is written:**
>
> **"The SPIRIT OF THE LORD IS ON ME, because he had anointed me to preach good news to the poor. He has sent me to proclaim freedom for the prisoners and recovery of sight for the blind, to release the oppressed, to proclaim the year of the LORD's favor . . ."** [Jesus read to this point, then quit right in the middle of a sentence. See Isaiah 61:1–2 from which He was quoting.]
>
> **Then he roled up the scroll, gave it back to the attendant and sat down. The eyes of everyone in the synagogue were fastened on him, and he began by saying to them, "TODAY THIS SCRIPTURE IS FULFILLED IN YOUR HEARING."** (Emphases mine.)

Everyone in the synagogue was startled by Jesus' strange behavior. It was not customary to read only a short passage of Scripture. And it was absolutely unprecedented for a reader in the synagogue to quit in the middle of a sentence without completing it, especially when it dealt with this subject. But the statement that should have immediately brought the house down on its knees was, **"Today this Scripture is fulfilled in your hearing."** It was such an enormous claim that its full meaning didn't hit them immediately. When a person makes a claim like this, from a passage that all recognized as predicting the Messiah, one either falls on his face and worships him, or stones him for blasphemy.

But another imperative lesson Jesus taught relates to His method of interpreting the prophecy of Isaiah chapter sixty-one. Jesus demonstrates for us how to lead forth from the text the meaning of these vital and sometimes difficult prophecies.

As noted in the quote above, Jesus stopped in the middle of a sentence and rolled up the scroll. The very next clause of that sentence says, **". . . and the day of vengence of our God . . ."** (Isaiah 61:2b) A careful study of the context, beginning with this clause, reveals that it is a prophecy of the events connected with the Second Coming of Christ. Had Jesus continued, He could not have said, **"Today this Scripture is fulfilled in your hearing."** Associated with **"the day of vengence of our God"** are such things as: (1) comforting and restoring the believing remnant of Israel to the land; (2) rebuilding Jerusalem and the other devastated cities of Israel; (3) making Israel's remnant into priests of the LORD; (4) the Messiah personally bringing devastating judgment on the nations of the world which have afflicted Israel.

Reconstructionists believe that passages like this one apply to the destruction of Jerusalem. But there is no way that this passage can be applied to the judgment against Israel in A.D. 70 without twisting it beyond recognition. Nor can this be applied to the Church without allegorizing the meaning of the words into nonsense.

This is a classic case to demonstrate that prophecies may be separated only by a comma, yet as far as the time of fulfillment is concerned, they may be separated by centuries.

The most important point of interpretation is that Isaiah predicted events of the First and Second Coming within one sentence without any obvious initial indication that this was the case. Those who looked for the coming of the Messiah before His First Coming were perplexed as to just how such different themes of prophecy could both be true of the same person.

This is why some rabbis before Jesus developed a theory that there would be two Messiahs. One would be a Conquering King who would come at a time of global disaster and save Israel. This one they identified as the son of David. The other Messiah would be a Suffering Servant who would come in lowly humility and give Himself for the sins of the people. He was identified as a Son of Joseph. They did not realize that there would be only one Messiah who would come at two separate times in two different roles.

We can learn a very important lesson about interpreting prophecy by raising the question, "Why did God arrange Old Testament prophecy in this way?"

I believe that God did this to force men to take prophecy literally by faith, even though it might not at the time "seem reasonable." If a person of that era realized that he was a sinner in need of a savior, then he would be open to the claims Jesus made about being the "Suffering Messiah" who had come to give His life as a ransom for mankind.

But if a person was self-righteous and convinced that his law-keeping had purchased him salvation, as was the case in the majority of religious Jews, then he would not see a need for a humble Suffering Messiah to die for his sins. His religious views would make him unobjective concerning those prophecies that predicted such a Messiah, for he would see no need for Him. To this type, the portrait of the King-Messiah, who would deliver Israel from the oppression of Rome and establish it as ruler over the nations, would have the greatest appeal. For this reason, the fanatically zealous religious groups, known as the Pharisees and the Sadduccees, could not be objective when the Lord Jesus presented evidence that He was the Suffering Messiah who had come to save them from their sins. Their very religious zeal and self-righteousness blinded them to the clear, literal predictions of passages like Isaiah 53:1–12 and 49:1–6. In fact, most of their descendants still have a veil over their hearts.

This should serve as a lesson and a warning to us today. Both the Dominionists and the Premillennialists interpret literally and allegorically. *The issue is to let the text dictate when to interpret allegorically instead of our theological presuppositions.*

We must come to the Word of God with a humble dependence upon the Holy Spirit as our teacher, and take each Scripture at face value. We must not allegorize a Scripture that is clearly intended to be normal and literal simply because it doesn't fit our presuppositions and peculiar doctrinal system.

Are You the One Who Was to Come, or Should We Expect Someone Else?

Another case history that illustrates how Jesus interpreted prophecies with double reference occurred when John the Baptist was thrown into jail. Even John was apparently confused as to just how the strange turn of recent events fit into the prophecies concerning the Messiah. With him, the Divinely predicted herald of the Messiah, in jail, with opposition against the Lord Jesus growing daily, these prophecies must have been baffling. John's faith didn't waver, but he did want and need some clarifications as to just how these events fit into the forecast pattern of events.

John sent some of his disciples to ask Jesus, **"Are you the one who was to come, or should we expect someone else?"** (Matthew 11:3) It is obvious that even the great John the Baptizer was confused. John had an excellent overall knowledge of the Messianic predictions, but he could not reconcile the idea that Jesus could be both a humble submissive servant as well as a great conquering deliverer. This was not an academic question to John. He could see how the opposition to Jesus by both the religious and political leaders was rapidly growing. And Jesus was still teaching about "turning the other cheek."

A key to John's confusion can be found in the very prophecy that spoke of his mission and purpose. When John was officially interrogated by an inquisition board from the High Priest as to who he was, and as to the ground of authority for his message, he answered, **"I am the voice of one crying in the wilderness: 'Make straight the way of the LORD,' as the prophet Isaiah said."** (John 1:23 NKJV) John's answer meant: I am the prophetic Voice predicted by Isaiah; my mission is to prepare the way for the LORD God of Israel to appear on earth; my authority is from God Himself.

But it must be carefully noted that the context of Isaiah chapter forty, from which John quoted, primarily speaks of events associated with the Messiah's role in the Second Coming as Israel's Liberator and Conquering King. John must have thought, "This doesn't match Jesus' present message and action." However, the part of Isaiah chapter forty that John actually quoted was fulfilled in the First Coming. The rest of the context can only be fulfilled in the Messiah's Second Coming.

Jesus reassured John the Baptist by sending back to him the

following message: **"Go back and report to John what you hear and see: the blind receive sight, the lame walk, those who have leprosy are cured, the deaf hear, the dead are raised, and the good news is preached to the poor. Blessed is the man who does not fall away on account of Me."** (Matthew 11:4–5)

The fascinating thing about Jesus' message of reassurance is that He quotes from another prophecy (Isaiah 35:5–6a) that had only a partial fulfillment in His First Advent. The whole context is couched in events that will be connected with the Second Advent. But Jesus appealed to John's faith and in essence said to him, "Though you don't understand it all now, John, these miracles predicted by Isaiah are My credentials. So just trust Me! Don't stumble over Me because you're having trouble understanding how all the prophecies fit together."

The Mystery of Elijah's Coming

Another example of how Jesus interpreted a double reference prophecy also has to do with John the Baptist. This time the disciples were confused about the relationship of John the Baptist to Elijah. They asked Jesus, **" 'Why then do the teachers of the law say that Elijah must come first?' Jesus replied, 'To be sure, Elijah COMES** [literally, **is going to come**] **and WILL RESTORE all things. But I tell you, Elijah has already come, and they did not recognize him, but have done to him everything they wished'** . . . **Then the disciples understood that he was talking to them about John the Baptist."** (Matthew 17:10–13)

Note carefully how Jesus clearly said, **"To be sure, Elijah is going to come and will restore all things."** So Jesus emphatically promises that the real Elijah will yet come and prepare the way for the Second Advent. The following prophecies clearly apply to Elijah and the events connected with the Second Coming:

> **"See, I will send my messenger, who will prepare the way before me. Then suddenly the Lord you are seeking will come to his temple; the messenger of the covenant, whom you desire, will come," says the LORD Almighty.**
>
> **But who can endure the day of his coming? Who can stand when he appears? For he will be like a refiner's fire or a launderer's soap. He will sit as a refiner and purifier of silver; he will purify the LEVITES and refine**

them like gold and silver. Then the LORD will have men who will bring offerings in righteousness, and the offerings of JUDAH and JERUSALEM will be acceptable to the LORD, as in days gone by, as in former years. (Malachai 3:1–4)

See, I will send you the prophet Elijah before that great and dreadful day of the LORD comes. He will turn the hearts of the fathers to their children and the hearts of children to their fathers; or else I will come and strike the land with a curse. (Malachai 4:5–6)

The prophecy in Isaiah chapter forty that spoke of John the Baptist's ministry as forerunner of the LORD carefully calls him simply, **"The VOICE of one crying in the wilderness."** God always knew that Israel would reject the Messiah in His First Coming, so He sent a bona fide substitute in the spirit and power of Elijah. As Jesus said, **"And IF you are willing to accept it, this is Elijah who was to come."** (Matthew 11:14) The majority of Israel was not willing to accept it, so Elijah must yet come to restore their hearts to the faith of their fathers and make the offerings of Judah and Jerusalem acceptable.

The lesson is this: Part of the predictions of Isaiah and Malachai were fulfilled in John the Baptist. But the full scope of these prophecies can only be fulfilled in the time of the Second Advent when the real Elijah will return. Nowhere is the beauty of God's foreknowledge more resplendent than in this kind of double reference prophecy.

The Dominionists flatly deny the possibility of double-reference prophecy. This factor is critical to their novel interpretation of passages like Matthew chapters twenty-four and twenty-five, as I will show in chapter ten of this book.

THE APOSTLES INTERPRETED LITERALLY

There are examples of how the Apostles interpreted the Old Testament throughout the Book of Acts and the Epistles. Paul built his whole case for justification through faith from the Old Testament. In witness of this he wrote, **"But now a righteousness from God, apart from law, has been made known, to which the Law and the Prophets testify."** (Romans 3:21)

Paul's summation argument on the guilt of all men before

God is made from direct quotes from the Psalms and Isaiah. Each quote is taken in its normal, literal sense. (See Romans 3:10–20 and 4:1–8.)

Paul's argument for salvation by faith alone is based not only on literal interpretation, but also on a careful analysis of Biblical history. When Abraham was about seventy-seven years old, he became discouraged because God had not yet fulfilled His promise that he would have a son through whom he would become a great nation and bless the world. So God spoke to Abraham in a vision and reassured him, and added this promise: **"'Look now toward heaven, and count the stars if you are able to number them.' And He said to him, 'So shall your descendants be.'"** Abraham's response was, **"And he believed in the LORD, and He accounted it to him for righteousness."** (Genesis 15:5–6 NKJV)

After this, Abraham got impatient again and decided that God needed His help to fulfill the promise. The whole episode was the result of unbelief. Since his wife Sarah seemed to be barren, he took her handmaid, as was the practice of the world of that time, and got her pregnant. God was very displeased with Abraham because he not only was trying to help Him fulfill His promise by human means, but also committed the sin of following the world's standards of morality rather than God's. Israel is still paying for this lapse of faith because the resulting illegitimate son, Ishmael, became the father of the Arabs. The original enmity that existed between Ishmael and Isaac has been perpetuated by their descendants to this present day.

Because of Abraham's lapse of faith, God delayed fulfilling His promise until he was ninety-nine years old (Genesis 17:1). It was at that time that God gave the covenant of circumcision to Abraham.

Paul draws upon these literal facts in Romans 4:9–14, where he shows that God declared Abraham righteous in His sight on the basis of faith alone, apart from works or rituals.

Again, my main point is that Paul interpreted the events as literal history.

Peter Interprets a Prophecy with Double Reference

When Peter stood up to preach the Gospel on the Day of Pentecost, he had not only to explain the miraculous phenomenon of the one hundred and twenty Jewish believers speaking in various languages they had never learned, but to demonstrate from the Old Testament that this very thing had been predicted

69

and that it was an evidence of three things: first it was an evidence that the general time known as **"the last days"** had begun; second, it was an evidence that the Holy Spirit had been poured out upon the true believers; third, it was an evidence that special grace was available for all those who would in faith call upon the name of the LORD to be saved. (See Acts 2:14–21.)

Peter drew upon and developed only these three points in his message. But when we put Peter's quote from Joel 2:28–32 back into its entire original context, it becomes clear that other prophetic aspects of this quote were not developed because there was no conceivable way they could have been fulfilled either at that time or in A.D. 70 as Dominion theologians contend. Read carefully the prophecy in its original context:

> I will show wonders in the heavens and on the earth, blood and fire and billows of smoke. The sun will be turned to darkness and the moon to blood BEFORE THE COMING OF THE GREAT AND DREADFUL DAY OF THE LORD. And everyone who calls on the name of the LORD will be saved; for on Mount Zion and in Jerusalem there will be deliverance, as the LORD has said, among the SURVIVORS whom the LORD calls.
>
> IN THOSE DAYS AND AT THAT TIME, when I restore the fortunes of Judah and Jerusalem, I WILL GATHER ALL NATIONS and bring them down to the Valley of Jehoshaphat. There I WILL ENTER JUDGMENT AGAINST THEM CONCERNING my inheritance, MY PEOPLE ISRAEL, for they scattered my people among the nations and divided up my land. They cast lots for my people and traded boys for prostitutes; they sold girls for wine that they might drink. (Joel 2:30–3:3)
>
> [And again in the same context] Proclaim this among the nations: Prepare for war! Rouse the warriors! Let all the fighting men draw near and attack. Beat your plowshares into swords and your pruning hooks into spears. Let the weakling say, "I am strong!" Come quickly, all you nations from every side, and assemble there.
>
> Bring down your warriors, O LORD!
>
> "Let the nations be roused; let them advance into the Valley of Jehoshaphat, for there I WILL SIT TO

70

JUDGE ALL THE NATIONS ON EVERY SIDE. [This refers to the same judgment as Matthew 25:31–46.]

"Swing the sickle, for the harvest is ripe. Come, trample the grapes, for the winepress is full and the vats overflow—so great is their wickedness!" [This is also predicted in Revelation 14:14–20.]

Multitudes, multitudes in the valley of decision! For THE DAY OF THE LORD IS NEAR IN THE VALLEY OF DECISION. The sun and moon will be darkened, and the stars no longer shine. The LORD will roar from Zion and thunder from Jerusalem; the earth and the sky will tremble. But the LORD will be a refuge for HIS PEOPLE, a stronghold for THE PEOPLE OF ISRAEL.

"THEN you will know that I the LORD your God, dwell in Zion, my holy hill. Jerusalem will be holy; never again WILL FOREIGNERS INVADE HER. [Jerusalem has seen multiple invasions since A.D. 70.]

"IN THAT DAY the mountains will drip new wine, and the hills will flow with milk; all the ravines of Judah will run with water. A fountain will flow out of the LORD's house and will water the valley of acacias [i.e., the Wadi al Arabah that extends from the Dead Sea to the Gulf of Eilat] [This is also predicted in Zechariah 14:8]. . . .

"Judah will be inhabited forever and Jerusalem through all generations. THEIR BLOODGUILT, WHICH I HAVE NOT PARDONED, I WILL PARDON." [This includes their guilt for rejecting the Messiah.]

The LORD dwells in Zion! (Joel 3:9–21) (Emphases mine.)

I quoted this lengthy passage because it is imperative to see in context all of the events that are necessary for its greater fulfillment. There is simply no way to be honest with the normal, literal meaning of the passage and say that it was ALL fulfilled on the Day of Pentecost, or in the destruction of Jerusalem in A.D. 70. This has to be another case of a prophecy with a double reference for some of the following reasons:

First, God did not darken the sun and turn the moon to the appearance of blood on the Day of Pentecost. Nor did he show astrological wonders in the heavens. There was no blood, fire, and billows of smoke.

All of these things are consistently associated with the great war of Divine judgment upon the NATIONS, which is stated in this prophetic context (Joel 3:2, 9–16), and in numerous other prophecies about this same event. Chilton writes that these things occurred during the destruction of Jerusalem in A.D. 70.[13] If this is so, then they occurred thirty-seven years after Peter said on the Day of Pentecost, "**This is what was spoken by the prophet Joel.**" This means that even in Chilton's interpretation, he admits that this is a prophecy with a double reference, which on other occasions he tries to deny exists in Scripture. About this, Chilton writes, "Contrary to some modern expositions of this text, Peter did not say that the miracles of Pentecost were *like* what Joel prophesied, or that they were some sort of 'proto-fulfillments' of Joel's prophecy; he said that this was the fulfillment: '*This* is *that* which was spoken of through the prophet Joel.' The last days were here: the Spirit had been poured out, God's people were prophesying and speaking in tongues, and Jerusalem *would be* destroyed with fire."[14] (Emphasis mine. Note the shift to future tense when he refers to the destruction of Jerusalem, thus admitting double reference.)

The difference is that Premillennialists say that the gap between the partial fulfillment on the Day of Pentecost, and its ultimate fulfillment on **the great and dreadful day of the LORD** is much longer than thirty-seven years.

Second, God did not *restore* the fortunes of Judah and Jerusalem in A.D. 70. He *removed* them. This prophecy clearly has to do with the fulfillment of the unconditional Palestinian Covenant to Israel's believing remnant at the Second Advent. (I will examine this covenant in detail in chapter five.)

Third, God did not bring all the nations to **the Valley of Jehoshaphat** (between Jerusalem and the Mount of Olives) and judge them for afflicting and scattering His people Israel. Chilton's contention that the prophecy of Joel was ultimately fulfilled in the A.D. 70 destruction of Jerusalem is impossible to fit into this context. Such an interpretation is ludicrous: the very opposite of what Chilton contends happened in A.D. 70. *This prophecy predicts the NATIONS will be judged for what they did to Jerusalem and for scattering Israel among the nations.* The Romans destroyed Jerusalem and scattered the survivors throughout the nations until this day. What they did in A.D. 70 *is the very thing* for which this prophecy declares the nations will be judged. In Joel's prophecy it is the GENTILE NATIONS that are going to be judged, *not* Israel.

72

This is just one of the numerous cases in which Chilton and the Dominionists disregard the original context of a prophecy quoted in the New Testament in order to superimpose their preconceived system upon it.

Fourth, Joel predicts that **"in those days and at that time"** God will RESTORE the fortunes of Judah and Jerusalem, not take them away and give them to the Church. Chilton says about the significance of the A.D. 70 holocaust:

> The divinely ordained cataclysm of A.D. 70 revealed that Christ had taken the Kingdom from Israel and given it to the Church; the desolation of the old Temple was the FINAL SIGN that God had deserted it and was now dwelling in a new Temple, the Church. These were all aspects of the First Advent of Christ, crucial parts of the work He came to accomplish by His death, resurrection, and ascension to the throne. This is why the Bible speaks of the outpouring of the Holy Spirit upon the Church and the destruction of Israel as being *the same event*, for they were intimately connected theologically. The prophet Joel foretold both the Day of Pentecost and the destruction of Jerusalem in one breath. . . . Peter's inspired interpretation of this text in Acts 2 determines the fact that Joel is speaking of the period from the initial outpouring of the Spirit to the destruction of Jerusalem, from Pentecost to Holocaust.[15] (Emphasis mine.)

If in fact Chilton's interpretation is correct, then God is a liar. This prophecy not only explicitly anticipated the destruction of Israel and the dispersion of its people, but predicted their restoration (Joel 3:1, 17–20), their forgiveness for bloodguilt (3:21), and the destruction of the nations who have mistreated them (3:2-3, 9–16).

This prophecy was fulfilled only in part on the Day of Pentecost. It will be completely fulfilled at the Second Coming of Jesus, the Messiah. So often in the Bible, prophecy is made in this way. The partial fulfillment actually becomes an illustration of the future greater fulfillment and helps to illuminate its ultimate fulfillment.

The Dominionists have made havoc of Biblical prophecy by refusing to interpret passages like this literally and in their Old Testament context.

The Apostolic Fathers Interpreted Literally

When we speak of the Apostolic Fathers, we are referring to those who were direct first and second generation disciples of the original Apostles. Their example of interpretation, especially of prophecy, is of great value since it reflects the method taught them by the Apostles.

Church historian Thomas Ice writes, "Premillennialism was the pervasive view of the earliest orthodox Fathers. This is the consensus of both liberal and conservative scholars in historical theology. J.N.D. Kelly, acknowledged internationally as an authority on patristic Christian thought, is typical of the scholarly opinion on this question and notes that the early Church was 'chiliastic' or millenarian in its eschatology."[16] Kelly, as quoted by Ice, observes concerning the eschatology of the second century:

> Millenarianism, or the theory that the returned Christ would reign on earth for a thousand years, came to find increasing support among Christian teachers. . . . This millenarian, or "chiliastic," doctrine was widely popular at this time.[17]

Kelly casts further light on the prophetic views of the Apostolic Fathers through the middle of the third century by observing:

> The great theologians who followed the Apologists, Irenaeus, Tertullian and Hippolytus, were primarily concerned to defend the traditional eschatological scheme against Gnosticism. . . . THEY WERE ALL EXPONENTS OF MILLENARIANISM.[18] (Emphasis added.)

Robert Clouse, a church historian who specializes in the history of eschatology, when speaking of the Premillennialism of the early Church wrote, "This hope [Premillennialism] seems to have been the prevailing eschatology during the first three centuries of the Christian era, and is found in the works of Papias, Irenaeus, Justin Martyr, Tertullian, Hippolytus, Methodius, Commodianus, and Latantius."[19]

Cambridge scholar and Church historian Henry Melvill Gwatkin (1844–1916) comments about Eusebius' quote of Bishop Papias' millennial view, "Papias, Bishop of Hierapolis in Phrygia (cir. 130), is chiefly known to us from the chapter of Eusebius [a well-known fourth-century historian] here given. It will be noted that Eusebius dislikes him for his Millenarianism, and probably does him less than justice."[20]

Gwatkin then gives Eusebius' quote on Papias, "The same writer [Papias] has recorded other notices as having come down to him from oral tradition, certain strange parables of the Savior's and teachings of His, and some other statements of rather mythical character. For example, he says that there will be a period of about a thousand years after the resurrection, and that the kingdom of Christ will be set up in material form on this earth."[21] Papias was a companion of Polycarp and had actually heard the Apostle John teach, so his testimony concerning the millennium surely reflects his views. Eusebius was a devout follower of Origen's allegorical school. He shared Origen's love for Greek philosophy, which viewed all physical things as evil. The idea of an earthly, physical Kingdom of God would have been especially offensive to him. This is the main reason why he spoke of Papias' view in a derogatory way.

Kelly again observes conclusive evidence that Premillennialism was the dominant view of the earliest Church Fathers:

> Irenaeus, for example, treats *the hope of a resplendent earthly Jerusalem as traditional orthodoxy*, and protests against attempts to allegorize away the great texts of the Old Testament and Revelation which appear to look forward to it. Tertullian likewise, after establishing the reality of Christ's heavenly kingdom, adds that this by no means excludes an earthly kingdom also. In fact, the latter is due to come before the former, and it will last for a thousand years.[22]

Irenaeus clearly believed in the literal promises of the Old Testament and the Book of Revelation concerning not only an earthly Messianic Kingdom, but also concerning the literal restoration and glorification of Jerusalem. The views of Irenaeus, the disciple of the great Apostolic Father Polycarp who was directly discipled by the Apostle John, must be given great importance.

Competent scholarship agrees that the first three and a half centuries of the Church held to a Premillennial view of eschatology. They interpreted the Old Testament prophecies and Revelation, especially chapter twenty, verses one through ten, in a normal, literal sense.

History reveals that Premillennialism was not contradicted by a single orthodox Church Father until the beginning of the third century, when Gaius first launched an attack against it. Gaius is the first one in recorded Church history who interpreted the thousand years symbolically. He also rejected the Book of Revelation because he held that it was written by the heretic Cerinthus.[23]

Sometimes you can tell the validity of a truth as much by its enemies as by its friends. Thomas Ice observes, "Premillennialism was attacked by the Alexandrian school in Egypt during the middle of the third century, and Augustine's influence prevailed against it by the fifth century. Clement of Alexandria and his pupil Origen popularized not so much another view as an antichiliastic polemic."[24]

Ice accurately observes the destructive effect upon the Church of Origen's anti-millenarian doctrines by quoting *Dutch Amillennialist* H. Hoekstra:

> The attack against Chiliasm by these dissenters cannot meet with our approval, for they placed their speculation above the Word of God and distorted it according to their grandiloquent ideas, denying the resurrection of the body and the future glorification of the material world, which was also created by God; for according to them the material world, matter, contained sin from which the spirit of man must liberate itself. It was only natural as a matter of course that they were very much against Chiliasm, but they threw away, as a German saying goes, with the bath water the baby also. They were a kind of Hymenaeus and Philetus who had departed from the truth, saying the resurrection was past already (2 Tim. 2:17). The success of the pernicious principles of this school was the first and chief cause of the decline of Chiliasm.[25]

In the light of these statements by scholars from both liberal, conservative, and Amillennial schools, it is extremely hard to know where David Chilton was coming from when he boldly said,

"The notion that the reign of Christ is something wholly future, to be brought in by some great social cataclysm, *is not a Christian doctrine*. It is an unorthodox teaching, generally espoused by heretical sects on the fringes of the Christian Church."[26] If Chilton is correct, then the Apostolic and Church Fathers from the first century through the middle of the third century "were all heretics on the fringes of the true Church."

Chilton even goes so far as to call Premillennialism a heresy. In so doing, he is even in disagreement with his mentor, Gary North, who sponsored him to write *Paradise Restored* and *Days of Vengeance*. North says concerning the origins of Premillennialism, "Historically, the church has had defenders of all three positions. *The early church fathers were mainly premillennial* or postmillennial. The Roman Catholics after Augustine [early fourth century] became amillennial, although there were occasional postmillennial revivals."[27] (Emphasis mine.) Although I haven't seen any evidence whatsoever for Postmillennialism in the early centuries, I do appreciate North's candor in admitting the early domination of Premillennialism in the Church. What all this does reveal is that Chilton interprets history with the same "allegorical elasticity" as he does the Scripture. He makes it mean what his presuppositions demand it should mean. Once again on another crucial point, the facts reveal Chilton's inaccuracy.

The Alexandrian Legacy

In summary, the Apostolic and early Church Fathers all interpreted prophecy literally. As a result, Premillennialism was the orthodox view of the Church through the middle of the third century. It was only disputed after the Alexandrian school began to teach allegorical interpretation of Scripture in order to introduce Greek philosophy into Christian doctrine.

Literal, grammatical, historical interpretation (which recognizes that there are parables and allegories in the Bible) was the method used by our Lord Jesus Christ, the Apostles, and the early Church Fathers. The Church plunged into the Dark Ages when the allegorical method of interpretation from the school of Alexandria became widely accepted. The Reformation occurred when the literal method was recovered. History teaches us a consistent and clear lesson in all of this.

Let us not allow history to repeat itself by going back to a method of interpretation that has not only been proven to be false in history, but the cause of terrible, inexcusable suffering for "the lost sheep of the house of Israel."

CHAPTER FOUR

When God Swears, Men Beware

When God made his promise to Abraham, since there was no one greater for him to swear by, he swore by himself, saying, "I will surely bless you and give you many descendants." . . . Because God wanted to make the unchanging nature of his purpose very clear to the heirs of what was promised, he confirmed it with an oath.

Hebrews 7:13, 14, 17

THE UNCONDITIONAL COVENANTS

From the twelfth chapter of Genesis onward, the rest of the Biblical message is related to four unconditional covenants which God made with Abraham and his descendants through Isaac and Jacob. Not only Israel's destiny, but indeed the destiny of the whole world is secured by these covenants. Without an understanding of these covenants, it is impossible to know what the Bible is all about.

A knowledge of these four unconditional covenants is necessary to understand whether or not Israel has a future as a special nation and people. A study of these covenants will also help to clarify the mission and purpose of the Church. It will require your prayerful concentration, but the rewards are great.

On a personal note, this review has given me a renewed confidence in God's Faithfulness to keep His Word even when we

79

fail. I believe that this kind of confidence is one of the most important factors in living a victorious Christian life. In these days of intense spiritual warfare, even the spiritual generals of the Church are being wounded, so it is more important than ever to learn about God's grace and faithfulness.

The Abrahamic Covenant

It is truly amazing that the whole history of the human race was affected by a private covenant that God made with one man and one specific line of his descendants. At a time when all nations were determined to push the knowledge of God out of their cultures and memories, God chose a man from whom He would create a nation and through which He would preserve the true knowledge of Himself. God's purpose was to reach out from this nation and provide salvation for all the other nations.

Here is a summary of the main reasons why God chose Israel:

First, to demonstrate to the world through Israel His existence, His reality, and the blessings of knowing Him. God accomplished this through Israel in times of both faith and faithlessness.

Second, Israel was to receive, write, and preserve God's Word for mankind.

Third, the Savior of the world was to be born physically as an Israelite.

Fourth, Israel was to spread God's message of salvation to the world.

The most important and foundational covenant in the Bible is the one God made with Abraham. God's plan for all mankind is laid out in broad outline within this covenant.

God made the original covenant with Abraham in the form of four direct and three understood **"I wills."** This is the LORD's consistent formula for expressing unconditional promises. The only requirement on Abraham's part was to, by faith, leave his country, his home, his family, and to travel to a land which God would show him (see Genesis 12:1).

This is the record of what God originally promised Abraham:

I WILL make you a great nation,	Promise of a Nation
I WILL bless you,	Promise of personal blessing
and make your name great,	
and so you shall be a blessing;	
I WILL bless those who bless you,	Promise against anti-Semitism

80

I WILL curse those who curse you. And IN YOU all the families of the earth shall be blessed (Genesis 12:2–3 NASB)

Promise of Divine blessing for the world through Abraham

God's ultimate purpose for calling Abraham and creating a nation from him was revealed in the original covenant. It was to bring Divine blessing upon all the families of the earth. This covenant was later expanded in all its facets.

In the first **"I WILL,"** God promises to make of Abraham **a great nation.** This inherently contained the promise of a son through whom this Nation could be created. It was also implicit that this covenant would extend to that Nation.

The second **"I WILL"** promised three things to Abraham personally. (1) God promised to bless him. God made Abraham a very rich man, blessed him with vibrant health even into old age, and prospered him in all his doings. (2) He promised to make his name great. The name of Abraham has been known and honored throughout the world for almost four thousand years. Three of the world's largest religions reverence him as a founder; Christianity, Judaism, and Islam. (3) Abraham's example of faith has been a blessing to millions.

God's Warning to Anti-Semites

The third and fourth **"I WILLS"** anticipated that Abraham and his seed would be the objects of Satanic attack. In view of their special mission of redemption, it is only logical that they would be singled out as prime targets by the devil. Anti-Semitism has been a consistent fact of history from the beginning of Abraham's family. Because of this, the LORD issued a strong promise of blessing to those who would help His people, and a severe warning to those who would deliberately harm them.

This same promise was restated by Isaac as he gave the Divine blessing to Jacob: **". . . Cursed be those who curse you, and blessed be those who bless you."** (Genesis 27:29b NASB) Almost four hundred years later, God made even the apostate prophet Balaam pronounce this solemn warning to King Balak, who had hired him to curse the Nation of Israel: **". . . How shall I curse, whom God has not cursed? And how can I denounce, whom the LORD has not denounced? . . . Blessed is everyone who blesses you [Israel], and cursed is everyone who curses you. "** (Numbers

23:8 and 24:9b NASB) These verses prove conclusively that this promise of Divine protection extended not only to Abraham, Isaac, and Jacob but to their descendants.

God has been faithful to carry out this promise throughout history. Egypt, Assyria, Babylon, Persia, and Greece, to mention only a few nations from ancient history, all in turn afflicted Israel and were destroyed.

In modern times, there are also demonstrable cases. When Napoléon began his conquests, he was favorable toward the Jews. Then he turned against them and his dreams of a Europe united under his control were buried under the snows of the Russian winter. He was finally defeated at Waterloo.

There was a time when the sun never sat upon the Union Jack of the British Empire. At the height of its power, the British Empire was a haven of protection for the dispersed Israelites. Then British policy-makers decided that their need for Arab oil was greater than their need to honor promises made in the Balfour Declaration, which provided for the establishment of a national homeland for the Jews in Palestine. The "White Paper" was issued in the early 1930s which prevented Jews from immigrating to Palestine. This helped assure that millions would be trapped in Hitler's "Final Solution." The British Empire was dismantled in the aftermath of World War II, and today it is only a shadow of its illustrious past. Hitler's Third Reich was to last "a thousand years." It was buried in the rubble of total defeat just over thirteen years after its birth.

Even though God has used nations to discipline Israel for sin, they have all been judged for their mistreatment of the Israelites. The subject of a great deal of prophetic Scripture is a warning to the Gentile nations that they are going to be judged for harming God's people, Israel.

The Curse Still Valid at the Second Advent

The LORD Jesus predicts the judgment He will conduct on earth at His Second Coming immediately after the cataclysmic events described in Matthew chapter twenty-four: **"But when the Son of Man comes in His glory, and all the angels with Him, then He will sit on His glorious throne. And all the nations [the Gentiles] will be gathered before Him; and He will separate them from one another, as the shepherd separates the sheep from the goats . . ."** (Matthew 25:31–32 NASB)

The context demands that the Greek words, τα εθνη, be translated **"the Gentiles"** instead of **"the nations."** This judgment determines whether the one judged receives eternal life with Christ or eternal damnation in the Lake of Fire. No people can have their eternal destinies judged corporately. This is something that can only be done with individuals. In the Bible, nations (plural) commonly means Gentiles in contradistinction to the Nation of Israel.

Even in Christ's judgment of the survivors of the Tribulation, the Gentiles are judged on the basis of how they helped or didn't help the ones Jesus calls **His brothers**.

About those who help **Jesus' brothers**, it is written, **"Then the King will say to those on his right, 'Come, you who are BLESSED by my Father; take your inheritance, the kingdom prepared for you since the creation of the world.'"** (Matthew 25:34) The LORD enumerates all of the things the righteous Gentiles are credited as doing for Him *personally.* Then they ask the LORD when they did all of these things for *Him,* and He replies, **". . . I tell you the truth, whatever you did for ONE OF THE LEAST OF THESE BROTHERS OF MINE, you did for me."** (Matthew 25:40)

About those who failed to help His brothers, Jesus warns, **"Then he will say to those on his left, 'Depart from me, you who are CURSED, into the eternal fire prepared for the devil and his angels.'"** (Matthew 25:41) After the LORD goes through the list of things they *did not do for Him personally,* these unbelievers reply, **"Lord, when did we see you hungry or thirsty or a stranger or needing clothes or sick or in prison, and did not help you?" "He will reply, 'I tell you the truth, whatever you did not do for ONE OF THE LEAST OF THESE** [i.e. His brothers], **you did not do for me.' Then they will go away to eternal punishment, but the righteous to eternal life."** (Matthew 25:44–46)

Who Are the Messiah's Brothers?

Who are the people Jesus calls **"these brothers of mine"**? The answer to this question is of utmost importance. Note that this is an exclusive judgment involving both believing and nonbelieving **"Gentiles"** who survive the terrible period described in Matthew chapter twenty-four. So the statement, **"these brothers of mine,"** cannot refer to believing Gentiles. And note that there are no Israelites involved at all in this judgment. The Israelites' judgment at this point in history is described as separate and segregated. (Ezekiel 20:33–40)

All the evidences of the context and parallel passages demand that the group the LORD Jesus calls "His brothers" are believing Israelites. No doubt this will be especially applicable to the 144,000 Israelites who will be the LORD's main evangelists during the seven-year Tribulation period that immediately precedes His Return.

They will be men with a price on their heads. The Antichrist and all his forces will target them for special wrath. It is also certain that they will be persecuted as few of the LORD's servants ever have been. It is easy to see how this group will suffer the hunger, thirst, estrangement, nakedness, sickness, and imprisonment described in Matthew 25:35–36. These conditions will come upon them because they will not only be exposing the deceptions of the Antichrist and his religion, but they will refuse his number. Without the number of his name, which is described as 666, they will not be able to buy, sell, or obtain money (Revelation 13:16–18). This will make them dependent upon the generosity of their converts. Only those who believe God's Word will dare to help this group, since to do so will endanger their lives. This is why helping them is considered proof of their true faith by the LORD.

It is important to note that this judgment will be administered according to the terms of the anti-Semitic article of the Abrahamic Covenant. The terminology the LORD Jesus uses in this judgment is the same as that used in the Abrahamic Covenant. The righteous are called **blessed** for blessing the Israelites, and the unrighteous are called **cursed** for cursing and not helping them.

So this remarkable prophecy by the LORD Jesus Christ Himself gives clear warning that all Gentiles will be judged on the basis of the anti-Semitic section of the Abrahamic Covenant. This also demonstrates that the covenant is in effect right up to the establishment of the Kingdom of God on earth.

A Word for the Rapture

It is important to note in passing that this also proves that the Church will not be in the Tribulation. If it were, there could be no segregated judgment, since in the Church there is no distinction between Jew and Gentile. The conditions reflected here are the same as those that existed during the past age of Israel's preeminence. This agrees with the conditions necessary to fulfill Daniel's predicted Seventieth Week (Daniel 9:24–27), in which Israel will receive her final allotment of seven years to complete her tests and receive her kingdom.

The Promise on Which World Salvation Hangs

The fifth **"I will"** in which the LORD promises to bless all the families of the earth through Abraham predicts in embryonic form the provision of salvation for the whole world through one of Abraham's seeds. It shows that the ultimate purpose of God through Abraham and his seed is redemptive. This is why the Lord Jesus later said, **". . . salvation is from the Jews."** (John 4:22)

The Promise of the Land and Descendants

In the only conditional part of the Abrahamic covenant, the LORD had said to Abram (whom God later renamed Abraham), **"Go forth from your country, and from your relatives and from your father's house, to the LAND which I will show you . . ."** **(Genesis 12:1 NASB)** When Abram obeyed this one condition, and arrived in the land, the LORD added these promises to the original covenant: **"And the LORD appeared to Abram and said, 'To YOUR DESCENDANTS I WILL give this LAND.'"** And, **". . . for all the LAND which you see, I WILL give it TO YOU and TO YOUR DESCENDANTS FOREVER. And I WILL make YOUR DESCENDANTS as the dust of the earth; so that if anyone can number the dust of the earth, then your descendants can also be numbered."** (Genesis 12:7 and 13:15–16 NASB)

This enlargement of the original covenant unconditionally promised three primary things. First, Abraham was promised innumerable *descendants*. Second, he was promised *a very specific plot of real estate*. Third, he was promised that both he and his descendants would possess that land *forever*.

The Two Most Important Questions

The big argument concerning this covenant has centered around three questions: Was this covenant in fact truly unconditional? Who are Abraham's true descendants? How long is forever? I will deal with the second and third questions in detail in the chapters six through eight of this book. The question of whether this

85

covenant was in fact unconditional was conclusively answered by Dr. John Walvoord as quoted by Pentecost:

(1) All Israel's covenants are unconditional except the Mosaic. The Abrahamic Covenant is expressly declared to be eternal and therefore unconditional in numerous passages (Gen. 17:7, 3, 13, 19; 1 Chron. 16:17; Psa. 105:10). The Palestinian Covenant is likewise declared to be everlasting (Ezek. 16:60). The Davidic Covenant is declared to be everlasting in the same terms (2 Sam. 7:13, 16, 19; 1 Chron. 17:12; 22:10; Isa. 55:3; Ezek. 37:25). The New Covenant with Israel is also eternal (Isa. 61:8; Jer. 32:40; 50:5; Heb. 13:20).

(2) Except for the original condition of leaving his homeland and going to the promised land, the covenant is made with no conditions whatever.

(3) The Abrahamic Covenant is confirmed repeatedly by reiteration and enlargement. In none of these instances are any of the added promises conditioned upon the faithfulness of Abraham's seed or of Abraham himself . . . nothing is said about its being conditioned upon the future faithfulness of either Abraham or his seed.

(4) The Abrahamic Covenant was solemnized by a divinely ordered ritual symbolizing the shedding of blood and passing between the parts of the sacrifice (Gen. 15:7–21; Jer. 34:18). This ceremony was given to Abraham as an assurance that his seed would inherit the land in the exact boundaries given to him in Genesis 15:18–21. No conditions whatever are attached to this promise in this context.

(5) To distinguish those who would inherit the promises as individuals from those who were only physical seed of Abraham, the visible sign of circumcision was given (Gen. 17:9–14). One not circumcised was considered outside the promised blessing. The ultimate fulfillment of the Abrahamic Covenant and possession of the land by the seed is not hinged, however, upon faithfulness in the matter of circumcision. In fact the promises of the land were given before the rite was introduced.

(6) The Abrahamic Covenant was confirmed by the

birth of Isaac and Jacob to both of whom the promises are repeated in their original form (Gen. 17:19; 28–13) . . .

(7) Notable is the fact that the reiterations of the covenant and the partial early fulfillment of the covenant *are in spite of acts of disobedience*. It is clear that on several instances Abraham strayed from the will of God. [Yet] in the very act [of disobedience], the promises are repeated to him.

(8) The later confirmations of the covenant are given in the midst of apostasy. Important is the promise given through Jeremiah that Israel as a nation will continue forever (Jer. 31:36) . . .

(9) The New Testament declares the Abrahamic Covenant immutable (Heb. 6:13–18; cf. Gen. 15:8–21). It was not only promised but solemnly confirmed by the oath of God.

(10) The entire Scriptural revelation concerning Israel and its future as contained in both the Old and New Testaments, if interpreted literally, confirms and sustains the unconditional character of the promises given to Abraham.[1]

Taken at face value and read normally, the Abrahamic Covenant and its enlargements should settle all arguments about the future of the nation of Israel. But Israel has had, and still has, some determined foes. It is for this reason that we will carefully analyze the other unconditional covenants God made with Abraham's descendants in the next chapter.

Remember, what is at stake is whether God keeps His promises, and that is of utmost importance to us all.

THE PALESTINIAN COVENANT

No other people's life and welfare has ever been so inseparably bound to a land in the way Israel is linked to the land of Palestine. Consider these facts:

- Being in the land is a sign of God's continued acceptance and blessing upon Israel. Israel out of the land is a sign of God's rejection and judgment.
- Israel can only be a Nation under God in the land He promised them.

- Israel can only receive the promised Kingdom of God while in possession of its ancient homeland.
- Israel's covenant blessings are inextricably woven together with specific places and conditions in the promised land.
- The Messiah's coming in Glory is specifically linked to geographical places in the promised land.
- A main feature in the promises of the Messiah's coming is that He will restore the believing remnant of Israel to the land.

These are some of the reasons why the Palestinian Covenant is one of the most important and strongly verified of all God's covenants. In it, God promised to Israel a very specific parcel of real estate which it has never yet possessed.

The promises in this covenant relating to the land of Israel give strong and objective proof that there must be a future Messianic Kingdom established for Israel *in history,* not just in eternity.

After Abram obeyed God and moved to what was then called the land of Canaan, God appeared to him and said, ". . . **To your OFFSPRING I will give this land."** (Genesis 12:7) The Palestinian Covenant was specifically made with Abraham's **offspring** from the very beginning of his sojourn in the land.

God soon gave more details concerning this covenant when Abraham demonstrated his faith in it. This was shown by the way he graciously allowed his nephew Lot to choose a parcel of land:

> **The LORD said to Abram after Lot had parted from him, "Lift up your eyes from where you are and look north and south, east and west. All the land that you see I will give to you and YOUR OFFSPRING FOREVER.**
>
> **I will make your offspring like the dust of the earth, so that if anyone could count the dust, then your offspring could be counted. Go, walk through the length and breadth of the land, for I am giving it to you."**
> (Genesis 13:14–17)

God's revelation to Abraham not only enlarged his understanding of how much land was to be given, but also introduced the fact that the gift would be everlasting.

The LORD also clarified and expanded His promise to give

Abraham children. Up until this point, the issue of offspring was only implicitly promised.

When Abraham became discouraged after a few years had passed and he still had no child, the LORD appeared and sought to encourage him, **"Do not be afraid, Abram. I am your shield, your very great reward."** But Abraham complained, **"How can you give me anything when I am childless and have no heir?"** (See Genesis 15:1–5.)

An Unusual Title-deed for Real Estate

Even after Abram believed the LORD concerning a promised son who would come from his own body, and offspring as numerous as the stars of heaven, he still wanted more assurance regarding the possession of the land: **"But Abram said, 'O Sovereign LORD, how can I know that I will gain possession of it** [the land]?'" (Genesis 15:8) God's response is one of the greatest demonstrations of just how patient and gracious He is. God chose to accommodate Abram's continuing need for strong reassurance. He did this by performing a strange covenant-making ritual that was the most solemn and binding known to man at that time. Here is how it happened:

> So the LORD said to him, "Bring me a heifer, a goat and a ram, each three years old, along with a dove and a young pigeon."
> Abram brought all these to him, cut them in two and arranged the halves opposite each other; the birds, however, he did not cut in half. Then birds of prey came down on the carcasses, but Abram drove them away.
> As the sun was setting, Abram fell into a deep sleep, and a thick and dreadful darkness came over him. Then the LORD said to him, "Know for certain that your descendants will be strangers in a country not their own [Egypt], and they will be enslaved and mistreated four hundred years. But I will punish the nation they serve as slave, and afterward they will come out with great possessions. You, however, will go to your fathers in peace and be buried at a good old age. In the fourth generation your descendants will come back here, for the sin of the Amorites has not yet reached its full measure."

> **When the sun had set and darkness had fallen, A SMOKING FIRE POT WITH A BLAZING TORCH appeared and passed between the pieces. On that day the LORD MADE A COVENANT WITH ABRAM and said, "To your descendants I give this land, from the river of Egypt to the great river, the Euphrates—the land of the Kenites, Kenizzites, Kadmonites, Hittites, Perizzites, Rephaites, Amorites, Canaanites, Girgashites and Jebusites." (Genesis 15:9–19)**

I quoted this lengthy passage because it gives important details concerning the irrevocable nature and the real estate boundaries of the covenant. This strange ritual gets at the heart of the meaning of the Hebrew word for covenant. It comes from the verb *barath*, which means "to cut." In Hebrew the expression for making a covenant is "to cut a covenant." The Hebrew scholar F. Delitzsch writes concerning this ritual:

> The proceeding corresponded rather to the custom, prevalent in many ancient nations, of slaughtering animals when concluding a covenant, and after dividing them into pieces, of laying the pieces opposite to one another, that the persons making the covenant might pass between them. . . . God condescended to follow the custom of the Chaldeans, that He might in the most solemn manner confirm His oath to Abram the Chaldean.[2]

What a gracious God we have. Once Abraham cut the animals, as the custom dictated, he laid the halves opposite to each other with a path in the middle. Usually the two parties making the covenant would join hands and walk between the pieces reciting the terms of the agreement. They would then take an oath stating they were to be hewed into pieces, just as the animals had been, if they ever broke the covenant. We are talking serious business here.

In this case, a most unusual thing happened. Abraham saw in a supernatural vision what the LORD did. Two symbols of the LORD pass between the animal pieces ALONE. God in gracious condescension took the most solemn oath known to Abraham from his Chaldean culture, and swore to it alone. Although covenants among humans always establish certain reciprocal obligations, this covenant depends only upon God's power and faithfulness.

Abraham's Understanding of the Covenant

Abraham's understanding of the covenant is stated under Divine inspiration when he sent his steward to get a wife for his son: **"The LORD, the God of heaven, who brought me out of my father's household and my native land and who spoke to me and promised me on oath, saying, 'To your offspring I will give this land'—he will send his angel before you so that you can get a wife for my son from there."** (Genesis 24:6–8)

To say, as the Dominionists do, that there was no unconditional covenant giving the land to Abraham's descendants is to accuse God of willfully deceiving Abraham. And it would be even more ludicrous to suppose that the LORD would record Abraham's *wrong* understanding of the covenant if in fact it was wrong. Nevertheless, David Chilton reflects the Dominionist view about the validity of this covenant when he wrote about conditions in the Kingdom of God: "The people of genetic Israel will be part of the covenantal tree of life, but there is no longer any religious significance belonging to Palestine."[3]

How Long is Forever?

One might think that an awareness of these unconditional covenant promises would end the controversy concerning Israel's future. But not so with the determined and inventive Dominionist interpreters. Some of them say that the expression "forever" in Genesis 13:15 simply means a long time. Others allegorize the meaning of "the land" and say that since it is forever, it must be symbolic for the New Heavens and New Earth.

Still others say the Palestinian covenant was fulfilled during Solomon's reign. But Solomon never had possession of all the land specified. And obviously, it was not an everlasting possession. Furthermore, virtually all of the prophets after Solomon's time confirmed the possession of the Promised Land was yet a future event. The coming of the Messiah is also connected with the repossession of the land.

Chilton clearly reveals the Dominionist's position on Israel's future: "Because Israel committed the supreme act of covenant-breaking when she rejected Christ, Israel herself was rejected by God. The awesome curses pronounced by Jesus, Moses, and the prophets were fulfilled in the terrible destruction of Jerusalem, with the desolation of the Temple and the obliteration of the nation in A.D. 70."[4]

The main thing that these allegorizers purposely overlook and ignore is that the very passages that predict Israel's apostasy, destruction, and global dispersion, also predict her future gracious forgiveness, restoration to the LAND, and restoration to nationhood and a Kingdom under the Messiah's reign.

Blessings Are Just as Binding as Curses

For instance, after Moses predicts the curses and judgments that will befall Israel for breaking their covenant (see Deuteronomy chapters twenty-eight and twenty-nine), he then predicts their ultimate restoration:

> **WHEN ALL THESE CURSES AND BLESSINGS I have set before you COME UPON YOU and you take them to heart wherever the LORD your God disperses you among the nations, and WHEN** [Note it doesn't say "if"] **you and your children return to the LORD your God and obey him with all your heart and with all your soul according to everything I command you today, THEN the LORD your God will restore your fortunes and have compassion on you and gather you again from all the nations WHERE HE HAS SCATTERED YOU. Even if you have been banished to the most distant land under the heavens, from there the LORD your God will gather you and bring you back. HE WILL bring you to the LAND THAT BELONGED TO YOUR FATHERS, and you will take possession of it. HE WILL make you more prosperous and numerous than your fathers.**
>
> **The LORD your God WILL circumcise your hearts and the hearts of your descendants, so that you may love him with all your heart and with all your soul, and live.** [This promise is expanded in the New Covenant.] **The LORD your God WILL put all these curses on your enemies who hate and persecute you. YOU WILL again obey the LORD and follow all his commandments I am giving you today.** (Deuteronomy 30:1–8)

Ezekiel speaks of this same situation:

This is what the Sovereign LORD says: "I will deal with you as you deserve, because you have despised my oath BY BREAKING THE COVENANT. YET [in spite of this] **I will remember the covenant I made with you as in the days of your youth, and I will establish an EVER-LASTING COVENANT with you. . . . So I will establish my covenant with you, and you will know that I am the LORD. THEN, when I make ATONEMENT for you FOR ALL YOU HAVE DONE, you will remember and be ashamed and never again open your mouth because of your humiliation, declares the Sovereign LORD."** (Ezekiel 16:59–63)

Moses and Ezekiel Confirm the Covenant

Deuteronomy chapter thirty does not introduce conditions to Israel's ultimate restoration. The conditional term **"if"** is not used, but rather the term of prophetic certainty, **"when."** Just as Moses predicted all the cursings that have been partially fulfilled in the destruction and the scattering of the nation by the term "when," so he predicts their restoration using the same term.

The Deuteronomy and Ezekiel passages predict the following points:

(1) Israel would break the covenant (Ezekiel 16:59). The Reconstructionists make the fact that Israel broke the covenant, the entire basis for their teaching that Israel was forever rejected. Yet God not only foreknew Israel's rejection, but predicted that He would restore them afterward.

(2) God would severely discipline Israel (Deuteronomy 28:63–68; 30:1 and Ezekiel 16:59).

(3) Israel will return to the LORD (Deuteronomy 30:1–3).

(4) It is God Himself who will take the initiative to restore them because He will remember the covenant with their fathers. On that basis, He will establish an everlasting covenant with Israel (Ezekiel 16:60).

(5) The Messiah will come to regather and restore Israel (Deuteronomy 30:3–6).

(6) The Israelites will be restored to the literal land specifically promised to their forefathers (Deuteronomy 30:5).

(7) Israel's enemies, who afflicted and persecuted them, will be judged (Deuteronomy 30:7).

All of the numerous Old Testament prophecies that deal with this same issue confirm these points. In fact, scores of references that confirm each of the seven points above could be added here. Ezekiel chapters thirty-six and thirty-seven explicitly confirm that Israel will be restored as a nation to their land under the Messiah's rule, as I will show in detail.

The Palestinian Covenant, then, promises and guarantees that Israel will have a national presence in the land of Israel, beginning in history and going on into eternity. The LORD is the One who went out of His way to make these promises certain to the descendants of Abraham, Isaac, and Jacob. The clear, simple, ordinary sense of the Words gave the Israelites the hope that they have clung to for over 3500 years. The fact that some have not believed in God's way of salvation does not nullify the promises to the believing remnant. If God does not keep these multiple, clear, and emphatic promises to the believing remnant, He would be a liar.

A PROMISE IS A PROMISE

The validity of both Dominion and Premillennial theology stands or falls with one key issue: Has the Nation of Israel been rejected forever and her promises given to the Church? Is the Church now and forever the true Israel of God?

David Levi and Isaac Da Costa, who were Christian Biblical scholars of the nineteenth century, clearly point out a great inconsistency in the Dominionists' interpretation of Old and New Testament prophecies concerning the Nation of Israel. David Levi wrote:

> What can be more absurd than to explain the prophecies, which foretell the calamity to befall the Jews, in a literal sense, and then those which bespeak their future blessing, in a mystic and spiritual sense.[5]

In the same vein, Isaac Da Costa wrote:

> Who gives us the right by arbitrary exegesis, to refer the predictions made to Israel, to the Christian Church,

when the judgments upon the same Israel evidently could not have been meant for the Church.[6]

Both Levi and Da Costa helped to defeat and throw off the dark cloud that Amillennialism and Postmillennialism had cast for centuries over the Church's understanding of prophecy. Da Costa was a Dutch Jew who became a believer in Jesus as his Messiah. Later, as a Dutch Reformed theologian, he became a Premillennialist and started a considerable movement for that view.

The main thrust of Levi's and Da Costa's argument is that just as the prophecies of judgment upon Israel were literally fulfilled, so must the prophecies of blessing be fulfilled. In almost every context where God predicted judgment upon Israel, He also promised that He would cause a remnant to repent, that He would forgive all their sins, and that He would then fulfill all the promises made to their fathers.

Now, since the judgments were literally fulfilled, how can anyone say that the prophecies of restoration, which are inseparably linked to the same people, are not going to be fulfilled in the same manner? The Dominionists cannot have it both ways. Either the prophecies concerning Israel's judgment and restoration are both allegorical, or they are both literal. But history proves that the judgments were indeed literal. So the only honest way to interpret the prophecies of Israel's restoration must be literal as well.

Here is one example of many that could be quoted that illustrates this issue. This prophecy comes from Ezekiel chapters thirty-six and thirty-seven. Note that Ezekiel used the prophetic perfect tense. This verb tense describes a future event as if it has already happened: it was frequently used to stress a prophecy's certain fulfillment.

The LORD explains through Ezekiel why He would judge Israel and disperse them throughout the nations of the world:

> **Again the Word of the LORD came to me: "Son of man, when the people of Israel were living in their own land, they defiled it by their conduct and their actions. Their conduct was like a woman's monthly uncleanness in my sight. So I poured out my wrath on them because they had shed blood in the land and because they had defiled it with idols." (36:17–19)**

Then God predicts that Israel would continue to sin even while in dispersion:

95

> **"And wherever they went among the nations they profaned my holy name, for it was said of them, 'These are the LORD's people, and yet they had to leave his land.'"** (36:20)

Yet, in spite of all their sins, God vows that He will forgive and restore them to their own land. The LORD makes it clear why He will restore them to their own land. It is NOT because of any merit in them, but in order to vindicate His great name by keeping His covenants to their fathers:

> **"I had concern for my holy name, which the house of Israel profaned among the nations where they had gone. Therefore say to the house of Israel, 'This is what the Sovereign LORD says: It is not for your sake, O house of Israel, that I am going to do these things, but for the sake of my holy name, which you have profaned among the nations where you have gone.'"** (36:21–22)

After stating His reason for restoring Israel, God promises that He will fulfill the *New Covenant* of Jeremiah 31:31–40 to them, which is only partially fulfilled to the church now:

> **"For I will gather you out of the nations; I will gather you from all the countries and bring you back into your own land. I will sprinkle clean water on you, and you will be clean; I will cleanse you from all your impurities and from all your idols. I will give you a new heart and put a new spirit in you; I will remove from you your heart of stone and give you a heart of flesh. And I will put my Spirit in you and move you to follow my decrees and be careful to keep my laws."** (36:24–27)

Continuing the same theme in the next chapter, the LORD predicts the Messiah, the greater David, will be king over both the restored northern kingdom of Israel and the southern kingdom of Judah. And most important, this section also shows that Israel is to be restored as a NATION. It is features like this that make it impossible for these predictions to be applied to the Church. God clearly predicts that Israel's repentance and restoration will be accomplished by His sovereign intervention *in spite of their sins*:

"I will take the Israelites out of the nations where they have gone. I will gather them from all around and bring them back into their own land. I will make them ONE NATION IN THE LAND, on the mountains of Israel. There will be ONE KING over all of them and THEY WILL NEVER AGAIN BE TWO NATIONS OR BE DIVIDED INTO TWO KINGDOMS. They will no longer defile themselves with their idols and vile images or with any of their offenses, for I WILL SAVE THEM FROM ALL THEIR SINFUL BACKSLIDING, and I WILL cleanse them. They will be my people, and I WILL be their God.

"My servant David will be king over them and they will all have one shepherd." (37:21–24)

God reveals precisely to which land they will be restored. It will be the same land promised to their forefathers. In fact, He will do these things solely because of His faithfulness to His covenants with Jacob and their forefathers:

"They will live in the land I GAVE to my servant Jacob, the land where your fathers lived." (Genesis 37:25)

Israel's Restoration Will be National and Eternal

The LORD makes it clear which dispersion and restoration is the subject of this prediction. He promises that this restoration will be the final and permanent one from which they will never again be scattered. This certainly couldn't be applied to the Babylonian dispersion from which they were restored temporarily and then judged and dispersed again in A.D. 70. Also, the two kingdoms were not restored and united in the return from the Babylonian captivity. In fact, this has never happened to date. But the LORD says about this future restoration:

"They and their children and their children's children will live there forever, and David My servant will be their prince forever. I will make a covenant of peace with them; it will be an everlasting covenant. I will establish them and increase their numbers, and I will

97

put my sanctuary among them forever. My dwelling place will be with them; I will be their God, and they will be my people. Then the NATIONS [Gentiles] will know that I the LORD make Israel holy, when my sanctuary is among them FOREVER." (37:26–28)

From this prophecy of Ezekiel, it is clear that God foresaw Israel's apostasy, the future judgment by the Romans in A.D. 70, their consequent scattering throughout the nations of the world, and their continued sin and unbelief during their dispersion. Then, in the same prophecy and inseparably connected with it, God predicts that for the sake of His great Name and the covenants made with the Fathers of Israel, He will restore them to the land as a Nation forever, and will rule over them through the Messiah.

If words mean anything, *this is an unconditional promise to restore the Israelites as a NATION in the same literal land promised to their forefathers.*

It also promises to establish a Theocratic Kingdom from which the greater son of David, Jesus the Messiah, will rule the world. If God did not intend for the Israelites to understand the obvious, clear sense of these words, then He deliberately misled and gave false hopes to the believing remnant of Israel for centuries.

The Dominionists try to explain this away by saying that Israel's sin of rejecting the Messiah made all of these promises null and void. To me, this kind of teaching blasphemes the character of God. First, because it fails to note that God, who foresees all things, not only foreknew Israel's sins, but also predicted them and made clear what He would do about them.

Second, instead of predicting Israel's rejection, God promises that He will cleanse them of ALL their transgressions.

Third, God clearly states that it is not because of any merit or faithfulness in the Israelites that He will act to cleanse them of sin and restore them to the promised land of Israel, BUT IN SPITE OF THEIR LACK OF IT. He makes it clear that it is His faithfulness to His Word alone that will accomplish all these things.

The Greater Issue at Stake

The same issues are at stake in God's saving of Israel as a Nation as are those involved in our individual salvation. God doesn't save anyone on the basis of merit. He saves solely on the basis of grace through faith, and even that is NOT OF OURSELVES. (See Ephesians 2:8–9.) This is why the LORD says concerning His sovereign election of Israel, **"And if by grace, then it is no longer by works; if it were, grace would no longer be grace."** (Romans 11:6) It is particularly ironic that the Reconstructionists are leading the pack of theological assassins who insist that Israel has lost its election, since they are all avowed Calvinists and supposedly believe in eternal security. Many Charismatics contend that believers *can* lose their salvation, so at least their view is consistent. But not so with the Reconstructionists.

Is God a Liar?

The Dominionists seem to feel that the only place to establish and verify Israel's future is the New Testament. I maintain that once God makes a definite promise that depends only upon His faithfulness, He *cannot* break it. If a promise is clearly stated in this manner in the Old Testament, then the New Testament cannot contradict it. If someone comes up with an interpretation that seems to contradict it, then rest assured their interpretation is wrong, not the Bible, because it cannot contradict itself.

This concept will be further developed in the next chapter, where we will examine God's promise of the King-Messiah and a New Covenant to replace the ineffective Mosaic Covenant.

CHAPTER FIVE

A King, A Kingdom, and Forgiveness

But the angel said to her, "Do not be afraid, Mary, you have found favor with God. You will be with child and give birth to a son, and you are to give him the name Jesus. He will be great and will be called the Son of the Most High. The LORD God will give him the THRONE OF HIS FATHER DAVID, and he will reign over the house of Jacob forever; his kingdom will never end."

The Angel Gabriel
Luke 1:30–33

THE DAVIDIC COVENANT

Many of the crucial issues addressed in this book are directly related to the promises contained in the Davidic Covenant. The most important prophetic aspects of the Abrahamic Covenant lie in the words *land* and *seed* or *offspring*. The Palestinian Covenant enlarged, clarified, and guaranteed the *land* promises to the Israelites. The Davidic Covenant does the same with the promises concerning Abraham's *seed*.

The Man After God's Own Heart

Nearly a thousand years after God made the Abrahamic and Palestinian Covenants with Abraham, God raised up a humble young shepherd to be Israel's greatest king.

David understood the grace of God and how to approach Him by faith in a way that no one else in the Old Testament did. Though David stumbled and fell into some terrible sins, He believed God's promises of forgiveness through confession. He knew that He never deserved anything from God, and that the only way he could ever approach a holy God was by faith in His provision for sin. He brought glory to God by this kind of faith. It was because of this that the LORD called him, **"A man after MY own heart"** (Acts 13:22).

After David was established as king, he told the LORD that he would like to build a house for Him and His ark of the covenant. In response, the LORD sent the prophet Nathan to give His Word to David. It is the clearest statement of what has come to be called the Davidic Covenant:

> **"'The LORD declares to you that the LORD himself WILL establish a HOUSE for you: When you rest with your fathers, I WILL raise up your offspring to succeed you, who will come from your own body, and I WILL establish his kingdom. He is the one who will build a house for my Name, and I WILL establish the THRONE of his kingdom forever. I WILL be HIS FATHER, and he will be MY SON. When he does wrong, I will punish him with the rod of men, with floggings inflicted by men. But my love WILL NEVER be taken away from him, as I took it away from Saul, whom I removed from before you. YOUR HOUSE and YOUR KINGDOM WILL ENDURE FOREVER BEFORE ME; YOUR THRONE will be ESTABLISHED FOREVER.'"**(2 Samuel 7:11–16) (Emphases added.)

There are many specific things promised to David and his descendants in this covenant. First, David was promised a son through whom the LORD would establish his kingdom.

Second, the LORD appointed this son, Solomon, to build the temple David desired to construct for the LORD.

Third, David's throne and kingdom was to be established forever.

Fourth, the throne would never be taken away permanently from Solomon and his seed, as it was from Saul, even though the LORD would discipline them for their sins.

Fifth, the LORD promised to unconditionally establish David's HOUSE, THRONE, and KINGDOM forever, *even though* it was prophesied that he and his descendants would be guilty of great sin and severely punished.

A Definition of the Important Covenant Words

The term **"David's House"** obviously didn't mean a building of stone and cedar. This term is often used to mean a family lineage, especially one of royalty. Webster's Third New International Dictionary gives a definition of *house* in this sense, "A family of ancestors, descendants, and kindred; a race of persons from the same stock, especially a noble family."[1]

The Epistle to the Hebrews uses *house* in a slightly different sense: **"He [Jesus] was faithful to the one who appointed him, just as Moses was faithful in all God's house."** (Hebrews 3:2) In this passage *house* is used to describe Israel collectively as God's special, chosen people.

God promised to build David an everlasting family and dynasty. This was later verified when the LORD called David's royal line the **House of David.** (See Isaiah 7:13.) Concerning the "House of David," God promised it would never be totally destroyed for any reason and that no other family would ever have a legitimate right to the throne.

In the same way, the promises related to David's **THRONE** are not referring to an ornate chair, but rather the authority, dignity, and sovereignty it represents. The throne of a king is a symbol of his royal authority and right to rule. David's descendants were assured of the everlasting right to rule by the promises of an **eternal throne.** All of these promises were literally fulfilled in David's line and ultimately fulfilled in the Lord Jesus Christ, who is the promised greater son of David.

David's promised **KINGDOM** referred to a *political kingdom*. This theocratic kingdom is promised to the remnant of the House of Judah and Israel on a restored earth in history. It will begin with the removal of nature's curse. (See Isaiah 11:1–16; 65:17–24; Micah 4:1–5; Zephhaniah 3:14–20; Zechariah 14:1–21, etc.)

The consistent witness of all the Prophets is that the establishment of this kingdom is inseparably linked to and dependent upon the cataclysmic intervention of the **KING MESSIAH**, the son of David, who judges all of Israel's enemies and then *restores* the believing remnant of Israel. (Deuteronomy 30:1–7; Ezekiel 36:1–12; Zechariah 12–14, etc.)

Did God Intend This Covenant to Be Understood Literally?

The Dominionists so allegorize this covenant that it ends up bearing no resemblance to the original statements. The way they interpret this covenant illustrates what I mean by literal versus allegorical interpretation. As noted before, all Premillennialists believe that the Scriptures contain both literal-narrative and allegorical sections. The main difference is that Premils don't take passages that are clearly literal and subjectively turn them into allegories.

Even though Dr. J. Dwight Pentecost's monumental work, *Things To Come,* was published in 1958, it is very relevant to the current controversy with the Reconstructionists and Dominionists. Despite the fact that it is one of the most scholarly works on predictive prophecy of this century, David Chilton doesn't refer to it even once in *Paradise Restored* and *Days of Vengeance.* This is like writing on the history of art and leaving out Michelangelo.

Dr. Pentecost demonstrates his mastery of prophetic Scripture in the following outline of the issues at stake in a correct understanding of the Davidic Covenant:

> Inherent in the Davidic covenant are many of the crucial issues facing the student of Eschatology. Will there be a literal millennium? Is the church the kingdom? What is God's kingdom? What is Christ's Kingdom? Will the nation Israel be regathered and restored under her Messiah? Is the kingdom present or future? These and many more crucial issues can be decided only by a correct interpretation of that which was covenanted to David.[2]

These questions are at the root of the controversy between the Premillennialists and the modern "improved version" of Postmillennialism. The interpretation of the Davidic Covenant is crucial to both positions.

The first clear promise that hinted of the things promised in the Davidic Covenant was given to Abraham when he received the rite of circumcision:

> **"I will confirm my covenant between me and you and will greatly increase your numbers. . . . As for me, this is my covenant with you: You will be the father**

**of many nations. No longer will you be called Abram
[Hebrew=High Father]; your name will be Abraham
[Hebrew=Father of many nations], for I have made you
a father of many nations. I will make you very fruitful;
I will make nations of you and KINGS will come from
you. I will establish my covenant as an EVERLASTING
COVENANT between me and you and YOUR DESCEN-
DANTS after you for the generations to come, to be your
God and the God of YOUR DESCENDANTS after you.
THE WHOLE LAND OF CANAAN, where you are now
an alien, I will give as an EVERLASTING POSSESSION
to you and your descendants after you; and I will be
their God. (Genesis 17:2–8)**

Though the LORD speaks of many nations coming from
Abraham (many did come from his sons Ismael, Medan, Midian,
Jokshan, etc.), He singled out one specific line of descendants
through Isaac. To this line he promised certain extraordinary
national blessings.

The most important features of this enlarged revelation of the
covenant to Abraham are these: (1) God made an everlasting
covenant with both Abraham and his descendants through Isaac
and Jacob to be their God forever (17:7); (2) He promised Abraham
and his descendants the whole land of Canaan (whose specific
borders were outlined in Genesis 15:18–21) as an everlasting
possession (17:8); (3) When the LORD said that **kings** would come
from Abraham, He was implicitly promising *a kingdom* as well.

A Battle to Be Remembered

The whole battle over the Amillennial-Postmillennial interpretation of prophecy was fought and decisively won by the greatest
theologians of the nineteenth and twentieth centuries. One of
these was Premillennialist Dr. George N. H. Peters who wrote *The
Theocratic Kingdom* in three volumes (originally published in 1884
by Funk and Wagnalls of New York). Dr. Wilbur M. Smith who
was a scholar and professor at Fuller Theological Seminary and
probably read more books that anyone of our times, called Peters's
volumes, "The most important single work on Biblical predictive
prophecy to appear in this country at any time during the
nineteenth century. The author of these volumes must have read
everything of importance in the major areas of history,

science, literature, and theology. From an examination of the index, one learns that over four thousand different authors are quoted, from the Church Fathers of the second century down to his own decade."[3]

I felt it necessary to reintroduce this great scholar to all those who desire to pursue an honest investigation of the exegetical basis for the Premillennial position. *The Theocratic Kingdom* has been reprinted many times throughout this century.

Peters argues that the Jewish expectation of a literal fulfillment of the Davidic Covenant to the Nation of Israel was and is accurate and completely justified:

> Before censuring the Jews, as many do, for believing that Jesus would *literally restore* the Davidic throne and Kingdom, we must consider, in fairness, that they were justified in so doing by the very language of the covenant.
>
> It is incredible that God should, in the most important matters affecting the interests and the happiness of man and nearly touching His veracity, clothe them in words, *which if not true in their obvious and common sense, would deceive the pious and God-fearing of many ages.*
>
> We cannot, dare not (however upheld by many eminent names), entertain an opinion *so dishonoring both to God and His ancient believing children.*
>
> The Jews are abundantly defended in their faith by the covenant itself; the correctness and justness of their fondly-entertained hopes appear from the particulars incorporated in it.
>
> (1) The words and sentences in their plain grammatical acceptance, do *expressly* teach their belief. *This is denied by no one, not even by those who then proceed to spiritualize the language.* Therefore already the Jews are excusable in believing what God so definitely declares.
>
> (2) The covenant is distinctly associated with *the Jewish nation* and none other. . . . In 2 Samuel 7:23, 24 (I Chron. 17:21, 22) he (David) expresses before God his consciousness of the magnitude of the blessing; that this covenant, in virtue of his throne and Kingdom being thus distinguished, embraces *"one nation,"* and this *the same* nation that was brought out of Egypt (i.e., Abraham's

descendants), who should be established in "thy (God's) land."

(3) It is called *a perpetual covenant*, i.e., one that shall endure forever. It may, indeed, require time before its fulfillment; it may even for a time be held, so far as the nation is concerned, in the background, but *it must be ultimately realized. . . .*

(4) It was *confirmed by oath* (Psalm 132:11, and 89:3, 4, 33), thus giving the strongest possible assurance of its ample fulfillment. Could the Jews do less than trust in language thus confirmed?

(5) To leave no doubt whatever, and to render unbelief utterly inexcusable God concisely and most forcibly presents His determination: **"My covenant will I not break, nor alter the thing that is gone out of my lips"** (Psalm 89:34). It would have been sheer presumption and blindness in the Jews to have altered (under the modern plea of spirituality) the words; and there is *a heavy responsibility* resting upon those who, even under the most pious intentions, *deliberately alter* the covenant words and attach to them *a foreign* meaning.[4]

The Certainties of David's Throne

In summary, the following specific promises within the Davidic Covenant cannot be broken:

First, God anticipated and predicted that David's royal descendants would become faithless and would be disciplined: **"If his sons forsake my law and do not follow my statutes, if they violate my decrees and fail to keep my commands, I will punish their sin with the rod, their iniquity with flogging . . ."** (Psalm 89:30 and 31)

Second, because of this anticipated sin, the Prophets predicted that David's throne would be without a king for a long period of time: **"For the Israelites will live many days without king or prince, without sacrifice or sacred stones, without ephod or idol. Afterward the Israelites will return and seek the LORD their God and DAVID THEIR KING. They will come trembling to the LORD and to his blessings in the last days."** (Hosea 3:4, 5)

Third, the people over which the King-Messiah, the son of David, will rule, can only be understood as a remnant of the physical descendants of Abraham, Isaac, and Jacob. The language used by several of the Prophets to confirm the ultimate fulfillment of the Davidic kingdom to Israel *cannot* be applied to the Church. Here is a specific case:

> "'This is what the Sovereign LORD says: I will take the Israelites out of the nations where they have gone. I will gather them from all around and bring them back into their own land. I will make them ONE nation in the land, on the mountains of Israel. There will be ONE KING over all of them and they will never again be TWO nations or be divided into TWO kingdoms. . . . They will be my people, and I will be their God. My servant David will be KING OVER THEM . . . DAVID MY PRINCE will be their prince FOREVER . . . I will put my sanctuary among them FOREVER. My dwelling place will be with them; I will be their God, and they will be my people. The GENTILES will know that I the LORD make Israel holy, when my sanctuary is among them forever.'" (Ezekiel 37:21–28)

Consider these important points from this Scripture: (1) The Church has never been scattered in discipline among the nations. (2) The Church has never been in a civil war that resulted in *two* kingdoms called Israel and Judah. (3) The Church has never been promised restoration to the land and mountains of Israel. (4) The Church *cannot* be in view when it says, **"They will live in the land I gave to my servant Jacob, the land where your fathers lived."** (5) If this were in any conceivable sense referring to the Church, why does it say that *the Gentiles will recognize who God really is when He makes Israel holy and His sanctuary is among them forever?*

Fourth, after the kingdom had been rejected by Israel, the Apostles asked the Lord Jesus the following question just before His ascension to heaven: **"So when they met together, they asked him, 'LORD, are you at this time going to restore the kingdom to ISRAEL?'"** (Acts 1:6) The LORD had just finished an intensive forty-day post-resurrection ministry to His disciples in which he taught them **"about the Kingdom of God."** (Acts 1:3) He would have surely told them if the kingdom were going to be forever removed from Israel in A.D. 70.

If the Church were going to permanently replace Israel, the LORD could have easily clarified their question. Instead, He told them it was not for them to know WHEN the kingdom would be restored to Israel. Jesus then gave an alternate program for the Church in the present age.

Contrary to Dominionists' theories, history testifies that the Apostles and the Apostolic Fathers believed that Jesus would return to restore Israel and to rule from David's throne over a theocratic kingdom for one thousand literal years. And the Apostolic Fathers continued to teach this for over a century *after* the A.D. 70 holocaust. It wasn't until Origen's time in the third century that this view began to change for reasons already given in chapter three.

The First Church Council Recognized a Future Davidic Kingdom

Fifth, the first Church council was convened in order to resolve the question of whether Gentile converts had to become Jews and keep the law of Moses to be saved. The Jerusalem Church Elders still thought that Gentiles had to become Jews to be accepted in the Church. The Apostle James resolved the issue by a quote from Amos:

> **After this I will return and rebuild David's fallen tent. Its ruins I will rebuild and I will restore it, that the remnant of men may seek the LORD, and all the GENTILES who bear my name, says the LORD, who does these things that have been known for ages.** (Amos 9:11–12 quoted in Acts 15.16–18)

In the context of Amos chapter nine, David's fallen tent or tabernacle is clearly referring to the reestablishment of the Davidic rule and kingdom. In the immediate context, the LORD predicts the destruction of Israel in discipline: **"'Surely the eyes of the Sovereign LORD are on the sinful kingdom. I will destroy it from the face of the earth . . . '"** (Amos 9:8a)

But in spite of this, the LORD promises, **"'. . . yet I will not totally destroy the house of Jacob,' declares the LORD. 'For I will give the command, and I will shake the house of Israel AMONG ALL THE NATIONS as a grain is shaken in a sieve, BUT NOT A KERNEL WILL FALL TO THE GROUND.'"** (9:8b–9) (Emphases added.)

It is at this time, *when* the LORD shakes the world and redeems a remnant of Israel which is scattered among all the nations, that He will restore the tabernacle of David. This is a clear reference to the Tribulation which immediately precedes the Second Coming of Christ. Jeremiah describes this same situation: **"How awful that day will be! NONE WILL BE LIKE IT. It will be a time of trouble for Jacob, BUT HE WILL BE SAVED OUT OF IT. . . . Though I completely destroy all the nations among which I scatter you, I will not completely destroy you. . . . I will restore the fortunes of Jacob's tents and have compassion on his dwellings; the city will be rebuilt on her ruins, and the palace will stand in its proper place."** (Jeremiah 30:7, 11, 18)

James only draws one point from this quote—the LORD will *first* **"take out from among the Gentiles a people for Himself,"** and then *afterward* the LORD **will return and restore the Davidic kingdom to Israel.** This answered the main problem the council was convened to solve—that a body of Gentiles must *first* be saved from among the nations, *then* the Messiah will return and fulfill His Covenants with the House of David and Israel.

Israel Is. . . !

One of the consistent traits of the great Premillennial interpreters of the nineteenth century was the expectation that the Nation of Israel would be reborn as the time of the Messiah's coming drew near. This was considered such an impossibility by the Amillennial and Postmillennial interpreters that it was held up as a case in point "to prove the folly" of the literal interpretation of the covenants and prophecies concerning a future for the Nation of Israel.

In this regard, Peters's following forecast concerning Israel's future, which was written in A.D. 1884, was remarkable:

> The convenanted Davidic throne and Kingdom, allied as it is with the Jewish nation (particularly with Judah and Benjamin), necessarily requires *a preservation* of the nation in order for a future restoration to take place. This has been done; and *to-day we see that nation wonderfully preserved down to the present* (in exile), although enemies, including the strongest nations and most powerful empires, have perished. *This is not a work of chance;* FOR IF OUR POSITION IS CORRECT, THIS IS DEMANDED, SEEING THAT WITHOUT A RESTORATION OF THE NATION IT IS IMPOSSIBLE TO RESTORE THE DAVIDIC KINGDOM.

The covenant language, the oath of God, the confirmation of the promise by the blood of Jesus, the prophetic utterances-*all*, notwithstanding the nation's unbelief, requires *its perpetuation*, that through it finally God's promises and faithfulness may be vindicated. God so provides that *His Word* may be fulfilled.

Every Jew . . . whom we meet on our streets is a living evidence that the Messiah will yet some day reign gloriously on David's throne and over his Kingdom, from which to extend a world-wide dominion.[5] (Emphases added.)

On May 14, 1948, the faith of these early modern-day Premillennialists was confirmed—against all odds, Israel became a Nation once more. Against all odds, it has continued to survive.

Israel has won four wars battling a determined collection of enemy nations with vastly superior numbers and equipment. After being destroyed and scattered throughout the whole world for almost two thousand years, relentlessly persecuted in virtually every place they settled, and with every reason to assimilate into the many cultures to which they were subjected, the Jews have miraculously remained a distinct Nation in exile.

Yet as predicted, Israel has not only become a Nation, but has become a central factor in the struggle of the world's super powers for Arab oil. This fits exactly into the scenario foretold by Ezekiel chapters thirty-six through thirty-eight.

The Dominionists remain consistent with their Postmillennial predecessors by refusing to recognize that the State of Israel has any prophetic significance. They believe that Israel's rebirth is simply a coincidence of history. Gary North has said on many occasions that he has a book already written, which he will publish within two weeks after Israel is either "pushed into the sea by the Arabs or converted." He has scorned the Premillennialists "for betting the farm on the Nation of Israel."

I throw out this challenge to the Dominionists: If Israel is indeed destroyed as a distinct people and nation, then I will acknowledge that my understanding of prophecy was wrong. I challenge Gary North to have the same kind of courage of his convictions and to publish his book on "Israel's future destruction" now. After all, wouldn't it be better to be labeled a "prophet" than to say "I-told-you-so"?

But for the time being, ISRAEL IS, in spite of the continuing obsession of 165 million Arabs and their Soviet sponsors to destroy them. I must also add that they continue in spite of the Dominionists' teaching that their hope is gone and they have no reason to remain a distinct people or a nation.

THE NEW COVENANT

The fourth unconditional covenant God made with Israel is called the New Covenant. At the same time God predicted the future institution of the New Covenant, He revealed that it would replace the Mosaic Covenant. The impossibility of keeping the Law Covenant, and Israel's failure under it, is the very reason God gives for replacing it with the New Covenant. The New Covenant operates entirely by the grace of God and the indwelling Holy Spirit.

The covenant is first introduced through Jeremiah. Here is a quote from part of the New Covenant:

> **"The time is coming," declares the LORD, "when I will make a NEW COVENANT with the house of ISRAEL and with the HOUSE OF JUDAH. It will not be like the covenant I made with their forefathers when I took them by the hand to lead them out of Egypt** [i.e., the Mosaic Covenant], **because THEY BROKE MY COVENANT, though I was a husband to them," declares the LORD.**
>
> **"This is the covenant I will make with THE HOUSE OF ISRAEL after that time," declares the LORD.**
>
> **"I WILL put my law in their minds and write it on their hearts. I WILL be their God, and they will be my people. No longer will a man teach his neighbor, or a man his brother, saying, 'Know the LORD,' because they will all know me, from the least of them to the greatest," declares the LORD.**
>
> **"For I WILL forgive their wickedness and WILL remember their sins no more."** (Jeremiah 31:31–34) (Emphases added.)

Even a casual reading of this covenant reveals that it was made very specifically with the House of Israel, the physical descendants of Abraham, Isaac, and Jacob. This is abundantly clear because of the following factors:

First, the covenant is made with the House of Israel and with the House of Judah. Though the Christians are called **the spiritual seed of Abraham** in the New Testament, they are never called **the House of Israel**. And most assuredly, the Church is never called **the House of Judah**.

Second, the fact that the natural children of Abraham are in view is made clear by this further description of those with whom the New Covenant was made: **"It** [the New Covenant] **will not be like the covenant I made with their forefathers when I took them by the hand to lead them out of Egypt . . ."** This could *only* refer to the physical Israelites. Even with the most dedicated "spiritualizing efforts," there is no way to legitimately place the Church in the Exodus from Egypt as required by this passage. The Church in no way can be identified with the Israelites who were led out of Egypt by God through Moses.

Charles C. Ryries's [6] excellent analysis of the New Covenant's provisions shows the following:

> (1) The new covenant is an unconditional, grace covenant resting on the **"I will"** of God. The frequency of the use of the phrase in Jeremiah 31:31–34 is striking. Cf. Ezekiel 16:60–62.
>
> (2) The new covenant is an everlasting covenant. This is closely related to the fact that it is unconditional and made in grace . . . (Isaiah 61:2, compared with Ezekiel 37:26; Jeremiah 31:35–37)
>
> (3) The new covenant also promises the impartation of a renewed mind and heart which we may call regeneration . . . (Jeremiah 31:33 compared with Isaiah 61:9)
>
> (4) The new covenant provides for restoration to the favor and blessing of God . . . (Hosea 2:19–20, compared with Isaiah 61:9)
>
> (5) Forgiveness of sin is also included in the covenant, **"for I will remove their iniquity, and I will remember their sin no more"** (Jeremiah 31:34b).
>
> (6) The indwelling of the Holy Spirit is also included. This is seen by comparing Jeremiah 31:33 with Ezekiel 36:27.
>
> (7) The teaching ministry of the Holy Spirit will be manifested, and the will of God will be known by obedient hearts . . . (Jeremiah 31:34)

(8) As is always the case when Israel is in the land, she will be blessed materially in accordance with the provisions of the new covenant . . . (Jeremiah 32:41; Isaiah 61:8; Ezekiel 34:25–27)

(9) The sanctuary will be rebuilt in Jerusalem, for it is written, **"I . . . will set my sanctuary in the midst of them for evermore. My tabernacle also shall be with them"** (Ezekiel 37:26–27a).

(10) War shall cease and peace shall reign according to Hosea 2:18. The fact that this is also a definite characteristic of the millennium (Isaiah 2:4) further supports the fact that the new covenant is millennial in its fulfillment.

(11) The blood of the Lord Jesus Christ is the foundation of all the blessings of the new covenant, for **"by the blood of thy covenant I have sent forth thy prisoners out of the pit wherein is no water"** (Zechariah 9:11).

By way of summary, it may be said that as far as the Old Testament teaching on the new covenant is concerned, the covenant was made with the Jewish people. Its period of fulfillment is yet future beginning when the Deliverer shall come and continuing throughout eternity. Its provisions for the nation Israel are glorious, and they all rest and depend on the very Word of God.[7]

The Dominionists use New Testament references, particularly verses in the Epistle to the Hebrews, to contend that this covenant is now fulfilled in the Church. The real problem comes when they allege that this is proof that there will be no future fulfillment to "rejected and displaced natural Israel."

The Church and the New Covenant

The truth is that the New Covenant *is partially* in force in this present age. But nowhere does the book of Hebrews teach that there will be no future fulfillment to natural Israel, to whom the promise was originally made.

The Christian is only allowed into the covenant's blessing through *union with Christ*, who, as a son of Abraham, inherited the blessings of the covenant.

The major purpose of the Epistle to the Hebrews is to prove four things from Old Testament prophecy: (1) that the conditional Mosaic Covenant has been replaced by the partial institution of the promised New Covenant; (2) that the New Covenant could not be instituted at all until it was made possible through the vastly superior sacrifice of the Messiah; (3) that the Messiah is the Son of God; (4) that Jesus is the only one who could be the Messiah.

The writer to the Hebrews carefully defines what part of the New Covenant is now in force to those who are grafted into Israel's covenant through union with Israel's Messiah:

For by one offering He has perfected for all time those who are sanctified. And the Holy Spirit also bears witness to us; for after saying,

> **"This the covenant that**
> **I will make with them**
> **After those days, says**
> **the LORD:**
> **I will put My laws upon**
> **their heart,**
> **And upon their mind I**
> **will write them."**
> **He then says,**
> **"And their sins and their**
> **lawless deeds**
> **I will remember no more."**

Now where there is forgiveness of these things, there is no longer any [need for another kind of] **offering for sin.** (Hebrews 10:14–18)

The two features of the New Covenant that are now in effect are these: (1) The LORD no longer remembers or holds against us our sins and lawless deeds because Jesus the Messiah has permanently atoned for our sins; (2) He puts His laws in our hearts, and writes them in our minds through the Holy Spirit who now dwells in every believer.

These two aspects of the New Covenant were never possible before the finished work of the LORD Jesus on the cross.

The first was made possible because the Messiah's perfect, once-and-for-all sacrifice removed sin as a barrier between God and man. Whereas the animal sacrifices only temporarily *covered our sins* (this is the meaning of the Hebrew word for atonement), the sacrifice of the Lord Jesus *took sin away* forever as a barrier for all who believe in Him.

The second was made possible because our sin natures were judged vicariously in Christ at the cross, making it possible for the Holy Spirit to take up permanent residence in us, even though our sin natures are still present. As a result, the Holy Spirit now changes us from the inside. He writes God's laws on our minds, which means that He causes us to understand what God's Will is. He also writes them on our hearts, which means that He causes us to desire to do His Will. The Holy Spirit empowers us to perform the things He causes us to desire through His *filling* ministry.

What Is Not Yet Fulfilled From the New Covenant

There are a number of specific promises made by oath in the New Covenant that are not yet fulfilled.

First, since this covenant was made specifically to a national remnant of the House of Israel and Judah, its ultimate fulfillment is still in the future. It was in connection with this feature of the covenant, and in its same context, that the LORD made one of His most binding oaths: **"This is what the LORD says, he who appoints the sun to shine by day, who decrees the moon and stars to shine by night, who stirs up the sea so that its waves roar—the LORD Almighty is his name: 'Only if these decrees vanish from my sight,' declares the LORD, 'WILL THE DESCENDANTS OF ISRAEL EVER CEASE TO BE A NATION BEFORE ME.'"** (Jeremiah 31:35–36) This is a clear, specific, and definite promise that Israel will be a distinct nation in God's plan as long as there is time, space, and history. I surely hope that Gary North and the Dominionists are wrong about the destruction of the State of Israel. I've grown accustomed to the sun and moon and would hate to see them disappear.

The LORD continues His confirming oath concerning Israel's national future under the New Covenant, **"This is what the LORD says: 'Only if the heavens above can be measured and the foundations of the earth below be searched out will I reject the descendants of Israel BECAUSE OF ALL THEY HAVE DONE,' declares the LORD."** (Jeremiah 31:37) This is about as heavy as oath-taking gets, folks. If God doesn't mean what He promised a remnant of physical Israel here, then He surely went to a lot of trouble to deceive them. This promise not only anticipates and takes into account the fact that Israel would backslide into terrible sin, it unconditionally promises a sovereign saving of a remnant of Israel afterward. This oath is an inseparable part of the New Covenant.

Second, God promises to be the personal God of Israel *after* the New Covenant is instituted with them.

Third, *in connection with the above*, the LORD specifically promises that all mankind living on earth will have a true knowledge of Him through the new ministries of the Holy Spirit. This promise is a prominent theme in the predictions of the millennium. Isaiah prophesied, **"They will neither harm nor destroy on all my holy mountain, for the earth will be full of the KNOWLEDGE OF THE LORD as the waters cover the sea."** (Isaiah 11:9) This verse is in a context that predicts the Messiah's personal presence, reigning over an earth that has the curse on nature removed.

This prediction is also vitally connected with the following theme of prophecy: **"In that day the LORD will reach out his hand a SECOND TIME to reclaim the REMNANT that is left of his people [Israel] from Assyria, from Lower Egypt, from Upper Egypt, from Cush [Africa], Elam, from Babylonia, from Hamath and from the islands [continents] of the sea."** (Isaiah 11:11) The first restoration was from the Babylonian Dispersion in the fifth century B.C. The *second restoration* can only refer to the remnant of the Roman holocaust which has been in a worldwide dispersion since A.D. 70.

The main point is that this part of the New Covenant cannot be fulfilled until the Messianic Kingdom has been given to Israel.

Fourth, although the promise that God would so deal with our sins that He could forgive and forget them is already partially in force with the Church because of our participation in Israel's covenants through our union with Christ, the original promise was specifically made to the physical remnant of Israel. Therefore the New Covenant cannot be fully in force until the numerous predictions of Israel's forgiveness and restoration are fulfilled.

Fifth, an integral part of the New Covenant is the graphic description of the rebuilding of Jerusalem to Millennial Kingdom specifications. Specific and exact geographical coordinates are given which all relate to the terrain of the earthly Jerusalem. (See Jeremiah 31:38–40.) Dominionists scoff at this teaching. Dominionist Richard Hogue said, "God is not interested in reigning on that peanut throne of physical Israel in an earthly Jerusalem."

The fact that this will occur right after the great judgments of the Tribulation is brought out by this promise in the New Covenant: **"The whole valley where DEAD BODIES AND ASHES are thrown, and all the terraces out to the Kidron Valley on the east as far as the Horse Gate, will be holy to the LORD. The city will never again be uprooted."** The mention of dead bodies correlates with the many other prophecies about the judgment that will occur in the Kidron Valley when Jesus the Messiah returns to set up His Kingdom (Joel 3:12; Zechariah 14:4–12). The Kidron Valley is also called the Valley of Jehoshaphat in some of these prophecies, which means *the valley of the LORD's judgment*. It is in this valley east of Jerusalem that the prophets forecast an awesome and special judgment of the Gentiles who invade Israel.

A MATTER OF GOD'S HONOR

If the four covenants we have reviewed in these last two chapters are read normally and taken at face value, we find that they were specifically made with the physical descendants of Abraham, Isaac, and Jacob. They are also clearly declared to be unconditional and everlasting. Their prominent theme is an earthly Messianic Kingdom which begins in history and is centered in the land of Israel.

If God fails to keep these covenants with a physical remnant of Israel, then He is a liar, no matter how the Dominionists seek to explain this difficulty away. The LORD would become guilty of consistently and deliberately deceiving Godly Israelites over a period of many centuries.

God will not reject His ancient people forever because of their sin. He anticipated and predicted their covenant-breaking and promised to forgive and restore them.

Israel's present sin and lack of faith presents God with a dilemma similar to the one with which He tested Moses during the Exodus. The incident occurred at a time when Israel had consistently and repeatedly failed to believe God's promises in spite of the many wonders He had performed to deliver them. God tested Moses by telling him that He was going to destroy Israel and make another nation out of his descendants. Moses cracked the faith barrier and repeated back to God what he had only recently been shown by God Himself about His character. He laid aside his own ego and self-interests, and sought only to protect God's honor and glory. Here is Moses in his greatest moment:

The LORD said to Moses, "How long will these people treat me with contempt? How long will they refuse to believe in me, in spite of all the miraculous signs I have performed among them? I will strike them down with a plague and destroy them, but I will make you into a nation greater and stronger than they."

Moses said to the LORD, "Then the Egyptians will hear about it! By your power you brought these people up from among them. And they will tell the inhabitants of this land about it. They have already heard that you, O LORD, are with these people and that you, O LORD, have been seen face to face, that your cloud stays over them, and that you go before them in a pillar of cloud by day and a pillar of fire by night. If you put these people to death all at one time, the nations who have heard this report about you will say, 'The LORD WAS NOT ABLE TO BRING THESE PEOPLE INTO THE LAND HE PROMISED THEM ON OATH; so He slaughtered them in the desert.'

"Now may the Lord's strength be displayed, just as you have declared [see Exodus 33:18–34:9]: 'The LORD is slow to anger, abounding in love and forgiving sin and rebellion.' . . . In accordance with your great love, forgive the sin of these people, just as you have pardoned them from the time they left Egypt until now."

The LORD replied, "I have forgiven them, as you asked." (Numbers 14:11–20)

Is the Lord Strong Enough?

Moses interceded for Israel on the basis of God's character and the Abrahamic and Palestinian Covenants. He reminded the LORD that He had promised an oath to bring them to the land of Canaan and give it to them. He also reminded the LORD that all the Gentiles would say that He was not strong enough to keep His Word if He failed to bring, not some other nation, but Abraham, Isaac, and Jacob's seed into the land.

Now, just consider this incident in the light of today's situation. If God has indeed permanently rejected the Nation of Israel and transferred to the Church her solemn covenants confirmed by oath, then all the world can say, with much greater justification than in Moses' day, "The LORD was not strong enough to keep His Word to His people Israel."

But against this unthinkable possibility that is alleged by the Dominionists, God swears concerning Israel,

> "It is not for your sake, O Israel, that I am going to do these things, but for the sake of MY HOLY NAME, which you have profaned among the nations where you have gone.
>
> I will show the holiness of my great name, which has been profaned among the nations . . .
>
> I am going to open your graves and bring you up from them; I will bring you back to the land of Israel. Then you, my people, will know that I am the LORD, when I open your graves and bring you up from them. . . . Then you will know that I the LORD have spoken, and I have done it, declares the LORD. . . .
>
> I will take the Israelites out of the nations where they have gone. I will gather them from all around and bring them back into their own land.
>
> I will make them one nation in the land, on the mountains of Israel. They will be my people, and I will be their God. My servant David will be king over them. . . . David my servant will be their prince forever. I will make a covenant of peace with them; it will be an everlasting covenant." (Ezekiel 36:22, 23; 37:12–26) (Emphasis added.)

In the light of what we have considered in these last two chapters concerning Israel's four unconditional covenants, how can the Dominionists honestly say:

- that the sins of physical Israel have caused God to reject them as His special people forever
- that the nation of Israel will never be restored to the land of Canaan and there given her promised Messianic Kingdom
- that the Messiah will not return to convert and restore the remnant of Israel from her worldwide dispersion
- that the LORD Jesus, the Messiah, will never personally reign over the world from a restored Jerusalem
- that Israel's covenants have been forfeited and permanently given to the Church
- that the Church is Israel now and forever

Let those who contend these things recognize that when God makes clear and repeated unconditional covenants confirmed by His own oath, He Himself cannot set them aside. God cannot break such clearly stated promises of this magnitude and remain true to His own character.

Let the Dominionists remember this Scripture and take it to heart:

> **God is not a man, that he**
> **should lie,**
> **nor a son of man, that he**
> **should change his mind.**
> **Does he speak and then not**
> **act?**
> **Does he promise and then not**
> **fulfill?**
>
> (Numbers 23:19)

CHAPTER SIX

Israel in the Past: Elected

Who is a God like you, who pardons sin and forgives the transgression of THE REMNANT OF HIS INHERI-TANCE? You do not stay angry forever but delight to show mercy.

You will again have compassion on us; you will tread our sins underfoot and hurl all our iniquities into the depths of the sea.

You will be true to Jacob, and show mercy to Abraham, AS YOU PLEDGED ON OATH TO OUR FATHERS IN DAYS LONG AGO.

> The Prophet Micah
> Micah 7:18–20
> (Emphases added.)

THE APOSTLE PAUL'S GREAT DISCOURSE ON ISRAEL

In the midst of his most important epistle to the Gentile world, the Apostle Paul took three chapters to answer the vital question: *What about Israel?* In his Epistle to the Romans, Paul gave the New Testament's only full and definitive answer to this question.

All other statements about Israel found in the New Testament must be understood in the light of Romans chapters nine through eleven. As discussed in chapter three, one of the most important rules of interpretation is that we must interpret the obscure passages of Scripture in the light of the most complete and clear passages that deal with the same subject. Interpretation must never be based on a parable, an allegory, or an isolated obscure verse. These kinds of Scriptures can illustrate the clear passages, but not interpret them. Otherwise one will produce, as so many cults have, novel and heretical doctrines that contradict the consistent and clear witness of the whole Bible.

Here is a brief analytical outline of these chapters: Romans 9, THE NATION OF ISRAEL IN THE PAST: ELECTED; Romans 10, THE NATION OF ISRAEL IN THE PRESENT: REJECTED; Romans 11, THE NATION OF ISRAEL IN THE FUTURE: AC-CEPTED. Since these are such important passages relating to the issue of Dominion Theology, I will use the next several chapters to analyze them.

Paul's Unceasing Grief Over Israel (Romans 9:1–3)

In the first eight chapters of Romans, Paul taught about the wonders of God's saving work through Christ that is given on the basis of grace through faith alone. As he concluded that section of his Epistle, he taught that once we are born as a child of God and put into living union with Christ, nothing in heaven, nor on earth, nor in the future, nor any created thing (including ourselves) can separate us from the love of God (8:38–39).

This brought up the issue of Israel's status. God made the same sort of promises to Abraham, Isaac, Jacob, and their descendants as He makes here to the Christians. In spite of this, Israel as a people and nation is now in apostasy. She has rejected the very Messiah that her prophets had predicted. At the time Paul wrote this letter, Israel was zealously persecuting those who believed in Jesus as the Messiah.

In the light of this, there were many logical questions that needed an answer. Has God's Word become ineffective? If God couldn't keep His covenant people from falling away into unbelief, how do we know that He can keep us? If indeed the LORD failed to keep His solemn word to Israel, will He keep His word to the Church and with me as an individual?

Paul begins his answer with a personal testimony about his superhuman love for his physical kinsmen, the people Israel. His grief is unceasing over them. He even declares that if such a thing were possible, he would gladly become separated from Christ if that would help open their eyes and save them (9:1–3).

The Ten Advantages of a Physical Israelite (Romans 9:4–5)

Paul actually began to speak about the Jews' advantages back in Romans 3:1–3. As was his style, he only introduced the subject and dropped it in order to pick it up later in more detail. Paul began by saying:

> **What advantage, then, is there in being a Jew, or what value is there in circumcision? MUCH IN EVERY WAY! First of all, they have been entrusted with the very words of God.**
>
> **What if some did not have faith? Will their lack of faith nullify God's faithfulness? Not at all! Let God be true, and every man a liar. As it is written: "So that you may be proved right in your words and prevail in your judging."** (Romans 3:1–4)

It is important to remember that Paul wrote this letter to a well-developed Gentile Church, and also that he had just taught in chapter two that a true Jew has a circumcised heart. A Gentile would naturally think, "Well, if the only important circumcision is that of the heart, what advantage is there to being a physical Jew?" Paul anticipates and answers this question emphatically— **"MUCH IN EVERY WAY."**

THE FIRST ADVANTAGE Paul lists the first of these advantages: the Jews were entrusted with the living words of God. What a privilege! God entrusted no other people to receive and write down His living Words. This is one of the major reasons they were chosen and miraculously made into a nation.

Paul then only touches upon the question that he answers in detail in chapters nine through eleven: **"What if SOME did not have faith? Will their lack of faith nullify God's faithfulness?"** God's faithfulness concerning what? In context, this must refer to His faithfulness to keep His unconditional promises to physical Israel. In the light of Israel's current blindness and unbelief, Paul had to explain how God would yet fulfill His unconditional promises to Israel.

In Romans chapter nine, Paul again begins to enumerate the advantages of being a physical descendant of Abraham, Isaac, and Jacob. He begins to recount these advantages out of great anguish of soul. His heart is broken over his kinsmen's tragedy. In spite of having such a great heritage, the Israelites are still failing to enter the promised eternal blessings because of unbelief.

THE SECOND ADVANTAGE (Romans 9:4a) The Jews have the advantage of being **Israelites** by the designation of God Himself. **Israel** came to mean *"prince of God,"* for Jacob strove with God and prevailed. As a result, he was given this name by God. Thereafter, God called his descendants Israel. No other race of people has ever been so designated by God.

THE THIRD ADVANTAGE (Romans 9:4b) Paul says, **"to them belongs the adoption as sons."** Again, this is unique to Israel as a nation. Christians are adopted individually into God's family through union with Christ. But Israel was adopted as a nation.

THE FOURTH ADVANTAGE (Romans 9:4c) Israel alone was given the visible, continuing manifestation of **"the glory"** of God. Throughout Israel's wanderings in the Sinai desert, God led them by a pillar of cloud by day and a pillar of fire at night. The pillar was connected to a great cloud that protected them from the blazing heat of the Sinai desert. At night, the pillar provided warmth against the sudden chill that comes upon that area. The fire of God's glory was again manifested in a special way at Mount Sinai with the giving of the Law. After the Exodus wanderings, God's glory, which was later called the Shekinah Glory, hovered over the mercy seat in the Holy of Holies of the Temple, and remained with the nation.

THE FIFTH ADVANTAGE (Romans 9:4d) **"The Covenants"** were made to only one people on earth—Israel. God made covenants (plural) with Abraham, Isaac, Jacob, and their descendants. These covenants promised an everlasting nation, the perpetual possession of a specific piece of real estate, an eternal Kingdom and King. I will deal with these covenants in detail in a moment, but I'd like to say here that it's only through our union with Christ, and on the basis of *His inheritance of the covenants,* that Gentiles are brought into salvation. (See Ephesians 2:11–13.) In other words, we get in on "Jesus' membership card to Israel's convenants." In this sense, the Christian is "a spiritual seed of Abraham." But the Church is never called the House of Israel, the House of Jacob, or the Nation of Israel. These terms are only used to refer to the physical Israelites.

THE SIXTH ADVANTAGE (Romans 9:4e) **God's Law,** commonly called the Law of Moses, was only given to the Nation of Israel. From the beginning God made it clear that this was a conditional, temporary covenant. One of the main reasons God made this covenant with Israel was to bring to light for all to see the impossibility of man's saving himself by his own efforts and merits. Its primary purpose was to show Israel and the world that the only way to be accepted with God is through faith in the Messiah.

THE SEVENTH ADVANTAGE (Romans 9:4f) Israel was given **"the Temple service."** Israel alone was given a Divine order of worship with the only God-given provision of sacrifice in the world for the forgiveness of sin.

THE EIGHTH ADVANTAGE (Romans 9:4g) To Israel as a nation were made unique **promises.** Israel was the only people who had promises of the Messiah and of direct blessings through Him. All other nations received blessings only through Israel. They were the only nation that was promised a specific plot of land, a city, and a kingdom on an earth from which the original curse would be removed.

THE NINTH ADVANTAGE (Romans 9:5a) **"Whose are the fathers."** Only Israel had as its fathers **Abraham**, the head of many nations and the "friend of God"; **Isaac**, who was born by supernatural power; and **Jacob**, who wrestled with God and prevailed. Other nations had great ancestors, but Abraham, Isaac, and Jacob have the honor of being not merely natural, but divinely chosen leaders.

THE TENTH ADVANTAGE (Romans 9:5b) When this clause is correctly translated, it presents a tremendous and climactic advantage for the Israelite. It literally says, **"from whom is the Messiah, according to the flesh, who is God overall, blessed forever. Amen."** The one who stepped out of eternity into time and forever joined Himself to a true human nature was none other than God, the second person of the Trinity. He honored Israel above all by choosing to be born into their family. The first words of the New Testament bring out this great honor: **"A record of the genealogy of Jesus Christ the son of David, the son of Abraham . . ."** So anti-Semites beware, *God the Son is a Jew.*

Who is a Jew?

One of the most perplexing questions today is, Who is a Jew? Even in the State of Israel, this question has not been satisfactorily answered. The orthodox rabbis are on the horns of a dilemma.

If they say that a Jew is simply a person whose mother was a

Jew and is circumcised (if a male), then being a Jew is only a physical thing.

But if they say that a Jew is one who also believes certain precepts of Judaism, there are even greater problems. First, there is an argument among the Orthodox, Conservative, and Reformed sects of Judaism as to just which precepts must be believed. Second, this would disqualify many of the citizens of the State of Israel from being considered Jews. A large percentage of them do not believe in the teachings of Judaism, whether it is Orthodox, Conservative, or Reformed. Many are agnostics and very secular-ized, especially those who originally established the state.

It must also be clarified that the name *Jew* was originally coined while the southern kingdom of Judah was in Babylonian captivity. It referred only to the tribes from the land of Judah, namely Judah, Benjamin, and Levi. However, in modern usage, it has been generally applied to all the survivors of the descendants of Abraham, Isaac, and Jacob.

An Even Greater Problem of Definition

Just who is a true Jew or Israelite is the most critical question in resolving the controversy between the Premillennialists and the Postmillennial-Dominionists. If the Church is now and forever Israel, and if Christians are permanently the only true Israelites, then the contentions of the Dominionists are justified.

But if there is still a future for national Israel, and if the Church is a distinct and separate program of God from them, then the Premil position is justified.

In the last two chapters we have considered why Premillen-nialists believe that the covenants made to physical Israel cannot be broken. But it is of equal importance to see that in the New Testament God says the same thing as in the Old concerning the immutability of His covenant relationship to ethnic Israel.

The Apostle Paul takes up this question immediately after he gives the ten advantages of the Israelites. Here is the Apostle Paul's inspired answer to the mystery as to just who is a true Israelite, and as to why they are now rejected.

ISRAEL IN THE PAST: ELECTED

Paul immediately gets to the real problem: the failure of Israel to believe in and receive her Messiah, and her consequent rejection, had to be answered. Paul raises an issue that he had apparently already encountered among the Gentile Christians when he says, **"It is not as though God's word had failed."** (Romans 9:6a) Apparently, some were already questioning whether God had failed to keep His Word to the Israelites. This whole issue has great relevance to the Christians. For what assurance can a Christian have that God will keep His Word to him if He didn't keep His numerous promises confirmed by oath to Israel? This is the real underlying question that the Holy Spirit answers in Romans chapters nine, ten, and eleven.

Case History Number One: Isaac and Ishmael

In answer to this, the Holy Spirit brings out an imperative factor that had always been implicit in the covenants with Abraham and his descendants: **"For NOT ALL who are descended FROM Israel ARE Israel. NOR because they are his descendants ARE THEY ALL Abraham's children. On the contrary, 'It is through Isaac that your offsprings will be reckoned.' In other words, it is not the natural children who are God's children, but it is the children of the promise who are regarded as Abraham's offspring. For this was how the promise was stated: 'At the Appointed time I will return, and Sarah will have a son.'"** (Romans 9:6b–9)

There are certain factors in this context which must be carefully observed. God DOES NOT say, **NOT ANY who are called Israel are Israel**, but rather, **Not ALL who are called Israel are Israel.** This context is ONLY dealing with the question of *who among physical Israel is true Israel*. The contrast is between believing Israel and unbelieving Israel, not between Israelites and Gentiles.

The only point that the Holy Spirit is developing here is that there has always been a *spiritual Israel* among *physical Israel* who are called **"the remnant."**

This point is further supported by the Holy Spirit's careful assertion that it is only **"the children of the promise"** who are true Israel. Then the **promise** that makes a true Israelite is specifically spelled out.

The case history of Isaac and Ishmael is given to prove the point. Ishmael was the son of Abraham, yet he was a Gentile. It was only Isaac that was promised to *both* Abraham and Sarah. He was miraculously conceived in response to their faith in God's promise, which made him *the child of promise*.

But the unbelieving Jew could say, "Of course Ishmael wasn't an Israelite. He was Abraham's illegitimate child through Sarah's Egyptian handmaid."

Case History Number Two: Jacob and Esau

The Holy Spirit, anticipating this line of reasoning, brings out another case history that should settle forever the question of who is a true Israelite: **"Not only that, but Rebecca's children had ONE and the SAME father, our father Isaac. Yet, before the twins were born or had done anything good or bad—in order that God's purpose in election might stand: not of works but by him who calls—she was told, 'The older will serve the younger.' Just as it is written: Jacob I loved, but Esau I hated."** (Romans 9:10–13)

This case is conclusive. Jacob and Esau were twins. Both were descendants of Abraham and Isaac. Both were circumcised. But Jacob became a believer, Esau did not. As a result, one was a true Israelite, the other was not.

THREE KINDS OF JEWS

History scholar and theologian Dr. Robert B. Thieme, Jr., in his excellent book *Anti-Semitism,* gave the best definition of an Israelite I have seen. He described three different kinds of Israelites.[1]

The First Distinction: Racial Israel

Israel, as we have seen, was created by a miracle. Sarah's womb was barren and Abraham's body was sexually dead. Yet by faith in God's promise, they were supernaturally enabled to have a son, Isaac, long after it was a physical impossibility (Romans 4:19–22). The line of promise was carried on through Isaac's son, Jacob. (It is interesting to note that God so renewed Abraham's youth that he had other children much later. But Isaac was the one to whom he willed all that he had. [Genesis 25:1–11])

From that time on, the Bible considers anyone to be racially an Israelite who possesses the genes of Abraham, Isaac, and Jacob. One does not have to be a full-blooded Israelite to be racially part of Israel. The Bible never taught that an Israelite was someone with absolute racial purity. This myth is blown out the window by even a casual study of Israel's Biblical history. Thieme accurately traces the history of physical Israel:

130

Racial purity is largely a myth! Consider the fact that the first Jew was a Gentile Chaldean and that the early Israelites as a rule chose their wives [from] within their [Gentile] family (Genesis 24:4; 28:2). Although the Mosaic Law later imposed marriage restrictions upon the Israelites (Deut. 7:3, 4; 23:3, 7, 8), mixed marriages were not unusual. For example, Joseph's wife was an Egyptian, the daughter of a gentile high priest in Pharaoh's court (Genesis 41:45). The two sons who issued from that union, Ephraim and Manasseh, were half Jew and half Gentile. They were to be numbered among the Israelites and not among the Egyptians (Gen. 48:15, 16), which caused the original twelve tribes to branch out into thirteen tribes (Gen. 48:20).

What qualified Ephraim and Manasseh for acceptance into the ancient Jewish tribal system? Certainly they had no Jewish mother! Was it deference for Joseph's exalted position? Was it because Joseph, as Jacob and Rachel's eldest son, had received the double portion of the family inheritance (Gen. 48:22)? No! The basis of their recognition as Jews was twofold: Personal relationship to the God of Abraham, Isaac and Jacob—a spiritual factor, which will be discussed under the category of the regenerate Jew—and secondly the fact that they possessed the genes of Israel; Jewish blood coursed in their veins!

One of the most revered Jews of all time is Moses. A true descendant of the tribe of Levi (Exodus 2:2), Moses married outside the Jewish tribal system. His first wife was a Midianite (Exodus 2:15, 21); his second, an Ethiopian (Numbers 12:1). Both were Gentiles. . . .

In the genealogy of our Lord appear the names of two notorious Gentile women: Rahab, a Canaanite, and Ruth, a Moabitess (Matthew 1:5)! While it is true that some records have been lost in the process of Israel's captivity in Babylon and during the dispersion of A.D. 70, the Jews have done a splendid job of keeping track of their genealogy over the centuries. This makes it relatively easy for people to determine whether or not they are racial Jews.[2]

I have met Jews in Israel who have immigrated from virtually every part of the world. On a flight to Israel aboard El Al Airlines, I was invited to visit with the crew in the cockpit. I spoke with the engineer who had a distinct Indian accent and a few of their physical characteristics. I found that he had in fact come to Israel from India. He said his family could trace their ancestry back more than 2500 years in India. He knew that he was descended from the tribe of Asher from carefully preserved records of the family history. Apparently, his family was originally dispersed in 722 B.C. by the Assyrian destruction of the Ten Tribes of the Northern Kingdom of Israel. Though there had obviously been some intermarriage, he knew that he was an Israelite. This is true of the millions of Israelites scattered throughout the world. After all, why would they suffer such persecution for being Jews if they in fact are not Jews?

One of the many false accusations leveled against the Jews by the anti-Semites is that there is no such thing as a racial Jew today. They claim that "most European Jews today are descended from a false race known as the 'Khazars,' and that there is no way for any 'Jew' to trace whether he is an Israelite or not." Thieme summarizes the Khazars' history:

> They were a Tataric (ancient Turkic) Greek-speaking people who first appeared in Transcaucasia in the second century A.D. In the fifth century they were subjugated by the Huns but rose to great power two centuries later. Charging across the Russian steppes, these greatly feared warriors conquered the Crimea and extended their empire from the western shores of the Caspian Sea to the River Don, from the southern Ukraine to the region north of the Black Sea and as far as Kiev. They had levied a heavy tribute on the eastern Slavs. They fought the Persians and the Armenians; they battled the Arabs, whose intent it was to convert them to Islam; and, on occasion, they fought the Byzantine Empire, which forcibly tried to make them Christian.
>
> In circa A.D. 740, the "khakan" (ruler) of the Khazars embraced Judaism. His conversion was a compromise between Christianity and the religion of Islam. Judaism became the official religion of the empire, and many people followed the example of the khakan. Others accepted what they presumed to be Christianity, only to practice a strange mixture of paganism and nominal

Christianity. All maintained their Tataric customs and warlike nature. The Khazar empire continued for 250 years and reached a high degree of civilization, which was characterized by religious tolerance.

In A.D. 969, the Khazars were defeated by the armies of Sviatoslav, Duke of Kiev, and incorporated into the new Russian state. Subsequently many of the Khazars were converted by the Russian orthodox church. Believed to be the ancestors of the Crimean Jews, the Khazars have been associated with Communist aspirations for world domination by the anti-Semites, who have thus found an additional outlet for their venomous attacks against the Jews.[3]

The Khazars who became prosylites to Judaism did so primarily as a matter of political expediency. Most were not really serious about practicing Judaism. Most did not have the kind of commitment that stood up under persecution. But the main point is that there is absolutely no reputable evidence to establish that the European Jews are primarily, or even partly, descended from the Khazars. It is another fiction built upon bits and pieces of deliberately distorted history.

The Second Distinction: Religious Israel

A religious Israelite is not a true Israelite. Religion is a word that is not used in a good light in the Bible. Strictly defined, religion is a system of works whereby a man seeks to earn God's acceptance. Satan uses religion more than any other means to blind people to the truth. The common denominator of all religion, whether it is Islam, Buddhism, Hinduism, Judaism, or a false form of Christianity, is that it assumes that man can do something to help God save him.

The Jewish religion called Judaism is primarily the product of centuries of rabbinic interpretations of the Old Testament. It is locked into a traditional form that is codified in the books of the Talmud. Modern Judaism is divided into three basic denominations.

The first and most influential denomination is ORTHODOX JUDAISM. This sect is primarily the heir of the first century Pharisees. Until modern times this was the predominant form of Judaism practiced by Jews in the dispersion. Their doctrines were

133

first formulated by the Pharisee scribes and priests who survived the A.D. 70 holocaust. They fled to a place called Yavneh (which is just southeast of modern Tel Aviv), where they reinterpreted Judaism so that it could be practiced without a Temple and animal sacrifices. In theory, this group fanatically holds to the Torah. But in reality they hold the rabbinical interpretations of the Torah as more authoritative. In my opinion, this tradition is the veil over the Israelite's heart that blinds him to the truth. At Yavneh, every prophecy concerning the Suffering Messiah was explained away.

The second denomination is CONSERVATIVE JUDAISM. Thieme wrote, "The conservative Jew observes the traditional rituals of Judaism but allows for a more liberal interpretation of the religious fundamentals and of the Jewish life. Conservative Judaism is, in fact, a compromise between Orthodox and Reform Judaism."[4]

The third denomination is REFORM JUDAISM. This developed during the modern times when the age of rationalism began to impact upon the Jewish community. It is both modernized and secularized. It does not enforce the ancient traditions and customs, and holds a very liberal view of the Bible.

These groups do not agree on most things. But all three denominations do agree on one thing; you cannot believe in Jesus of Nazareth as the Messiah of Israel and be a true Jew. Most agree about supporting the State of Israel. But even on this issue there is some disagreement. Some fanatical Orthodox Jews believe that the present State is false, and that only the Messiah can establish the true State of Israel.

There is a saying in Israel that appropriately describes the relationship between these different sects: "If you have two Jews arguing, you will have three opinions."

The Third Distinction: Regenerate Israel

The Regenerate Israelite has always been the True Israelite. This group combines together both the racial and spiritual factors that the Bible describes as **"the remnant of Israel."** It was to a sincere and devoutly religious and racially pure Israelite named Nicodemus that the Lord Jesus declared: **"I tell you the truth, unless a man is born again** [from above], **he cannot see** [understand] **the kingdom of God"**; and, **". . . unless a man is born of water and the Spirit, he cannot enter the kingdom of God. Flesh gives birth to flesh, but the Spirit gives birth to spirit. You should not be** surprised at my saying, 'YOU ALL must be born again.'" (John 3:3, 5, 6, 7) And remember, this was not said to Nicodemus under the conditions of the New Testament, but during the age of the Law.

Only an Israelite who believed in God's revelation of the way of forgiveness was born spiritually. The Old Testament Israelite believed in the available revelation of the coming Messiah. Jesus revealed that **Abraham** foresaw His coming as the Messiah and rejoiced. (John 8:56) The Holy Spirit reveals that **Moses** turned down the throne of Egypt because **"he regarded disgrace for the sake of the Messiah as of greater value than the treasures of Egypt."** (Hebrews 11:26) Moses had to have had a very real understanding of the Messiah to turn down the throne of Egypt.

The Bible reveals the insufficiency of being only a racial and religious Jew: **"A man is not a Jew if he is only one outwardly, nor is circumcision merely outward and physical. No, a man is a Jew if he is one inwardly; and circumcision is circumcision of the heart, by the Spirit, not by the written code. Such a man's praise is not from men, but from God."** (Romans 2:28–29) The Holy Spirit reminded the Jews that Abraham was declared righteous before God on the basis of his faith alone fifteen years before he received the sign of circumcision. (Romans 4:9–12) Most Dominionists, however, divorce this passage from its context and interpret it to mean that the Christians have permanently replaced the Israelites in God's plan because we are circumcised in the heart by the Spirit. They believe that this made Israel's covenant of physical circumcision irrelevant. But the Holy Spirit refutes this false conclusion when he asks in the very same context, **"What advantage, then, is there in being a Jew, or what value is there in circumcision? MUCH IN EVERY WAY!"** (Romans 3:1, 2). He declares unequivocally that there is *still* an advantage to being part of the Jewish race.

The Bible teaches that no ritual has ever had meaning unless accompanied by true faith. All the members of Abraham's household were circumcised. This in and of itself didn't make them true Israelites. Both Ishmael and Esau were circumcised, but were Gentiles. Neither one was a true descendant of Abraham because neither was born spiritually.

In conclusion then, the Bible has always taught that only the racial Israelite who is born spiritually is a true Israelite and heir to the eternal promises.

When a Jew believes in Jesus as his Messiah in this present

age, he enters into union with Him and becomes a member of His Body, the Church. In the same way, when a Gentile believes in Jesus as his Savior, he ceases to be a Gentile. He also becomes a member of the Body of Christ. In this relationship, both Jew and Gentile become one in Christ where there are no more racial distinctions. Together we become members of one Royal Family, and are made citizens of a Heavenly Nation and Kingdom. (Galatians 3:28–29; 1 Peter 2:9; Philippians 3:20–21) But the time is soon coming when the Body of Christ will be completed and God will turn back the focus of His grace to His ancient people, Israel. (Romans 11:25–29) He will then keep all His unfulfilled covenants with them as a believing nation. This will be established when we consider Romans chapter eleven.

THE MYSTERY OF GOD'S ELECTION

There is an issue here that reaches into the deepest mysteries of God's Word. It is a subject which I have agonized to understand for nearly the entire thirty-five years I have been a Christian. It must be dealt with, because it is at the very heart of the answer as to why God will yet forgive and restore a remnant of physical Israel, and secure to them all the unfulfilled covenants and promises made to their forefathers.

Why is it that some believe in Christ and others do not? What makes one seek after God and another not? The Scriptures say, **"There is NO ONE righteous, not even one; there is NO ONE who understands, NO ONE SEEKS GOD. ALL have turned away, they have together become worthless; there is NO ONE who does good, not even one."** (Romans 3:10–11) These are all inclusive and unequivocal statements. No human being understands God, nor seeks after Him.

Since this is so, and the Scriptures cannot lie, why is it that some do seek after God? The Lord Jesus Himself gives us the answer: **"ALL that the Father gives to me will come to me, and whoever comes to me I will never drive away. . . . No one can come to me unless the Father who sent me draws him, and I will raise him up at the last day."** (John 6:37, 44) According to the Scriptures, faith is the *result* of God drawing us, not the *cause* of God drawing us.

This naturally brings up the questions, "What about free will?" "Don't we have the freedom to chose God?" The answer is,

"Yes, we do, but we use it to chose against God unless He draws us to Him!" Let me explain.

When Adam and Eve sinned, their spiritual natures died instantly. The one part of their being that could know and understand God as a person died. Without spiritual life, we are like a television set without electrical power. The TV signals can be all about us, but unless we turn on the power, the set can't pick them up.

When mankind, represented by Adam and Eve, chose to reject their relationship with God, He was under no moral obligation to do anything about it. But because the LORD loved us, He chose to provide a way of forgiveness in the only way that would be acceptable to His righteous and just character; He did all the work of salvation Himself and offered it to us as a gift. This way, no human merit was involved. The moment we try in any way to earn salvation, we put ourselves on a merit system, and the standard becomes God's perfect righteousness.

The Origin of Spiritual Death

Adam and Eve illustrated in the Garden a phenomenon that has been going on ever since. After they sinned, they not only didn't seek God, they hid from Him. But God sought them, and performed a sacrifice to provide a covering for their guilt. He provided them with animal skins to cover their nakedness, pointing to a greater future sacrifice—first the Passover lamb, then the Messiah. When the LORD killed an animal to get its skin, it was the first time Adam and Eve had ever seen anything die. They realized by this that their sin could only be forgiven by the death of a Divinely provided substitute. They learned about the way of faith through accepting this provision for their sin.

From that time onward, all humans have been born physically alive but spiritually dead. The only way we can regain spiritual life is by a miraculous birth. This is why Jesus taught, **"Unless one is born again [from above], he cannot understand nor enter the Kingdom of God."** (See John 3:1–16.)

When Ezekiel predicted the future restoration of faith of the Nation of Israel, he spoke of this same spiritual rebirth for each individual: **"For I WILL take you from the nations, gather you from all the lands, and bring you into your own land. THEN I WILL sprinkle clean water on you, and you will be clean. . . . Moreover, I WILL give you a NEW HEART and put** a NEW SPIRIT within you; and I WILL remove the heart of stone from your flesh and give you a heart of flesh. And I WILL put MY SPIRIT within you and cause you to walk in My statutes, and you will be careful to observe My ordinances." (Ezekiel 36:24–27 NASB)

From birth we are incapable of understanding either God or His Word. God says, "But a natural [soulish] man does not accept the things of the Spirit of God; for they are foolishness to him, and he cannot understand them, because they are spiritually appraised." (1 Corinthians 2:14 NASB) The original Greek word *psychikos* (ψυχικος) translated *natural* emphasizes that we are born as **soulish** beings without a spirit. We have a **soul**, *psyche* (ψυχη), that can only understand physical phenomena. But we have no spiritual nature with which to perceive Divine phenomena. We can see evidences of God's existence in nature, but we can't know Him as a person. The soul may become highly educated in the natural, material realm, but it cannot comprehend even the elementary things of God's spiritual realm.

Since we are born spiritually dead, incapable of understanding God as a person, there is one consistent and universal experience. All mankind uses his freedom of choice to *reject* God. God doesn't make us reject Him. It is the natural decision of a being who is separated and alienated from God, without the kind of life to know Him as a person.

Because God loved us, He became a man in the person of Jesus Christ. He came to die for the sins of every person who would ever live, even the sins of those whom He foreknew would reject Him (1 John 2:1–2). By His substitutionary death in our place, He removed sin as a barrier between God and mankind. The only barrier between us and God today is our failure to receive by faith the pardon He purchased for us. Jesus stressed this point when He promised to send the Holy Spirit: ". . . But if I go, I will send him [the Holy Spirit] to you. When he comes, he will convict the world of guilt in regard to sin and righteousness and judgment: in regard to sin, because MEN DO NOT BELIEVE IN ME. . . ." (John 16:9–11) The Holy Spirit *convicts* the world *of the one issue that keeps us from salvation,* that of refusing to believe in the Lord Jesus Christ and receiving His gift of forgiveness.

Herein is the terrible tragedy. Every human being freely chooses to reject the LORD's gracious gift of forgiveness and eternal life. God doesn't make us do that. We freely choose to reject it.

The Proper Question to Ask

According to the Bible, God stepped into this mass of hostile and unbelieving humanity, and drew some to Himself. Therefore, in the light of all this, the question that we should ask is not, "Why doesn't God save everyone?", but rather, *"Why does God save anyone?"* No one deserves to be saved. No one, unaided, seeks God. But praise Him, He draws some of us to Himself in spite of our alienation and rejection. The Bible says, **"For it is by grace you have been saved, through faith—and this is not from yourselves, it is the gift of God—not by works, so that no one can boast."** (Ephesians 2:8, 9)

Once again, God does not make anyone reject Him. We all choose to do that of our own free will. The fact that some do believe is because God graciously draws them to Himself and gives them the gift of faith. Dr. Ironsides, a great Bible teacher of the early twentieth century, had a simple way of explaining this mystery. He said that as we approach the gates of heaven, it says "Whosoever will may come"; and after we enter and look back, there is written, "Chosen from the foundation of the earth."

God's Illustration of Election Through Jacob and Esau

Over a thousand years after Esau's lifetime, God looked back upon him and said through the prophet Malachai, **"Jacob I loved, but Esau I hated."** (Malachai 1:2) Esau despised God. Both he and his descendants lived lives of rebellion against the LORD. They became known as the Edomites. The Edomites persecuted Israel and were later destroyed as a nation.

Jacob, humanly speaking, was no better than Esau. In fact, Jacob's name means *supplanter,* or *one who takes something by deception.* But Jacob had a heart for God and desired the spiritual-rights of the firstborn. Esau, who was the firstborn, had such a low regard for his birthright that in a moment of hunger, he traded it to Jacob for a pot of lentil stew.

Why did Jacob seek God and Esau not seek Him? The LORD answers this very clearly, **"Yet before the twins were born or HAD DONE ANYTHING GOOD OR BAD—in order that GOD'S PURPOSE IN ELECTION MIGHT STAND: not by works but by him who calls—she [Rebecca] was told, 'The older [Esau] will serve the younger [Jacob].'"** (Romans 9:11–12) If words mean anything, God chose Jacob before he was born—before he had done anything good or evil.

From what we read in the Scriptures, Esau must have been an all around great guy. Certainly his father Isaac favored him over Jacob. But God does not call us on the basis of some innate goodness or charm, but because of His grace that works freely through Christ's atonement on our behalf. If the LORD saved only "good people," no one would be saved.

Is God Unjust?

The LORD anticipates the question of all who study this section of the book of Romans:

> **What then shall we say? Is God unjust? Not at all! For he says to Moses,**
>
> > **"I will have mercy on whom I have mercy,**
> > **and I will have compassion on whom I have compassion."**
>
> **It [God's election] does not, therefore, depend on man's desire or effort, but on God's mercy."** (Romans 9:14–16)

Why Introduce Election Here?

The really important question to answer at this point is, "Why does the LORD introduce this subject in a context that is answering whether physical Israel has a future as a nation?"

I believe that it is because Divine election answers the whole problem of whether Israel is finished as God's distinct covenant people, or still has a unique and distinct national future in God's plan.

If we contend, as the Dominionists do, that Israel has forever forfeited her covenants for rejecting her Messiah, then we must ultimately say that Israel lost her election as a nation because of a lack of merit. Of course, this will pose no problem for many Charismatics, since they believe that a believer can lose his salvation. But this poses a monumental problem for the Reconstructionists, since most of them correctly believe in the eternal security of the believer.

The Holy Spirit's logic here is inescapable. He shows that God's election of Israel is the same as His election of individuals. In fact, God's dealing with Israel as a Nation is a picture of how he deals with us as individuals.

Since the Nation of Israel was elected and created on the basis of pure grace and not human merit, then it cannot be rejected because of human failure. What do the Scriptures say about Israel's election? This is certainly clear in the case of Isaac and Jacob. This is also brought out very clearly in chapter eleven where God shows that even today, Israel's rejection is not total: **"So too, at the present time there is a REMNANT CHOSEN BY GRACE. And if by grace, then it is no longer by works; if it were, grace would no longer be grace."** (Romans 11:5–6) This clearly shows that within physical Israel, there is a spiritual Israel called *the believing remnant*. Their election is and always has been on the basis of grace alone, not human works or merit—otherwise, grace would be no more grace. Grace and human merit are mutually exclusive. Where you have one, you cannot have the other. It is to this remnant of true Israel, who is from the physical descendants of Abraham, Isaac, and Jacob, that God has sworn to fulfill His promises.

Case History Number Three: Moses and Pharaoh

The LORD further illustrates the truth of election with the case of the Pharaoh of the Exodus. He demonstrates how the hardness of Pharaoh's heart was used to spread the message of His reality and glory to the nations. This Pharaoh grew up in the same court as Moses did. He had the same opportunity to learn about God as Moses did. But Pharaoh freely chose to reject God and His revelation. So God used his rejection and hardened his heart even more, so that through Pharaoh's resistance and obstinance, He could reveal more of His miraculous power and glory. Those miracles were not only a witness to the nations of that day, but through the record of them in the Word of God, they have continued to witness to millions down through the centuries.

A wrong inference might be drawn against God's character on this point. So the Holy Spirit anticipates it by saying, **"One of you will say to me: 'Then why does God still blame us? For who resists his will?' But who are you, O man, to talk back to God?**

Shall what is formed say to him who formed it, 'Why did you make me like this?'" (Romans 9:19–20) You see, the LORD doesn't have to make us do evil; it comes naturally through our sin natures. God restrains evil so that the unbeliever doesn't destroy His people along with the world. If the Holy Spirit had not been restraining evil to some degree, man would have destroyed the world long ago. (2 Thessalonians 2:4–12) Apart from God's restraint, natural man does evil continuously, so God is not unjust for using man's rebellion for His own purposes.

God gives the real answer to this issue in the following verse: **"What if God, choosing to show his wrath and make his power known, bore with great patience the objects of his wrath— prepared for destruction [or, who prepared themselves for destruction]."** (Romans 9:22)

The key to understanding the mystery of why God holds the unbeliever responsible is in the correct interpretation of the grammatical voice of the verb **to prepare.** The original word (κατηρτισμενα) is in a form that can be interpreted either as a passive voice or a middle voice. The context has to determine which. If it is passive, then it means that *God prepares the unbelievers for destruction*. If it is middle voice, then it means that the *unbeliever prepares himself for destruction*.

Both God's character and the context indicate that it should be interpreted as a *middle voice*. The unbeliever chooses to reject God's free gift of salvation. He chooses to live in rebellion against God and all that He stands for. In so doing, he prepares himself for judgment. After God endures the unbeliever with great patience, He may choose to use his very rebellion as a means of revealing Himself to those who will believe.

The Believing Remnant of Israel Is the True Israel

Paul now reveals that the Old Testament Prophets forecast the rejection of the Nation of Israel because of sin, and the salvation of Gentiles. But the Holy Spirit also reveals through these same Prophets that there will always be a remnant of Israel to whom the covenants made with their forefathers will be fulfilled. Paul reasons concerning this:

Isaiah cries out concerning ISRAEL:

"Though the number of the
    Israelites be like the sand
    by the sea,
    only the REMNANT will be
    saved.
For the LORD will carry out
    his sentence on earth with
    speed and finality." [Isaiah 10:22–23]

It is just as Isaiah said previously:

"Unless the LORD Almighty
    had left us DESCENDANTS,
we would have become like
    Sodom,
and we would have been like
    Gomorrah."   [Isaiah 1:9]

(Romans 9:27–29)

Paul, through inspiration of the Spirit, clearly reveals that true Israel has been and always will be the believing remnant from among the physical Israelites, and that they continue to be God's special people.

It is especially important to note the context of Isaiah chapter ten, from which the quote in Romans 9:27–28 is taken. It predicts God's judgment upon Assyria for afflicting Israel. Yet the prophecy quoted above concerning **the remnant** that will return is applied by the Holy Spirit to the time of the Messiah's coming. This further demonstrates a very important factor in the interpretation of Bible prophecy which was discussed in chapter three. Prophecies concerning events that are in the distant future are often couched in the midst of a message that is about contemporary events, or events in the near future. Carefully note also that right after the LORD predicts the restoration of the remnant of Israel and the destruction of the Assyrian enemy (which must be applied to a yet future enemy), He says, **"VERY SOON my anger against you will end and my wrath will be directed to their**

[Israel's enemies] **destruction."** (Isaiah 10:25) What the LORD called **Very soon** has already been some 2700 years. Many prophecies in the Bible speak of the Second Coming as if it were to come immediately. But this is intended to mean that Jesus could come at any moment, so that the believer is kept in a state of constant expectancy. If the Dominionists ever admit that this kind of prophecy exists, their whole system of prophetic interpretation will fall apart.

An Imperative Lesson in Prophetic Interpretation

These are principles of interpreting prophecy that Dominionists, especially David Chilton, try to discount. Chilton, for instance, argues that the predictions of the Book of Revelation had to be fulfilled within the first century because chapter one, verse three says, **"for the time is near."** The adverb **near** is ἐγγυς in the original Greek. It literally means something close by or near in point of time. Paul uses it in an exhortation to holy living: **"Let your forebearing spirit be known to all men. The LORD is NEAR."** (Philippians 4:5 NASB) According to the best Greek lexicon, *eggus* (ἐγγυς) in this verse refers to the nearness of the LORD's Second Coming.[5] The *imminence* of His return is used as the motivation for living in the Spirit. Obviously, the LORD has not returned yet. But ἐγγυς is used in this case to mean that the LORD's return is an *any moment* or *imminent* possibility. It is used in the same way in Revelation 1:3.

Israel's Remnant in History

There are innumerable prophecies about Israel's believing remnant from among physical Israel which show that the spiritual eternal blessings in the covenants were always intended for them:

> **The LORD will scatter you among the peoples, and ONLY A FEW OF YOU WILL SURVIVE** [the remnant] **among the nations to which the LORD will drive you** [the dispersion of A.D. 70] **. . . WHEN you are in distress and all these things have happened to you** [the Tribulation period], **THEN in the latter days you will return to the LORD your God and obey him. For the LORD your God is a merciful God; HE WILL NOT abandon or destroy you or FORGET THE COVENANT**

144

with YOUR FOREFATHERS, which HE CONFIRMED TO THEM BY OATH. (Deuteronomy 4:27, 30–31)

In that day the LORD will reach out his hand a second time to reclaim THE REMNANT that is left of his people. . . . (Isaiah 11:11)

There will be a highway for THE REMNANT OF HIS PEOPLE that is left from Assyria, as there was for Israel when they came up from Egypt. (Isaiah 11:16) [Since this speaks of the remnant from the Assyrian dispersion, it must refer to the restoration of the ten northern tribes, who were scattered by the Assyrians. The context clearly shows that the prophetic time of fulfillment is in the establishment of the Millennial Kingdom on earth.]

I myself will gather THE REMNANT OF MY FLOCK out of all the countries where I have driven them and will bring them back to their pasture, where they will be fruitful and increase in number. (Jeremiah 23:3) [This can only refer to a remnant from literal ethnic Israel being restored to their land. It is clearly not referring to eternity since they will bear children.]

I will surely gather all of you, O Jacob; I will surely bring together THE REMNANT OF ISRAEL. I will bring them together like sheep in a pen, like a flock in its pasture; the place will throng with people. I will make the lame A REMNANT, those driven away a strong nation. The LORD will rule over them in Mount Zion from that day and forever. (Micah 5:6–7) [This can only refer to the Millennial Messianic Kingdom.]

Thus says the LORD, "I will return to Zion and will dwell in the midst of Jerusalem. Then Jerusalem will be called the City of Truth, and the mountain of the LORD of hosts will be called the Holy Mountain." Thus says the LORD of hosts, "Old men and old women will again sit in the streets of Jerusalem, each man with his staff in his hand because of age. And the streets of the city will be filled with boys and girls playing in its streets."

Thus says the LORD of hosts, "If it is too difficult in the sight of THE REMNANT of this people in those days, will it also be too difficult in My sight?" declares the LORD of hosts.

Thus says the LORD of hosts, "Behold, I am going

to save My people from the land of the east and from the land of the west; and I will bring them back, and they will live in the midst of Jerusalem, and they will be My people and I will be their God in truth and righteousness." (Zechariah 8:3–8 NASB)

"In those days, at that time," declares the LORD, "search will be made for ISRAEL'S GUILT, but there will be none, and for THE SINS OF JUDAH, but none will be found, for I WILL FORGIVE THE REMNANT I spare." (Ezekiel 50:20) [The emphasis of many prophecies about the remnant's final restoration is the forgiveness of their sins.]

Who is a God like you, who PARDONS sin and FORGIVES the transgression of THE REMNANT of his inheritance? You do not stay angry forever but delight to show mercy. You will again have compassion on us; you will tread our sins underfoot and hurl all our iniquities into the depths of the sea. You will be true to Jacob, and show mercy to Abraham, as YOU PLEDGED ON OATH to our FATHERS in days long ago. (Micah 7:18–20) [Note that forgiveness of the remnant is tied to God's faithfulness to Israel's unconditional covenants.]

THEN I will go back to MY place [the ascension of the Lord Jesus] until they admit their guilt. And they will seek MY face; in their misery they will earnestly seek ME. "Come let us return to the LORD. He has torn us to pieces but HE will heal us; HE has injured us but HE will bind up our wounds. After TWO DAYS HE will revive us; on the THIRD DAY HE will restore us, that we may live in HIS presence. Let us acknowledge the LORD; let us press on to acknowledge HIM. As surely as the sun rises, HE will appear [Second Coming]; HE will come to us like the winter rains, like the spring rains that water the earth." (Hosea 5:15–6:3)

The Real Marvel!

How anyone can read through verses like these and say that God is finished with Israel is completely beyond me. Though Israel is for the present rejected, God has sworn on oath that He will cause a national remnant from Israel to believe in the Messiah. To this remnant, He will fulfill all the covenants made with the Nation through their fathers.

Although *all* Israel is not the *true* Israel, there has always been and always will be a believing remnant from among them that constitutes the true Israel. God's very Word and Character are at stake in the restoration of this remnant from the seed of Abraham, Isaac, and Jacob in the Messiah's Second Coming.

Even in this present age, the LORD still recognizes a distinction between His ancient people and Gentiles. Paul brings out this distinction: **"Give no offense either to Jews or Greeks or to the church of God. . . ."** (1 Corinthians 10:32) In this important verse, we see that God recognizes even in this age three kinds of people. Unbelievers are viewed as Jews and Greeks (or Gentiles). A believer, whether Jew or Gentile, is simply a member of the Church, because all are made one in Christ in this age.

But the time is coming when Gentiles will no longer be in the main focus of God's blessing. For just as that focus of blessing was taken from the Jews and turned upon the Gentiles, even so it will soon be refocused upon a remnant of Israel.

CHAPTER SEVEN

Israel in the Present: Rejected

"For I will be like a lion to Ephraim, like a great lion to Judah. I will tear them to pieces and go away; I will carry them off, with no one to rescue them. Then I will go back to MY place [the Ascension of the Messiah] UNTIL they admit their guilt. And they will seek my face; in their misery [the Tribulation] they will earnestly seek ME.

"Come, let us return to the LORD. He has injured us but HE WILL bind up our wounds. *AFTER* two days [the period of dispersion] HE WILL revive us; *ON* the third day [the beginning of the millennium] HE WILL restore us."

The Prophet Hosea
Hosea 5:14–6:2
(Emphases mine.)

Why the Nation of Israel Is Rejected Today (Romans 9:30–10:21)

The inspired Apostle Paul carefully explained why Israel, as a Nation, is rejected today. The Israelites sought to establish their own righteousness through keeping the Law. They did this because of ignorance concerning the one thing they prided themselves on knowing best, the true purpose of the Law of Moses. The moral code of the Law was never given as a way of salvation, but rather to show the Israelite how good he would have to be if

149

he were going to earn God's acceptance through his own works and human merit.

Paul reveals that the Israelite's failure under the Law was also due to an even more basic ignorance—they did not understand *the righteousness of God*. Had they understood the true spiritual meaning of the Law, they would have perceived that God's righteousness, which was revealed in the Law, is so far beyond the best of human righteousness that it is unattainable by the most sincere and concerted human effort.

The Apostle Paul succinctly summarizes the reason Israel failed to see the need for a suffering Messiah who would die to deliver them from their sins:

> **What then shall we say? That the Gentiles, who did not pursue righteousness, have obtained it, a righteousness that is by faith; but Israel, who pursued a law of righteousness, has not attained it. Why not? Because they pursued it not by faith but as if it were by works. They stumbled over the "stumbling stone." As it is written:**
>
> **"See, I lay in Zion a stone [the Messiah] that causes**
> **men to stumble and a rock that makes them fall,**
> **and the one who trusts in him**
> **will never be put to shame." [Isaiah 8:14, 28:16]**
>
> **Brothers, my heart's desire and prayer to God for the Israelites is that they may be saved. For I can testify about them that THEY ARE ZEALOUS FOR GOD, but their zeal is not based on knowledge. Since they did not know the righteousness that comes from God and sought to establish their own, they did not submit to God's righteousness.**
> **CHRIST IS THE END OF THE LAW so that there may be RIGHTEOUSNESS FOR EVERYONE WHO BELIEVES. (Romans 9:30–10:4) (Emphases added.)**

The Law was given to drive men to faith in God's provision for sin in the Messiah. God instituted a system of sacrifice for sin (the ceremonial code of the Law) at the same time He gave the moral code. This in itself was a clear revelation that men could not keep the Law without breaking it and therefore needed a Divine provision for forgiveness. As the Holy Spirit reasons in the Epistle to the Hebrews, the fact that animal sacrifices had to be continuously offered pointed to the fact that they were not God's ultimate solution for sin. Animal sacrifices only temporarily covered sin until the suffering Messiah, who was portrayed with breathtaking accuracy in Isaiah's fifty-third chapter, would come to permanently remove sin as a barrier to God.

But the Bible reveals that all men are born blind to the fact that we can never be good enough to earn God's acceptance. So the Law was given to reveal four basic truths to Israel, and through Israel to the whole world.

The Purpose of the Law

First, the Law was given to show man what sin is: **"Because by the works of the Law no flesh will be justified in His sight; for by the Law COMES THE KNOWLEDGE OF SIN."** (Romans 3:20 NASB)

Second, the Law was given to make man sin more: **"And the Law came in that the transgression might INCREASE; but where sin increased, grace abounded all the more."** (Romans 5:20 NASB) Now I realize that it sounds almost blasphemous to say that God gave something to man that would actually make him sin more. But that is exactly what the Scriptures say. The more a person trys to keep the Law, the more his old sin nature is incited to rebellion. This is absolutely contrary to our human viewpoint, but God says, **"The sting of death is sin, and THE POWER OF SIN [nature] IS THE LAW."** (1 Corinthians 15:56) The sin nature actually gets its power over us when we put ourselves under the principle of Law, because it is a works system that depends upon human strength and merit. The principle of grace depends upon God's power through the indwelling Holy Spirit. Grace is all that God set Himself free to give us through the atoning death of Christ. As someone correctly said, grace means God's Riches At Christ's Expense. On the basis of grace, which operates through faith, the Holy Spirit produces inside of us a righteousness that fulfills the Law.

The Law forces us to recognize how hopelessly sinful our natures really are. It makes us see that we cannot produce a life acceptable to God by our own human strength, no matter how sincerely we try. Our old sin nature is unreformable. This is why God doesn't even try to reform it. He simply puts a new nature inside of us and commands us to live according to its desires.

Third, the Law was given to drive man to despair of self-effort: **"All who rely on observing the law are under a curse, for it is written: 'Cursed is everyone who does not CONTINUE to do EVERYTHING written in the Book of the Law.' Clearly NO ONE is justified before God by the law, because, 'The righteous will live by faith.' THE LAW IS NOT BASED ON FAITH; on the contrary, 'The man who does these things will live by them.'"** (Galatians 3:10–12)

God doesn't grade our law-keeping on the curve. The standard is His own absolute righteousness, not man's relative righteousness. Man will not be judged by a "Gallup poll" at the last judgment. This is why the above Scriptures say that if we are to be justified by human effort, the standard is to continuously keep everything written in the entire Book of the Law. If we break even one point of the Law, we are guilty of breaking it all. (James 2:10)

Two Inevitable Responses to the Law

Inevitably, a person who tries to come to God by keeping the Law, or any other system of self-effort, will invariably come to one of two positions. He will either be driven to despair, as was Paul when he exclaimed, **"Wretched man that I am! Who will set me free from the body of this death?"** (Romans 7:24 NASB) Or he will become self-deceived and a hypocrite, as were the Pharisees. The self-deceived externalize the commandments so that they can be brought down to man's level of performance. This in essence is the meaning of religion. As I've mentioned, the common denominator of all religions is the idea that man can gain God's acceptance by human effort and merit. Jesus condemned all who try this approach when he said to the religious zealots of His day, **"Woe to you, scribes and Pharisees, hypocrites! For you are like whitewashed tombs which on the outside appear beautiful, but inside they are full of dead men's bones and all uncleanness. Even so you too outwardly appear righteous to men, but inwardly you are full of hypocrisy and lawlessness."** (Matthew 23:27–28 NASB) Note that Jesus testified of these religious men, **". . . you outwardly appear righteous to men**."

The purpose of the Sermon on the Mount was to rip off this veil of religious self-deception and to restore the Law to its full and awful convicting power. Jesus revealed the true purpose of the Law when He demonstrated that God doesn't just judge our external law-keeping, but the motives of our hearts.

It was to the sincere and outwardly righteous religious leaders that Jesus said, **"You have heard that it was said, 'Do not commit adultery.' But I tell you that anyone who looks at a woman lustfully has already committed adultery with her in his heart."** (Matthew 5:27) He also taught that to be angry with a brother without cause is equal to murder in God's sight. When anyone sincerely tries to keep this kind of standard, he is either driven to despair of self-effort or to self-deceiving hypocrisy. The Sermon on the Mount, which is simply God's interpretation of the true meaning of the Law, was designed to crush all hope of coming to God by human merit.

Few of us will ever be as religiously sincere and zealous as the Pharisees, yet listen to what Jesus said about them, **"For I tell you that unless your righteousness surpasses that of the Pharisees and the teachers of the law, you will certainly not enter the kingdom of heaven."** (Matthew 5:20)

Fourth, the Law was given to lead us to faith in the Messiah. **"Therefore the Law has become our tutor to lead us to Christ, that we may be justified by faith."** (Galatians 3:24 NASB) Once the Law has convinced us that we cannot be saved by trying to keep it, or any other system of human merit, then it points us to the One who has paid the penalty for our lawbreaking, the LORD Jesus, the Messiah.

The Law of Moses was specifically given *only* to the Nation of Israel. More than 150,000 of the first believers in Jesus as Messiah were all Israelites. When these early Jewish believers first had to deal with the problem of Gentile converts, many were still confused about the purpose of the Law. They tried to put the Gentiles under the Mosaic Law. The first Church council clearly interpreted the significance of Israel's historical failure under the Law and applied its significance to this age:

> **Then some of the believers who belonged to the party of the Pharisees stood up and said, "The Gentiles must be circumcised and required to obey the law of Moses."**
>
> **The apostles and elders met to consider this question. After much discussion, Peter got up and addressed them: "Brothers, you know that some time ago God made a choice among you that the Gentiles might hear from my lips the message of the gospel and BELIEVE.**

God, who knows the heart, showed that he ACCEPTED them by giving the Holy Spirit to them, just as he did to us. He made no distinction between us and them, for he purified their hearts by FAITH. Now then, why do you try to test God by putting on the necks of the disciples a yoke [the Law] that neither we nor our fathers have been able to bear? No! We believe it is through the GRACE of our Lord Jesus that we are saved, just as they are." (Acts 15:5–11)

Israel's failure under the Law serves as an historical lesson to all of us today that religion of all kinds blinds us to the truth. Christianity is not a "religion." Remember, religion, regardless of which brand, says that man can earn his salvation by his own merit. True Biblical Christianity says that man can do nothing acceptable to God except to receive by faith a gift of forgiveness purchased by the death of the Messiah. Christianity is a personal relationship with God which is entered by faith in Jesus as Savior.

The Modern-day "Pharisees"

The issue of whether the Christian is still under the Law of Moses is at the center of the current controversy with the Dominionists. The Dominionists are seeking to put the Church back under the Law as a way of life. But the Christian under grace is called to live a supernatural life that is beyond anything the Law could ever produce, weak as it is because of the flesh. The Holy Spirit produces in the yielded believer a righteous life that fulfills the requirements of the external written code, **"For the law of the Spirit of** [who gives] **life in Christ Jesus has set you free from the law of** [that produces] **sin and death . . . in order that the requirement of the law might be fulfilled in us, who do not walk according to the flesh, but according to the Spirit."** (Romans 8:2, 4 NASB)

The Holy Spirit gives the believer the desire to follow God's will, and then gives the power to perform it. But He does it from the inside. The desire of a believer to live for God by external commandments not only does not produce a righteous life, but rather incites the old sin nature to greater rebellion. Paul clearly reveals this as he writes of his own early Christian experience, **"Once I was alive apart from the law; but when the commandment came, sin sprang to life and I died. I found that the very** commandment that was intended to bring life actually brought death. For sin, seizing the opportunity afforded by the commandment, deceived me, and through the commandment put me to death." (Romans 7:9–10)

There are many kinds of death in the Bible. But the death referred to in Romans 7:10 is a kind of operational death. It refers to the temporary loss of fellowship and the empowering ministry of the Holy Spirit. A Christian who is out of fellowship with the LORD is operationally dead. Nothing he does in that state will count for eternity.

The Law Produces Spiritual Schizophrenia

Paul as a young believer was growing in his new faith until he started to try to keep the Law again. He made the most common error of Christianity by trying *to mix Law and Grace*. The moment that he tried to keep the Law, the old sin nature was stirred to life and quickly defeated his best human efforts to control it. The commandment that crushed Paul was the only one in the Ten Commandments that dealt exclusively with an internal sin. The tenth commandment says, **"You shall not covet your neighbor's house, You shall not covet your neighbor's wife, or his manservant or maidservant, his ox or donkey, or ANYTHING that belongs to your neighbor."** (Exodus 20:17) It is interesting to note that although the Rabbis have written thousands of pages on how to keep the six hundred plus commandments in the Law of Moses, there is very little about the tenth one. The reason is obvious. It is hard to externalize coveting. That is something a person does in his heart.

After Paul received a new spiritual nature and the Holy Spirit came to dwell in him, he truly understood for the first time the meaning of the tenth commandment. Paul testifies, **"What shall we say, then? Is the law sin? Certainly not! Indeed I would not have known what sin was except through the law. For I would not have known what it was to covet if the law had not said, 'Do not covet.' But sin** [the sin nature], **taking opportunity afforded by the commandment, produced in me every kind of covetous desire. For apart from the law, sin** [the sin nature] **is dead."** (Romans 7:7–8) When Paul began to try not to covet, he coveted all over the place.

This passage reveals that the Law does to the Christian exactly the same thing that it does to the unbeliever, it drives him to despair of self-effort. Once the Law drives the believer to this point in trying to live the Christian life, it should lead him to total dependence upon the Holy Spirit. Our responsibility is to say "No!" to the desires of the sin nature, and then to depend upon the Holy Spirit to produce God's kind of righteousness *in us*.

You see, the Holy Spirit produces righteousness in us as long as we walk by grace through faith. But the Law is a works system that is not of faith. Once again, Paul wrote, **"THE LAW IS NOT BASED ON FAITH; on the contrary, 'The man who does these things** [i.e., seeks to live by the Law principle] **will live by them.'"** (Galatians 3:12) In other words, if you seek to keep the Law, then you must live by all that is written in it. And God must judge you on the basis of His *absolute* standard. Even the slightest failure makes you guilty of breaking the whole Law. If we live by grace, the Holy Spirit fills our hearts with God's kind of love which makes us not want to kill or steal or defraud our fellow man. When we are filled with the Spirit, we don't covet what someone else has, rather we rejoice with him. God says of this kind of behavior, **". . . Against such things there is no law."** (Galatians 5:23b)

How relevant this argument is to the problems in the Church today. Man's nature has not changed, and Israel is not the only one with the problem of failure to understand the Law. Mankind has by nature always sought to establish his own righteousness before God. It takes Divine revelation to remove the congenital blindness we all have to our hopelessly fallen condition. Coming to God on the basis of grace (which excludes all human merit) through faith (which is an act with no merit), is completely contrary to the human viewpoint. Only God could have devised such a scheme. It is not the sort of thing man would dream up, even if he could.

This whole account of Israel's failure should be a sober warning, not only to the Christian, but to the world. Christians in every generation get tricked into trying to live by the Law of Moses and man-made systems of legalism. These only short-circuit the higher way of life provided by walking in the Spirit.

The Dominionists' View of the Law

One of the major doctrines of the Dominionist Movement is called *Theonomy*, which means "God's Law." The leading Dominionist thinkers on this are all in the Reconstructionist wing of the movement. Remember, they are called Reconstructionists because they want to *reconstruct* society by instituting God's Law as the civil law for all the governments of the world. This is fundamental to bringing about the Dominionists' vision of the Millennial Kingdom. The Church is to bring in the Kingdom of God by establishing authority over the governments of the world and ruling by the Law of Moses.

The Reconstructionists' view of *Theonomy* is stated by one of their leading thinkers, Greg Bahnsen: "The Old Testament Law applies today in exhaustive and minutial detail. Every single stroke of the law must be seen by the Christian as applicable to this very age between the advents of Christ."[1] There is real confusion in the Reconstructionists' doctrine of Theonomy as to just how the Law applies to the Christian. It is correct to say that Biblical Law should serve as a *pattern* for civil law as John Calvin taught. But they teach that the Theocracy God established with Israel is a "blueprint" for how Christians will ultimately establish the governments of the world.

Even more serious, they teach that the Law of Moses is the *modus operandi* of the Christian life. The patriarch of modern Reconstructionism, Rousas Rushdoony, defines sanctification as, "submission through the grace of God in Jesus Christ to the law of God."[2] He says on the one hand that we can be morally reformed by growing through a personal relationship with Jesus Christ, yet adds that Christians are "under the law as a way of life."[3] This was no slip of the pen. The love affair the Reconstructionists have with the Law permeates their writings. Rushdoony adds, "So central is the law to God, that the demands of the law are fulfilled as the necessary condition of grace."[4] In other words, we earn grace by keeping the Law. Talk about putting the cart before the horse! Any attempt to earn grace destroys its very meaning. God says, **"And if [our relationship to God is] by grace, then it is no longer by works; if it were, grace would no longer be grace."** (Romans 11:6)

The Scriptures teach, **"As you therefore have received Christ Jesus the Lord, so keep walking in Him . . ."** (Colossians 2:6 HL) How did we receive Christ?—**"By grace through faith."** (Ephesians 2:8–9) So we are to walk moment by moment in dependence upon the Holy Spirit by grace through faith. This produces a life **"against which there is no law."** (Galatians 5:14–23)

Rushdoony revealed the basis of his thinking when he argued, ". . . Man, having been created in the image of the righteous God, requires *justice* EVEN MORE THAN LOVE. The basic requirement of man's being is thus justice rather than love."[5] (Emphasis mine.) This statement speaks volumes. God help us if such men ever gain control over the Church, much less the world. What man needs is not justice, but the grace of God. If God ever dealt with us on the basis of justice, He would immediately destroy the world and mankind with it. It was an awareness of this that drove the inspired King David to write: **"Do not bring your servant into judgment, for no one living is righteous before you"** (Psalm 143:2); and again, **"If you, O LORD, kept a record of sins, O Lord, who could stand? But with you there is forgiveness; therefore you are feared** [reverently trusted]." (Psalm 130:3–4) If God dealt with us on the basis of justice, He would have to bring us into judgment and keep a record of our sins. It is a paradox that these men, who so adamantly condemn Israel for its historical failure, are guilty of the same kind of thinking that led to Israel's failure. They are equally ignorant concerning the "righteousness of God."

The Reconstructionists call those who dispute with them concerning the principles of Theonomy *antinomianists* (i.e., a person who is lawless). They have missed the basic reasons for which the Law was given. The Reconstructionists label those who seek to live by grace through the filling of the Spirit "escapists, pietists, mystics, and antinomianists."[6] They also believe that the main difference between the New and the Old Testament way of life is that we now have the Holy Spirit to help us keep the Law, but that most of the Law remains in full force.

The Holy Spirit Did Not Come to Help Us Keep the Law

As we have seen, Jesus did not send the Holy Spirit to help us keep the Law, but to give us a whole new power for living that results in an entirely new nature with God's desires. We are called by faith to depend upon the indwelling Spirit who gives us new desires that are God's desires. This is what God meant when he said, **". . . I will put my laws in their hearts, and I will write them on their minds."** (Hebrews 10:16)

How does the Holy Spirit write God's commandments on our hearts? This means that He implants His Word in our hearts and then gives the desire and the power to live it. Paul described the whole beautiful process: **"But we all with unveiled face beholding as in a mirror the glory of the LORD, are being transformed** into the same image from glory to glory, just as from the LORD, the Spirit." (2 Corinthians 3:18 NASB) The symbol of an Israelite with a veil over his heart meant that he was blind to the true purpose of the Law. The Christian is said to have an **unveiled face**. This means that he understands that he is not under law, but rather under grace by which the Spirit is free to work in him through faith. The Christian empowered by the Spirit beholds the LORD Jesus in the **mirror** of the Word of God as he reads it. The Holy Spirit reveals to his heart the image of Christ and gives the desire to be like Him. Then the Spirit progressively transforms him into the image of Jesus, from one degree of glory to another. This is why the Christian, though not under the Law, is not lawless. But those who do not understand how to be filled with the Spirit are quick to label this kind of teaching "antinomianism" and "mysticism." The true Christian life is a moment by moment miracle that works on the basis of faith through the motive of love by the Holy Spirit's power.

Through this supernatural process, Christ is formed in us. (Galatians 4:19) The more we become like Jesus, the better able we are to deal with the world's problems. The world does not need another generation of "Pharisees" who seek to put it under the Law, professing to have the answers to life while they can't even get along with one another. Rushdoony hasn't spoken to his son-in-law, Gary North, in several years, even though they have been in the same room together during meetings. Love and a forgiving spirit is the first and foremost evidence of a Spirit-filled Christian. (1 Corinthians 13 and Galatians 5:22–23)

When the Apostle Paul taught this higher way of life, he was also called an *antinomianist* by the Pharisees of his day. It is obvious that Paul taught that we are *not* under Law as a way of life by the accusations of his adversaries. They accused Paul of teaching, **"Let us do evil that good may come."** (Romans 3:8b NASB) Grace is a principle of living that is simply impossible to understand by a mind that is not controlled by the Holy Spirit.

The Real Irony

It is ironic that the Dominionists, who teach that Israel has been forever cast away for rejecting Jesus as Messiah, are seeking to enforce upon the Church through their *Theonomics* that very system that blinded Israel to their need for a Suffering Savior who would die for their sins.

The LORD Jesus taught, **"Do not think that I have come to abolish the Law or the Prophets; I have not come to abolish them but TO FULFILL them. I tell you the truth, until heaven and earth disappear, not the smallest letter, not the least stroke of a pen, will by any means disappear from the Law UNTIL everything is accomplished."** (Matthew 5:17–18) The Lord Jesus *did fulfill* the Law for us. That is why the word **UNTIL** is in verse eighteen. The Law was binding UNTIL Jesus took its penalty of death from us and bore it upon the cross.

The Apostle Paul taught why we are no longer under the Law: **"For through the law I died to the law so that I might live for God. I have been crucified with Christ and I no longer live, but Christ lives in me. The life I live in the body, I live by faith in the Son of God, who loves me and gave himself for me. I do not set aside the grace of God, for if righteousness could be gained through the law, Christ died for nothing!"** (Galatians 2:19–21) The Law can only do two things, demand perfect obedience or demand death for all who break it. We could never keep it perfectly, so the Law put us to death through our union with Christ in His death. Through this same union with Christ, we have been raised into His new resurrection life over which the Law has no authority. Our debt has already been fully paid. Now the only issue is to live moment by moment in faith-dependence upon the LORD Jesus who permanently lives within us. If we go back and seek to relate to God through the principle of Law, we are saying that Christ died for nothing.

The Debt No Man Could Pay

How our debt to the Law was paid is so important that Paul illustrated it again in the most graphic terms known to the people of that time. We owed God perfect obedience to His Law. We couldn't pay, so Jesus died in our place, **". . . having canceled out the CERTIFICATE OF DEBT consisting of DECREES against us [the Law] and which was hostile to us; and He has taken it out of the way, having nailed it to the cross."** (Colossians 2:14 NASB)

The term "**certificate of debt**" was well known in the Roman world. This was a legal paper that was prepared when someone was convicted of crimes. Each crime was considered a debt owed to Caesar's justice and was listed on the "certificate of debt." This accompanied the prisoner to jail and was nailed to his cell door. When the sentence was served, they would write the Greek word *tetelestai* across the certificate of debt and give it to the released prisoner. *Tetelestai* (τετελεσται) meant "paid in full." The prisoner could never again be punished for those crimes. This is the word that Jesus shouted out in triumph as He died upon the cross (John 19:30). He had taken our certificate of debt, consisting of every time we break God's Law, and nailed it to His cross. As He died, He proclaimed that our total debt to the Law of God was paid. This is why the Holy Spirit can now proclaim, **"Christ is the END OF THE LAW so that there may be righteousness for everyone who believes."** (Romans 10:4) **"I do not set aside the grace of God, for if righteousness could be gained through the law, Christ died for nothing!"** (Galatians 2:21)

The Law Is All or Nothing

A Christian *cannot* seek to live by one part of the Law, and leave out any other part. The Law is a complete system. If you put yourself under any part of the Law, you are obligated to keep it all. Paul brought this out when a group of Galatians was circumcised in order to keep the Law of Moses: **"Again I declare to every man who lets himself be circumcised that he is obligated to obey the WHOLE LAW. You who are TRYING TO BE JUSTIFIED BY LAW have been alienated from Christ; you have fallen away from grace [i.e., as the means of living for God]. But by faith we eagerly await through THE SPIRIT the righteousness for which we hope. For in Christ Jesus neither circumcision nor uncircumcision has any value. The only thing that counts is faith expressing itself through love."** (Galatians 5:3–6)

It is certainly all right to be circumcised for health reasons. But if you are circumcised in order to keep the Law, you are obligated to keep the whole Law perfectly. The Galatian Christians by this act had put themselves under the Law. The most serious charge that Paul brought against them is that the act of circumcision to keep the Law constituted seeking to be justified by Law. Law and Grace are two completely different systems of approaching God. They are antithetical to each other. We must approach God by one or the other, but we can't mix them. If we try to live by any part of the Law system, we are obligated to keep the whole system.

The principle of walking in the Spirit by faith, which works through love, is one that has apparently been missed by some Reconstructionists. A number of their main leaders have had such arguments that they no longer speak to each other. This reveals a failure to walk in the Spirit. The Scriptures teach, **"Let no debt remain outstanding, except the continuing debt TO LOVE ONE ANOTHER, FOR THE ONE WHO LOVES HIS FELLOW MAN HAS FULFILLED THE LAW. The commandments, 'Do not commit adultery,' 'Do not murder,' 'Do not steal,' 'Do not covet,' and WHATEVER OTHER COMMANDMENT THERE MAY BE, are all summed up in this one rule: 'LOVE YOUR NEIGHBOR AS YOURSELF.' Love does no harm to its neighbor. Therefore LOVE IS THE FULFILLMENT OF THE LAW."** (Romans 13:8–10)

The Law Cannot Give Life

If the Holy Spirit could have been given to all believers in the Old Testament era, there would have been no need for the Law. But any written code, even God's, can't give us the power to keep its commandments. The problem is not with God's Law; it is perfect. The Holy Spirit pinpoints the problem: **". . . For if a law had been given that could impart [spiritual] life, then righteousness would certainly have come by the law."** (Galatians 3:21b) No law can give us that dynamic spiritual life that effectively operates through the filling of the Spirit in producing God's kind of love. This love is declared to be the first fruit and evidence of being filled with the Spirit: **"So I say, live by the Spirit, and you will not gratify the desires of the sinful nature. . . . But the fruit of the Spirit is LOVE, joy, peace, patience, kindness, goodness, faithfulness, gentleness and self-control. AGAINST SUCH THINGS THERE IS NO LAW."** (Galatians 5:16, 22, 23)

The problem in the Galatian Church was the same as Israel's historic problem. The Galatians were trying to live for God by a system that depends entirely upon human strength and merit. The LORD offers us two plans of approaching Him. Both operate in the same way, whether it is in obtaining salvation or living the Christian life. I call the two approaches plan A and plan B.

Under plan A, all you have to do is keep the Law of Moses perfectly in your thoughts as well as in deeds. If you are trying to work your way to God by plan A, good luck. No one but the Lord Jesus has ever kept the Law perfectly.

But under plan B, you are saved by receiving a total provision of salvation as a gift through faith in the atonement of the Lord Jesus. This whole transaction is declared by God to be not of ourselves. (Ephesians 2:8–10) Everyone who approaches God by plan B succeeds, because it depends upon the Lord Jesus Christ's merit, not his. Right now you can receive by faith the forgiveness Christ died to provide for you.

The Moment-by-Moment Miracle

The Law can neither save nor sanctify us. ("Sanctification" is used in the progressive sense of living a holy life.) The Galatian error was committed by believers who were trying to live the Christian life by keeping the Law. Paul revealed the folly of this.

> **You foolish Galatians! Who has bewitched you? Before your very eyes Jesus Christ was clearly portrayed as crucified. I would like to learn just one thing from you: Did you receive the Spirit by observing the law, or by believing what you heard? Are you so foolish? After beginning with the Spirit** [the new birth], **are you now trying to attain your goal** [personal sanctification] **by human effort? Have you suffered so much for nothing— if it really was for nothing? Does God give you his Spirit and work miracles among you because you observe the law, or because you believe what you heard?** (Galatians 3:1–5)

The Holy Spirit's logic is irrefutable. His whole point here is this: "If human effort couldn't save us, then it certainly can't make us holy." We began our life with God through an instantaneous, miraculous new birth produced by the Holy Spirit by grace through faith.

Israel's Present Rejection Is a Warning

Israel's present rejection as a nation stands as an inescapable lesson to all who would seek to approach God by the Law. This should particularly warn the *Theonomists*. Romans chapter ten teaches that Israel is without excuse because the Old Testament taught that we must come to the Lord by faith and not by works. The Law is a system that totally depends upon works and assumes human merit. Because of this, the Scriptures say that **"the Law is not of faith"** and **"can only bring wrath."** (Galatians 3:12 and Romans 4:15)

The LORD saw Israel's blindness to the way of faith and predicted that the time would come when they would be severely

163

disciplined. God then predicted that in their exile, He would motivate them to come back: **"I will make you envious by those who are not a nation; I will make you angry by a nation that has no understanding."** (Deuteronomy 32:21 as quoted in Romans 10:19)

Let us not miss the point of Paul's quote of this prophecy. The present focus of God's special grace upon us Gentiles has as one of its major purposes the moving of Israel as a Nation to salvation. This clearly demonstrates that God still has a distinct future purpose for the descendants of Abraham, Isaac, and Jacob as a Nation.

Let us not miss another imperative lesson. The Reconstructionists' failure to correctly interpret an issue as clearly revealed in the New Testament as Law and Grace is a major doctrinal error. We are not talking about some peripheral side issue here. We are talking about the very Gospel itself. They have embraced as one of their central teachings one of the most serious doctrinal errors about which the New Testament warns—rejecting the Grace principle of living for God for the Law principle. The Apostle Paul declared this error serious enough to call those who taught it "accursed." (Galatians 1:6–9 NASB)

If these men are this far off on their interpretation of something that is a main theme of the New Testament (i.e., Law vs. Grace), is it any wonder they are so far off on something as complex as Biblical prophecy? Christians who have leaped on the Reconstructionist bandwagon had better take a good long look at *all* they are teaching.

CHAPTER EIGHT

Israel in the Future: Accepted

The word of the LORD came to Jeremiah: "Have you not noticed that these people are saying, 'The LORD has rejected the two kingdoms he chose'? [Israel and Judah] So they despise my people and NO LONGER REGARD THEM AS A NATION. This is what the LORD says: 'If I have not established my covenant with day and night and the fixed laws of heaven and earth, then I will reject the descendants of Jacob and David my servant and will not choose one of his sons to rule over the descendants of Abraham, Isaac and Jacob. For I WILL restore their fortunes and have compassion on them.'"

The Prophet Jeremiah
Jeremiah 33:23–26

The mystery of Israel's future destiny as a nation is resolved in Romans chapter eleven. The ninth chapter of Romans declared that the nation of Israel was sovereignly chosen in grace with God's complete foreknowledge of their future sin. It clarified that the true nation of Israel has always consisted not just of physical descendants of Abraham, Isaac, and Jacob, but of physical descendants who also *believed*. These are called *"the remnant of Israel"* throughout the Prophets.

The tenth chapter of Romans revealed the factors that led to Israel's failure to believe in Jesus as the Messiah. The Holy Spirit charged that Israel's failure to believe in the Messiah was inexcusable because of the clear revelation of the way of faith in the Old Testament. Israel failed to understand that God's righteousness is unattainable through any form of human merit. God's righteousness can only be received as a gift by grace through faith. The Law was given to force them to see this. Israel's failure to grasp these truths led to a progressive blindness that culminated in the rejection of their long-awaited Messiah.

Dr. Everett F. Harrison gave an accurate summary of Romans chapter nine and ten.

> Thus far, Paul has treated the problem of Israel from two standpoints. In chapter 9 he has emphasized the sovereignty of God in choosing this people for himself in a special sense. In chapter 10 he has dealt with Israel's failure to respond to God's righteousness, ending with the verdict that she is "a disobedient and obstinate people" (10:21). These two presentations involve a serious tension. (1) Will Israel's sin and stubbornness defeat the purpose of God, or (2) will God find a way to deal effectively with the situation so as to safeguard his purpose? To this question Paul now turns. His answer will dip into Israel's past, encompass her present, and reveal her future.[1]

ISRAEL'S PRESENT REJECTION IS NOT TOTAL (ROMANS 11:1–10)

In the light of this great national failure, the Holy Spirit raises a critical question: **"I say then, God has not rejected His people, has He?"** (11:1 NASB)

"Then" refers back to all that was said about the nation of Israel's failure in the tenth chapter of Romans. In view of national Israel's unbelief in spite of clear Old Testament revelation, has the LORD finally rejected them as **"His people"**?

A critical question is, "To whom exactly does **'His people'** refer?" It *cannot* refer only to the present elect remnant that are part of the Church. If that were the case, Romans nine, ten, and eleven would be meaningless. The whole focus of these three chapters is concerned with the plight of that mass of Israelites who are in this present age *unbelievers*. It was well known and elaborately taught in other Epistles that an Israelite could believe and become part of the Church. In these chapters, it is God's honor and veracity that is defended. For the Church recognized the dilemma posed by Israel's present rejection and God's unconditional promises concerning Israel's national future. Romans chapter eleven spells out how the LORD will solve this dilemma.

This is the main issue raised in Romans chapter eleven. Even the way the question is worded reveals that God *still*, in a very special sense, considers unbelieving Israel to be **"His people."** If the LORD had intended to convey that He had rejected *national* Israel forever, He would have made that clear by saying, **"God has not rejected the Israelites, has He?"** But instead He emphasizes their continuing special relationship by calling the unbelieving nation **"His people."** Dr. F. Godet, in his classic commentary on Romans, writes concerning this issue, "The expression *His people* does not refer, as some have thought, to the *elect* part of the people *only*, but, as the expression itself shows, to the *nation* as a whole. It is evident, indeed, that the rest of the chapter treats not of the lot of the Israelites who have believed in Jesus, but of the lot of the nation in its *entirety*."[2]

The answer the Holy Spirit gives to this hypothetical question is begun with the strongest negative expression in the Greek language, *me genoito* (μη γενοιτο), which literally means, *"May such a thing never be!"* When this kind of vehement denial is used to answer a hypothetical question, it is intended to convey the utter impossibility of the answer being *yes*.

The Apostle Paul supplies only one historical precedent to prove his case: **"For I too am an Israelite, a descendant of Abraham, of the tribe of Benjamin."** (11:1b NASB) Paul's answer to his own hypothetical question is full of meaning that must be carefully analyzed.

First, it could simply mean that Paul considered his own salvation to be an example that God hasn't rejected *all* Israelites. I don't believe that this adequately explains the context, because: (1) Paul would not have just used himself as an example to prove this point. If this were his point, he could have made a much stronger case by citing the well-known fact that there were thousands of Jewish believers in the Church. Indeed, the original Church was *all* Jewish. (2) It would not have been consistent with Paul's humility to have put himself forth as the only proof of such a point. (3) The strongest Greek negative, **"May it never be,"** is used to deny something far more serious than the idea, "God hasn't rejected 'His people' because some are being saved and put into the Church." When an Israelite is saved in this age, in one sense he loses his national identity. Therefore, he is not considered one of God's people because he is an Israelite, but because he is in the Church. So this idea doesn't answer the basic question, "Has God rejected **His people?**"

The second possibility is that Paul meant, "If God has rejected forever His people on a *national* basis, then He has rejected me also, since I too am from that *nation*." This is the view of the Greek scholar Kenneth S. Wuest. Wuest writes,

> If such an hypothesis were to be conceded, it would exclude from God's kingdom the *writer himself*, as an *Israelite*. This seems better to agree with "God forbid," as deprecating the consequence of such an assertion. But a question even more important arises, not connected with that just discussed: namely, Who are "His people"? In order for the sentence "For I also am an Israelite," to bear the meaning just assigned to it, it is obvious that "His people" must mean the people of God *nationally* considered. If Paul deprecated such a proposition as the rejection of *God's people*, because he himself would thus be *as an Israelite* cut off from God's favor, the rejection assumed in the hypothesis must be *a national rejection*. It is against *this* that he puts in his strong protest. It is *this* which he disproves by a cogent historical parallel from Scripture, showing that there is a remnant even at this present time according to the election of grace: and not only so, but that part of Israel (considered as having continuity of national existence) which is for a time hardened, shall ultimately come in, and so all Israel (nationally considered again, *Israel as a nation*) shall be saved. Thus the covenant of God with Israel, having been *national*, shall ultimately be fulfilled to them *as a nation:* not by the gathering in merely of *individual* Jews, or of *all* the Jews individually, into the Christian Church—but by the *national restoration* of the Jews, not in unbelief, but as a *believing nation*, to *all that can, under the gospel, represent their ancient preeminence*, and to the fullness of those promises which have *never yet in their plain sense been accomplished to them*.[3]

God Cannot Undo His Own Unilateral Choice of Israel (11:2)

For God to reject His people would require repudiation of His deliberate, unilateral choice of Israel. Verse two infers that such a thing is impossible on the basis of God's foreknowledge and sovereignty. Paul strengthens this idea in this verse: **"God has not rejected His people whom He foreknew."** (11:2a) This drives home the impossibility of God rejecting Israel since He **"foreknew"** them as a *nation*. Note that they are again called **"His people."** "Foreknew" is *proginosko* (προγινωσκω) in the Greek. It means to foreknow something in such a way that it is certain. Wuest quotes two other Greek authorities on this word:

> Alford explains the word, "which, in His own eternal decree before the world, He selected as the chosen nation, to be His own, the depository of His law, the vehicle of the theocracy, from its first revelation to its completion in Christ's future kingdom." Denney says: "'Which He foreknew' must contain a reason which makes their rejection incredible or impossible."[4]

This in essence means that Israel's unbelief and apostasy did not take God by surprise. He knew all about it before He ever chose to create the nation. This is a point that I have made many times from Old Testament prophecies about Israel. Nevertheless, the LORD not only predicted their national failure, but promised to restore them as a nation from this very failure. This is why I previously went into detail on Israel's convenants. It is impossible for the all-knowing God to make such detailed and explicit *unconditional* promises concerning Israel's ultimate future restoration *from apostasy* and then to change His mind. God clearly and deliberately placed Himself in such a position so that if He does not restore Israel as a Nation, He is a liar.

The Importance of Israel's Remnant

The Holy Spirit brings up a most convincing case from Israel's history to establish that even in their worst times of apostasy, God has always kept *a believing remnant* from the seed of Abraham, Isaac, and Jacob. God's sovereign preservation of a believing remnant during the worst periods of Israel's history is offered as *proof* that there will always be a nucleus from which God can establish a future believing nation to whom He will fulfill all that has been promised to them.

> **Or do you not know what the Scripture says in the passage about Elijah, how he pleads AGAINST Israel? "LORD, they have killed Thy Prophets, they have torn down Thine altars, and I alone am left, and they are seeking my life." But what is the divine response to him? "I have kept for Myself seven thousand men who have not bowed the knee to Baal." (Romans 11:2–4 NASB)**

There is a parallel made between God's past election of Israel as a Nation and His present election of individuals to salvation. The Reconstructionists' doctrine of Salvation (Soteriology) is totally inconsistent with their doctrine of Prophecy (Eschatology). They correctly interpret the Scriptures in saying that an individual's salvation is completely apart from human merit from start to finish; that it is forever based on the completed redemptive work of Christ alone; that we must receive salvation by faith alone; and that God sees to it that all who believe in Christ are not lost (John 6:37–40). But they are incorrect and inconsistent when they read into the Scriptures that Israel as a nation has been rejected forever because of disobedience, and that all of Israel's convenant blessings have been given to the Church, but not her curses. If the predicted curses have been valid for the nation of Israel, then the blessings that were predicted to follow the curses are also valid for the nation.

As I've mentioned, this issue presents no problem for some Dominionists who come from the Pentecostal tradition, for they believe that a Christian can lose his salvation. But this presents an enormous problem for the Reconstructionists. In effect it makes them *Calvinists* (who believe that you *cannot* lose your salvation) in their doctrine of Salvation, but *Arminians* (who believe you *can* lose your salvation) in their doctrine of Prophecy. A Calvinist believes that a person saved by Divine choice cannot thereafter be lost.[5] An Arminian believes that a person's salvation always hangs upon his choices and behavior.[6] The point is that once God chose Israel as His own elect nation and gave them unconditional promises guaranteeing that they would always be His elect nation, He cannot thereafter disown them because of their sin.

The Remnant of Israel in the Present Age

Paul continues to reason, **"In the same way then** [as in Elijah's time], **there has also come to be at the present time a remnant according to GOD'S GRACIOUS CHOICE. But if it is by grace, it is no longer on the basis of works, otherwise grace is no longer grace."** (Romans 11:5–6 NASB)

There is a most profound point introduced here as far as the question of Israel's future. It is simply this: The only reason that Israel has ever had a believing remnant is because of *God's sovereign grace*. A remnant has always been elected to salvation by the unmerited favor of God even in the midst of the worst times of unfaithfulness and apostasy. Paul's argument in Romans chapter eleven is that God will again on the basis of *this same grace* bring the nation back to faith and fulfill His promises to them as a nation. God has clearly promised this very thing in many passages we have already considered.

If the Dominionists argue with this, on what basis can they argue? If they say this can't be because Israel doesn't deserve to be restored, then what do we do with this passage? Their election, according to God, has always been on the basis of *grace alone*. If the nation of Israel doesn't deserve to have God keep solemn promises confirmed by His oath to them, then by what right do we Christians deserve it more? God deals with all of us, Israel as a Nation and individuals today, on the same basis—grace: **"For God has bound all men over to disobedience so that he may have mercy on them all."** (Romans 11:32) The whole book of Romans focuses on this point, that all mankind is *equally undeserving* of a relationship with God. **"But now apart from the Law** [both the Law of Moses and the principle of Law] **the RIGHTEOUSNESS OF GOD has been manifested, being witnessed by the Law and the Prophets, even the RIGHTEOUSNESS OF GOD THROUGH FAITH IN JESUS CHRIST for ALL those who believe; for there is NO DISTINCTION; for ALL have sinned and fall** [keep falling] **short of the glory of God."** (Romans 3:21–23 NASB)

Most Dominionists profess to believe these things as far as they pertain to salvation of individuals today, but they fail to see that according to the Scriptures, the same principles apply to God's election, forgiveness, and restoration of the *Nation* of Israel.

The Curse of a Hardened Heart (Romans 11:7–10)

In this paragraph the Holy Spirit sums up the real cause for Israel's failure:

> **What then? What Israel sought so earnestly it did not obtain, but the elect did. The others were hardened, as it is written:**
>
> **"God gave them a spirit of stupor,**
> **eyes so that they could not see**
> **and ears so that they could not hear,**
> **to this day."** [Deuteronomy 29:4; Isaiah 29:10]
>
> **And David says** [concerning Israel]:
>
> **"May their table become a snare and a trap,**
> **a stumbling block and a retribution for them.**
> **May their eyes be darkened so they cannot see,**
> **and their backs be bent forever."** [Psalm 69:22, 23]
> (Romans 11:7–10)

"What then?" means "How does the case stand now?" In this present age, Israel as a nation has not obtained the righteousness it so earnestly sought. The reason was given in Romans 9:30–10:21: they tried to produce a righteousness acceptable to God by keeping the very Law that was given to prove that such a thing was impossible.

But the elect did obtain God's righteousness because they received it by faith. This is the elect who are chosen on the basis of grace alone (11:5, 6).

The statement **"the rest were hardened"** is a difficult truth to receive. This is a warning of a deadly process that we must avoid at all costs: the more light a person rejects, the more blind he becomes. The majority of the nation of Israel rejected the light God gave them. As they did, they progressively hardened their hearts. There came a point when the LORD added to their hardened hearts an additional judicial hardening. Their case is the same as that of Pharaoh. They definitely hardened their own hearts first, then the LORD placed them in situations where they rebelled all the more.

Dr. James M. Stifler's comment is helpful: **"'And the rest** [the mass of natural Israel] **were hardened.'** Since the remnant was saved by grace, there was no justice done to the **'rest.'** For who can complain if salvation came to *some* where *none* deserved it? And if the undeserving remnant was saved *because* God would and *when* He would, WHY NOT THE **'REST'** BE SAVED IN HIS OWN TIME AND BY THE SAME FREE GRACE?"[7] (Emphases mine.) Stifler accurately brings out why Paul introduced again the subject of election here. It clearly demonstrates God's right to again save the mass of Israel as a nation in the future. This is emphatically asserted in several ways in Romans chapter eleven.

The Old Testament verses Paul quoted in Romans 11:8–10 described the spiritual condition of the majority of Israel even in the days of Moses, David, and Isaiah. This failure to understand the real purpose of the Law continued to plague one generation after another. *It was this failure to understand the grace of God, which was caused by their persistent efforts to establish their own righteousness through law-keeping, that resulted in such a terrible hardening of the majority.*

What the Dominionists Should Learn From Israel

As we considered in chapter seven, it is the Reconstructionists' failure to understand the true purpose of the Law that has blinded them to God's real purpose in the future of Israel and the Millennial Kingdom. Their writings reveal a tragic ignorance of the grace of God, particularly as it relates to living the Christian life. Their doctrine of *Theonomy* is a modern version of the same error that Paul fought so vehemently against in the Epistle to the Galatians—i.e., seeking to live the Christian life by a mixture of Law and Grace. Law and Grace are antithetical systems that cannot be mixed. The righteousness of the Law is produced *in* a believer who is walking in dependence upon the Holy Spirit by faith. But the moment a believer sets up the Law as his standard and then seeks to keep it, even with the help of the Holy Spirit, the old sin nature gains control of him and he plummets into a spiral of continuous failure. Romans chapter seven details the miserable failure of a believer who sincerely tries to live by the Law.

NATIONAL ISRAEL'S REJECTION IS NOT FINAL (ROMANS 11:11–32)

Paul considers the question of the future of Israel as a nation in this concluding section concerning Israel. He has already proven that there is a believing remnant from the nation in the present age. But in clear contrast to the issue of the remnant, he now deals with the weighty question of whether God will, at some future point, keep His covenant promises to Israel as a national entity. At stake in this question is the veracity of God Himself.

As was characteristic of Paul's rabbinical style, he begins his answer with a question, **"Again I ask, Did they stumble so as to fall beyond recovery? Not at all** [μη γενοιτο—may it never be]!**"** (Romans 11:11a) The question is asked in such a way in the original Greek that it demands a negative answer. In addition, the most emphatic negative, *me genoito* (μη γενοιτο), is used again here. The New International Version quoted here faithfully brings out the meaning of Paul's question.

Even if Paul were to go no further on this issue, this one statement would be enough to prove that God is not through with Israel as a national people. The contrast here (which sets up the main point for the rest of the chapter) is between the minority who have believed and lost their national identity, and the lost majority who are nevertheless still identified as God's people. As we will see, it is out of this lost majority that God will in the future bring forth a saved nation (11:25–26).

There are several critical questions raised in this section. Was the nation of Israel's history intended to end with their present rejection? Was this present calamity God's ultimate purpose for miraculously creating the nation? Could the people who are the central subject of most of the Bible be cast away forever? All of these ideas are inherent in Paul's question in verse eleven. To all of these questions the Holy Spirit answers with a resounding NO!

An Overlooked Purpose Clause

God reveals His overall purpose and strategy in history: **"Rather, because of their** [the nation's] **transgression, salvation has come to the Gentiles** [for the purpose of making] **to make Israel envious."** (Romans 11:11b)

The main point of the rest of this chapter is given in the last half of verse eleven, particularly in the purpose clause, **". . . salvation has come to the Gentiles** *for the purpose of* **making Israel envious."** Paul probes into the mystery of God's eternal purposes and reveals that far from Israel's fall being beyond recovery, God has worked the tragedy of their fall together for good and through it brought the Gospel to the mass of unsaved Gentiles. Throughout the Biblical history, the LORD has continuously turned cursing into blessing. In this case the principle is once again beautifully displayed. Israel's failure has turned the focus of God's grace from their nation to the Gentiles.

The LORD continues to demonstrate His overall purpose, wisdom, and mercy by using the present grace that is being poured out upon the Gentiles *to make the nation of Israel jealous.* It is designed to provoke Israel to believe in their Messiah. In the original Greek (as well as in the English translation) **"to make Israel envious"** is a purpose clause. This means that even the very salvation of the Gentiles has as its ultimate purpose the future salvation of the nation of Israel.

Remember Who the Audience Was

It must not be forgotten to whom Paul was speaking and his primary purpose for explaining the question of Israel's future. Paul was explaining God's continuing purpose for Israel to the large Gentile Church in Rome. He was showing them what their attitude toward Israel should be in the light of that purpose. There were already anti-Jewish feelings throughout the Gentile churches. These feelings were well deserved since many Orthodox Jews had vigorously persecuted both Jewish and Gentile Christians. But the Holy Spirit carefully developed why the Church must never promote nor tolerate anti-Jewish attitudes or actions.

It is also imperative to keep in mind throughout the whole section of Romans 11:11–32 that the subject is the Gentiles as a *corporate whole* and Israel as a *corporate whole.* At no place in this crucially important passage of Scripture is the individual Gentile or Israelite in view. It is strictly concerned with how God deals with each group. Failure to keep this factor in focus has resulted in gross misinterpretations, especially in the field of the doctrines of salvation.

Ultimate World Blessing Contingent on Israel's Fullness

Paul gives some logical reasons why Gentiles should have an attitude of grace toward the Israelites: **"But if their transgression means riches for the world, and their loss means riches for the Gentiles, how much greater riches will their fullness bring!"** (Romans 11:12) Paul introduces his proposition by using a first class conditional clause in the original Greek. This means that the condition raised is viewed as true. It should be translated, "Since their transgression means riches for the world . . ." Israel failed in her responsibility to spread the Gospel to the world, so God used this very **transgression** and **loss** to spread the riches of His salvation to the Gentile world.

Great emphasis is placed upon the term **"riches,"** since it is repeated three times. This is to drive home the fact that the present **"riches"** of God's blessings which have been turned upon the Gentiles has occurred because of the nation of Israel's calamity. This being so, God wants us to lift up our eyes of hope to the **"riches"** that must be in store for the world when the nation of Israel comes into her **"fullness."** In other words, if the LORD can bring such blessing to the Gentile world through Israel's tragedy, how much more will He do for the world when Israel's convenant promises are fulfilled to her?

This clearly reveals that God's ultimate blessings for the world are contingent upon the nation of Israel's being restored to her fullness. Even the Postmillennial scholar John Murray partially agrees with this: "There should be no question but *this is the fullness of Israel as a people.* The *stumbling* was theirs, the *fall* was theirs, theirs was the *trespass*, and theirs the *loss*. The *fullness*, therefore, can have no other reference."[8]

Sadly, Murray later confuses the issue by teaching that **the fullness of Israel** refers to *a mass of Israelites* who will be suddenly converted and brought into the Church. The whole point of this passage revolves around Israel's being restored to a position of preeminence as a believing nation. This could not be true if those who are converted in the future are made part of the Church, since the national distinction would be lost. Furthermore, it would be no different than the current situation and would need no elaborate explanation such as we have in Romans chapter nine, ten, and eleven.

The exact meaning of the future **"riches for the world"** and of the **"fullness for national Israel"** is of utmost importance.

The Bible does not leave us in the dark as to what the future **"riches for the world"** means. It is elaborately described in the numerous prophecies that promise the Millennial Kingdom which the Messiah Jesus will establish when He returns to restore Israel. The following is only a sample of what is promised:

(1) Such great numbers of Gentiles will be saved during the Tribulation that they can't be numbered

(Revelation 7:9–17). Those who survive that period will go into the Millennial Kingdom and participate in its blessings. Those who die will be resurrected at the Second Coming (Revelation 20:4–6; Daniel 12:1–3).

(2) The curse on nature and the animal kingdom will be removed (Isaiah 11:6-8; 65:17–25).

(3) The whole earth will be filled with the knowledge of the LORD (Isaiah 11:9).

(4) The Messiah will reign over all the earth from Jerusalem (Zechariah 14:9–21; Ezekiel 37:24–28; Jeremiah 33:14–16).

(5) Life will be greatly extended (Isaiah 65:20–22). There will be unending world peace (Micah 4:3).

(6) There will be justice for all (Isaiah 42:1-7; 11:3–5).

(7) There will be permanent prosperity for all (Isaiah 65:21–23).

These represent only a few of the **"riches"** that all who live in the coming Millennial world will enjoy, but they at least illustrate the point.

Even a Premillennialist couldn't explain to whom the phrase **"Israel's fullness"** applied better than John Murray: "Whatever might be the precise term by which to express the import here, it is obvious that the condition or state denoted is one that stands in sharp contrast with the unbelief, the trespass, and the loss characterizing Israel when the apostle wrote. It points, therefore, to a condition marked by antithesis in these respects. This means that ISRAEL is contemplated as characterized *by the faith of Christ, by the attainment of righteousness,* and *by restoration to the blessing of God's kingdom as conspicuously as Israel then was marked by UNBE-LIEF, TRESPASS,* and *LOSS."*[9] (Emphases mine.) I agree with Murray's logic of antithesis, but he does not hold consistent with his own premise. What I mean is that since they fell as a Nation, they must be restored as a Nation. For within the very prophecies that predicted the Nation of Israel's fall are predictions of that same Nation's ultimate restoration.

The word **"fullness"** is *pleroma* ($\pi\lambda\eta\rho\omega\mu\alpha$). In this context it means "to complete the full number." All of the great covenant promises made by oath to Israel as a nation have never been completed or fulfilled. This completeness speaks of that future time when *the full measure of all* that God has promised to the Nation of Israel will be completed. The promises of the Messiah as her King, of being preeminent in the Kingdom of Heaven on earth, and of becoming a nation filled with godly priests will all come true. This will bring such blessing upon the earth that we can only exclaim, "**. . . how much greater riches will Israel's fullness bring!"**

Reaching Israel Through the Back Door (Romans 11:12–13)

Paul enlarges upon the purpose of making Israel envious expressed in verse eleven: **"I am talking to you Gentiles. Inasmuch as I am the apostle to the Gentiles, I make much of my ministry in the hope that I may somehow arouse my own people to envy and save some of them."** (11:12–13) Even though Paul was sent as a missionary to the Gentile world, he still sees a way to provoke **"his own people"** to faith. He proposed to use the very riches of salvation and the new ministries of the Holy Spirit primarily bestowed upon the Gentiles in this age to provoke Israel to faith through envy. Even Paul's zealous ministry among the Gentiles was viewed by him as a means to save some of his own beloved people.

From Rejection to Resurrection (Romans 11:15)

The thought begun in verse twelve is resumed here: **"For if their rejection is the reconciliation of the world, what will their acceptance be but life from the dead?"** Once again, Paul argues from lesser to greater. If the tragedy of Israel's rejection could be utilized by God to produce the reconciliation of the world, then how much more will the LORD be able to do when Israel is again accepted?

Israel's rejection has made **reconciliation** with God available to the whole Gentile world. The channel of God's special grace was diverted from Israel to the Gentiles. Gentile believers replaced Israel as God's chosen instruments to spread the Gospel. In this age, Israel has had to come to a Gentile-dominated Church in order to enter a relationship with God where all are one body in Christ. This is exactly the reverse of the Old Testament order. During the Mosaic age, a Gentile had to become a Jewish proselyte in order to come to God.

Three views have been suggested as to the meaning of the phrase **"life from the dead,"** which seems to be a parallel thought with **"riches for the Gentiles and the world"** in verse twelve. First, it could mean an unprecedented spiritual awakening in the world.

178

Second, it could mean the consummation of redemption at the resurrection of the dead. Third, it could refer to a figurative expression describing the conversion of national Israel as a joyful glorious event (like resurrection)—which will result in even greater blessing for the world.

Of these three views the first seems least likely, since, before Israel's spiritual rebirth, the fullness of the Gentiles will already have come in (Romans 11:25). Since the Gentile mission will then be complete, there seems to be no place for a period of unprecedented spiritual awakening.

The second view also seems unlikely, since the context suggests nothing of bodily resurrection.

Ezekiel's Prophecy of the Nation's Resurrection

I believe the third view is the one that fits the whole context of Biblical prophecy. When Israel is again accepted as God's special nation, it will result in bringing "life out of death" for the whole world because the long-awaited Kingdom of God will be instituted on earth under the Lord Jesus Christ's personal Theocratic rule.

This momentous future event is dramatically predicted in Ezekiel's prophetic allegory of "The Valley of Dry Bones." Read carefully this important prophecy:

> **The hand of the LORD was upon me, and he brought me out by the Spirit of the LORD and set me in the middle of a valley; it was full of bones. He led me back and forth among them, and I saw a great many bones on the floor of the valley, bones that were very dry. He asked me, "Son of man, CAN THESE BONES LIVE?" I said, "Sovereign LORD, you alone know."** (Ezekiel 37:1–3)
>
> **Then he said to me, "Prophesy to these bones and say to them, 'Dry bones, hear the word of the LORD! This is what the Sovereign LORD says to these bones: I WILL MAKE BREATH ENTER YOU, AND YOU WILL COME TO LIFE.'"** (Ezekiel 37:4–5)
>
> **So I prophesied as I was commanded. And as I was prophesying, there was noise, a rattling sound, and the bones came together, bone to bone. I looked, and tendons and flesh appeared on them and skin covered them, BUT THERE WAS NO BREATH IN THEM.**

179

(Ezekiel 37:7–8) (This is phase *one* of the prophecy which predicts the *PHYSICAL RESTORATION* of the Nation *without* Spiritual life which began May 14, 1948.)

Then he said to me, "Prophesy to the BREATH; prophesy, son of man, and say to it, 'This is what the Sovereign LORD says: Come from the four winds, O BREATH, and BREATHE INTO THESE SLAIN, THAT THEY MAY LIVE.'" So I prophesied as he commanded me, and BREATH ENTERED THEM; THEY CAME TO LIFE (as per Romans 11:15) **and stood on their feet—a vast army.** (Ezekiel 37:9–10)

(This is phase two of the prophecy which predicts the *SPIRITUAL REBIRTH* of the nation *AFTER* they are physically restored to the land as a nation.)

God's Interpretation of the Allegory

Then he said to me: "Son of man, THESE BONES ARE THE WHOLE HOUSE OF ISRAEL. They say, 'Our bones are dried up and OUR HOPE IS GONE; WE ARE CUT OFF.'" (Ezekiel 37:11) (What **"they say"** in this verse sounds like a direct quote from many of the modern-day Dominionists. They teach that the Nation of Israel is finished and has no future as a distinct people or nation. The LORD identifies the bones in the allegory as representing **"the whole house of Israel."** It is crystal clear that this is literally predicting the *restoration* and *rebirth* of the *whole nation* at the time of the Messiah's coming [Ezekiel 37:21– 27].)

Their Acceptance Will Be *Life From the Dead*

"Therefore prophesy and say to them: 'This is what the Sovereign LORD says: O MY PEOPLE, I am going to OPEN YOUR GRAVES [i.e., the *nations* into which Israel is scattered] **and bring you up from them; I WILL BRING YOU BACK TO THE LAND OF ISRAEL. THEN you, MY PEOPLE, will know that I am the LORD, when I open your GRAVES and BRING YOU UP FROM THEM. I WILL put my Spirit in you and YOU SHALL LIVE, and I will settle you in your own land. Then you**

**will know that I the LORD have spoken, and I have
done it, declares the LORD.'"** (Ezekiel 37:12–14)

The allegory is straightforward and easy to interpret. The
scattered dry bones are the whole House of Israel. The Nation is
presently scattered and disjointed with no national life. It appears
to be as impossible for Israel to be regathered and Spiritually
reborn as a Nation as the restoring to life of a disjointed skeleton.

The graves symbolize the nations where the Israelites are
scattered. Each nation is like a tomb to the disjointed members of
the Nation.

The coming together of the bones and the miracle of flesh
coming upon them so that they stand up as a great army
symbolizes the miracle of Israel's restoration to the land of Israel as
a nation.

The fact that they have **no breath** is symbolic of having no
Spiritual life as yet. **The breath** symbolizes the Holy Spirit. The
breath coming into them portrays the Spiritual rebirth of the
people.

The LORD swears to bring Israel back to life from the graves
of the nations where they are scattered. They are brought back to
life as a Nation by two factors: first, when God puts His Spirit in
them; and second, when they are not just returned to the land of
Israel, as they are now, but permanently *settled* there by the
LORD. It really shouldn't be necessary to remind you that this has
never happened as yet.

But the most important point is this: the world-system and
nature itself cannot be delivered from the bondage of the original
curse until the Nation of Israel is spiritually resurrected. Isaiah
predicts that at the same time the curse is removed from nature,
Israel will be restored as a believing nation. (See Isaiah 65:17–24
and compare it with Romans 8:18–25.)

Israel's Two-Stage Restoration

There is a remarkable statement concerning the predictions of a
two-stage restoration of Israel which was made by a Jewish
convert to Christianity. David Baron was a Hebrew scholar who
was trained from childhood to be a Rabbi. After he came to believe
in Jesus as his Messiah, he became a great Christian theologian.
Consider carefully what Dr. Baron wrote in 1906 concerning

Ezekiel chapters thirty-six and thirty-seven and other prophetic passages about Israel.

On reading this and similar prophecies we must bear in mind—

First, that they refer to a restoration in blessing subsequent to the dark cloud of Israel's final apostasy and final sufferings. Some seem puzzled at the apparent contradiction in the Scriptures in reference to this subject; *for while some prophecies speak of a return of the Jews to Palestine in a condition of unbelief, there are other Scriptures which announce, in unmistakable terms, that Israel will be brought back in a condition of repentance and faith.*

The solution of the apparent difficulty is to be found, I believe, in the fact that the future restoration will be accomplished in different sections and at different stages, even as was the case with their dispersion.

It seems from Scripture that *in relation to Israel and the land there will be a restoration, before the second advent of our Lord, of the state of things as they existed at the time of His first advent, when the threads of God's dealing with them nationally were finally dropped, not to be taken up again "until the times of the Gentiles shall be fulfilled."*

There was at that time a number of Jews in Palestine representative of the nation; but compared with the number of their brethren, who were already a diaspora among the nations, they were mere minority, and not in a politically independent condition.

SO IT WILL BE AGAIN. There will be at first, as compared with the whole nation, only a representative minority in Palestine, and a Jewish state will be formed, probably under a Gentile suzerainty. . . .

But what follows? After a brief interval of outward prosperity there comes a night of anguish. **"Alas! for that day is great, so that none is like it; it is even the time of Jacob's trouble; but he shall be saved out of it** (Jeremiah 30:7)" . . .

But, simultaneously with their outward deliverance, there takes place also Israel's spiritual redemption: **"And I will pour upon the House of David, and upon the inhabitants of Jerusalem, the spirit of grace and of supplication; and they shall look upon Me whom they**

have pierced: and they shall mourn for him as one mourns for his only son, and shall be in bitterness for him as one that is in bitterness for his firstborn. (Zechariah 12:10.) . . .

And the spared remnant of the dispersed of Israel will, like their brethren in Jerusalem, hail Him—though at first, it may be, from a distance—whom they crucified, and turn to Him in true repentance and love. These will, at the lifting up of God's standard to the nations, return in a condition of faith, and such Scriptures as Deut. 30:1–10; Jer. 31:6–13, which speak of their restoration *as subsequent to their conversion, and conditional upon it, shall be literally fulfilled.*[10]

The insight that students of prophecy like David Baron had is truly amazing. Almost all of these scholars who interpreted by the literal method were able to foresee clearly the coming establishment of the State of Israel. It is also important to note that Baron clearly saw in these prophetic Scriptures that the restoration of the Nation of Israel would be *first physical and then later, spiritual.*

Israel Is Still Considered Holy by the LORD (Romans 11:16)

Paul reveals the basis of why God still loves Israel as a special people and the logical necessity of why they must be reborn as a nation: **"If [since] the part of the dough offered as firstfruits is HOLY, then the whole batch is HOLY; if [since] the root is HOLY, so are the branches."** (Romans 11:16)

Two different symbols are used to illustrate a profound truth. The first symbol is taken from a ritual instituted to Israel by the LORD in Numbers 15:18–21. The Israelites were commanded to *set apart* a portion of dough from *each baking of bread* and to offer it as the **"firstfruit"** to the LORD. It was considered to be of equal importance and of the same kind as the firstfruit offering from the harvest. The handful offered to the LORD was evidence of the worthiness of the whole mass from which it was taken.

In this illustration, **"the firstfruit"** represents the Patriarchs (Abraham, Isaac, and Jacob) to whom the unconditional convenants were given.

The **"dough"** represents the nation which was founded by those covenants and descended from the Patriarchs. Just as the LORD considered the **dough** to be made *holy* by the **firstfruit**

183

offering taken from it, so the Israelites, even though in apostasy at present, are still considered to be *holy* because of both their physical and convenantal relationship to the Patriarchs.

The term **"holy"** does not mean behavior here. The primary meaning of the original word, *hagios* (ἅγιος), is *something that is set apart to God for a special use*. It is obviously used in this sense here, since the **"dough"** is not **"holy"** because of behavior but because of being set apart as an offering to the LORD. The Patriarchs and their descendants have been set apart to God as a chosen nation through which salvation could be produced and channeled to the rest of the human race.

The second symbol sets the stage for one of the most important allegories in the Word of God, which follows this verse. It is the metaphor of the **olive tree**. This allegory builds upon the basic point of the first, but it is more comprehensive because it allows for an application that illustrates the conversion of the Gentiles. Let me identify the important features of this allegory at this point:

The **"root"** is a symbol of the Patriarchs and the covenants given to them. It corresponds to the symbol of the **"firstfruit."**

The **"tree"** is a symbol of that special company of people who are set apart as God's channel to spread salvation to the world. Much more will be developed from this allegory in the next chapter.

The LORD sovereignly chose (elected) to create the nation of Israel as His instrument of salvation at a time when the world had rejected Him and was pushing the knowledge of God from its memory. He made a special nation so that through it He could save the other nations. God is presently carrying on His redemptive plan for the world through a heavenly nation, the Church, which is composed of converts from all the nations.

But let us Gentiles never forget, **". . . as far as election is concerned, they [Israel] are loved on account of the patriarchs, for God's gifts and his call are irrevocable."** (Romans 11:28b–29)

CHAPTER NINE

Hope Hidden
in an Olive Tree

Do not gloat over ME [the Nation of Israel], my enemy!
THOUGH I HAVE FALLEN, I WILL RISE. Though I sit
in darkness, the LORD will be my light.
BECAUSE I HAVE SINNED AGAINST HIM, I will
bear the LORD's wrath [Israel's current rejection], UN-
TIL HE PLEADS MY CASE and establishes my right. He
will bring me out into the light; I will see his justice [at
the Second Advent].
Then my enemy will see it and will be covered with
shame, she who said to me, "WHERE IS THE LORD
YOUR GOD?" My eyes will see her downfall; even now
she will be trampled underfoot like mire in the streets.

The Prophet Micah
Micah 7:8–10

I believe that many prophecies concerning the events that will
precede the return of the Lord Jesus have specific application to
the current conflict that is developing within the Church. The
passage above from Micah foresaw that Israel would be attacked at
a time when they were under Divine discipline for sinning against
the LORD. The statement **"Where is the LORD your God?"**
sounds much like the Dominionists' attitude toward Israel today.
The prophecy of Ezekiel, **"They say, 'Our bones are dried up
and our hope is gone; we are cut off,'"** also sounds similar to what

is being preached from many Dominionists' pulpits. (Ezekiel 37:11)

Jeremiah's prediction sounds equally familiar, **"Have you noticed that these people are saying, 'The LORD has rejected the two kingdoms he chose'? So they despise MY PEOPLE and NO LONGER REGARD THEM AS A NATION."** (Jeremiah 33:24)

How appropriate Jeremiah's prophetic insight is to this current controversy. Many of the Dominionist preachers do not believe that there will be a future spiritual awakening among the Israelites. However, the Reconstructionist teachers generally admit that there will be a significant number of Israelites converted during the general time that the Church establishes God's Kingdom on earth.

It would be hard to read Romans chapter eleven and not at least admit that there is predicted therein a future conversion of some kind for the Israelites. But they do not see this as a *national* conversion. Chilton denies any future for Israel as a distinct, special nation.[1] Dominionists teach that the Jews will be converted and brought into the Church, which is now "Israel." This would, of course, eliminate all national distinctions for Israel. This would also render null and void all the unconditional covenants, because they were made *only* with the physical descendants of Abraham, Isaac, and Jacob as a unique nation.

They in effect do exactly what Jeremiah predicted, **"they despise God's people and NO LONGER REGARD THEM AS A NATION."**

Paul's allegory of God's Olive Tree sounds forth a severe warning to people who think this way. Let's carefully consider this Divine allegory.

GOD'S OLIVE TREE

The Apostle Paul's first question in Romans 11:1 leads into a discussion concerning the *minority* of Israelites who had not stumbled in unbelief. His second question in Romans 11:11 leads into a discussion of the *majority* of Israelites who have stumbled in unbelief. The following allegory unveils their future.

Read carefully this allegory of the Olive Tree:

> **If the part of the dough offered as firstfruits is holy, then the whole batch is holy; if the root is holy, so are the branches.**

186

If some of the branches have been broken off, and you [Gentiles], though a wild olive shoot, have been grafted in among the others and now share in the nourishing sap from the olive root, do not boast over those branches. If you do, consider this: YOU DO NOT SUPPORT THE ROOT, BUT THE ROOT SUPPORTS YOU.

You will say then, "Branches [national Israel] were broken off so that I [the Gentiles] could be grafted in." Granted. But they [Israel] were broken off because of UNBELIEF, and you [Gentiles] stand by FAITH. DO NOT BE ARROGANT, but be afraid. For if God did not spare the natural branches [national Israel], HE WILL NOT SPARE YOU [Gentiles] EITHER.

Consider therefore the kindness and sternness of God: sternness to those who fell, but kindness to you [Gentiles], provided that you continue in his kindness. Otherwise, you [Gentiles as a corporate group] ALSO WILL BE CUT OFF. And if they [Israel as a Nation] do not persist in unbelief, THEY WILL BE GRAFTED IN, FOR GOD IS ABLE TO GRAFT THEM IN AGAIN.

After all, if you [Gentiles] were cut out of an olive tree that is wild by nature, and contrary to nature were grafted into a cultivated olive tree, how much more readily will these, the natural branches [National Israel], be grafted into THEIR OWN OLIVE TREE! [i.e., the place of blessing under their *own* covenants] (Romans 11:16–24) (Emphases and explanations added.)

IDENTIFYING THE SYMBOLS

We began to consider this allegory in the last chapter as we examined the meaning of Romans 11:16. It is important to note the difference between an allegory and a parable. A parable is designed to convey one basic point. But an allegory is designed to convey many truths with point by point analogies. Let us identify the important symbols of this allegory.

The **"root"** of the tree is symbolic of the Patriarchs in possession of the covenants and promises with which God created the Nation of Israel and through which salvation was brought to the world. This is why Jesus said, **"You Samaritans worship what you** do not know; we worship what we do know, **FOR SALVATION IS FROM THE JEWS."** (John 4:22)

The **"cultivated olive tree"** symbolizes the place of blessing through those covenants and promises. Whoever is *in the tree* partakes of those covenants and promises. Whichever group (composed of either Israelites or Gentiles) is predominant in the tree becomes God's preeminent corporate vessel for evangelizing the world.

The **"natural branches"** symbolize Israel as the covenanted national people physically descended from the Patriarchs.

The **"wild olive branches"** symbolize the Gentiles as a corporate people. The symbol emphasizes that the Gentiles are unnatural partakers in Israel's covenants and promises. Indeed, Gentile salvation is clearly presented as dependent on Israel's covenant relationship to God, since their **"root"** and **"their tree"** give us salvation and not vice versa.

The figure of **"grafting branches into the cultivated olive tree"** symbolizes *a corporate group being placed into the covenant blessings and established as the principle channel for God's work on earth.* Gentiles could be saved in the old economy, but they had to come through Israel, who were God's predominant and preeminent servants. Now the reverse is true. An Israelite can be saved today, but he must come to a Church in which Gentiles are the predominant and preeminent servants of God. The focus of this chapter is how the Israelites will return to their place of preeminence as a nation.

God is the Husbandman who supernaturally grafts in or removes both Israel and the Gentiles.

The figure of **"the branches being broken off from the tree"** *means to be removed corporately as a group from the place of God's covenant blessing.*

There are two points that must be kept constantly in mind. (1) This allegory *does not have in view individual Israelites or Gentiles, but rather each general group as a whole.* (2) All through this inspired allegory, the Church and Israel are presented as two distinct programs of God.

Everett F. Harrison writes clearly about this issue: "Paul treats the Gentile element in the church as a unit, addressing it as 'you' (singular in Greek). This should not be understood on an individual basis as though Paul were questioning their personal salvation. The matter in hand is the current Gentile prominence in the church made possible by the rejection of the gospel on the part of the nation of Israel as a whole."[2]

Preeminence Is Precarious

The main point of Paul's argument is: Gentiles beware, because your predominance in God's community will come to an end just as the Israelites' did.

From the call of Abraham until Israel's official rejection of Jesus as the Messiah at the time of His triumphal entry to Jerusalem (commonly known as Palm Sunday), the nation of Israel was viewed by God as His special representative to bring His message to the world. Israel was the recipient of God's revelation and the focus of His special grace. Though a few Gentiles were saved during this period, Israelites were predominant and preeminent in His plan.

But from the birth of the Church at the Advent of the Holy Spirit on the Day of Pentecost the situation has been reversed. The Church, which is called God's *holy nation*, has replaced the Nation of Israel as God's channel of blessing for the world. In the Church, Gentiles are predominant and preeminent. During this age, Israel's covenant blessings, conveyed on the believer through union with Christ, and God's special grace are both focused on the Gentiles. (More about this in chapter twelve.)

Postmillennialist John Murray, as he commented on Romans 11:16, gave a surprisingly accurate analysis of the basic import of this allegory:

> The **root** is surely the patriarchs. Furthermore, in verse 28 (unbelieving) Israel are said to be **"beloved for the father's sake."** In the one case it is the consecration belonging to Israel, in the other it is the love borne to Israel. But both are derived from the patriarchal parentage. . . . *This fact of consecration derived from the patriarchs is introduced here by the apostle as support for the ultimate recovery of Israel. There cannot be an irremediable rejection of Israel;* the holiness of theocratic consecration is not abolished and will one day be vindicated in *Israel's fullness and restoration.*[3] (Emphases added.)

Premillennialist Kenneth Wuest rightly shows the *national* character of Israel as represented by the allegory:

The Jewish nation is a **tree** from which some **branches** have been cut, but which remains living because **the root** (and therefore all the **wild branches** connected with it) is still alive. Into this living tree the wild branch, the Gentile (corporately considered), is grafted among the living branches, and thus draws life from the root. The insertion of the wild branches takes place in connection with the cutting off of the **natural branches** (the bringing in of the Gentiles in connection with the rejection of the Jews). But the grafted branches should not glory over the natural branches because of the cutting off of some of the latter, since they derive their life from the common root. *The life-force and the blessing are received by the Gentile through the Jew, and not the Jew through the Gentile.* The spiritual plan moves from the Abrahamic covenant downward, and from the Israelitish nation outward.[4] (Emphases added.)

Overall Observations

Before going into further interpretation of this allegory, here are some observations that are obvious.

First, the Apostle Paul's emphasis is that it is most appropriate for the natural branches to be grafted back into *their own tree.* It is unnatural for the branches of a wild olive tree to be in a cultivated olive tree. This emphasizes that it is much more natural for Israel to be restored to the covenants that were specifically made to them, than for the Gentiles to remain in the place of preeminence under them. Gentiles are only received on the basis of our union with the Lord Jesus Christ who inherited the rights of those covenants. Paul unmistakably teaches by this allegory that the Gentile's position of preeminence is much more *precarious* than Israel's was. (See Romans 11:22–24.)

Second, in order for the wild branches to be grafted in, the majority of natural branches had to be broken off. Conversely, in order for the natural branches to be grafted back in, the majority of the wild branches must be broken off. Throughout this allegory, only one group is viewed as preeminent at any given period in God's administration of the world.

Translated, this aspect of the allegory means that there will come a time when the Gentiles will be taken out of their place of preeminence in God's purpose, and the Israelites will be restored to it. This is exactly the condition about which the Apostle warns the Gentiles when he says, ". . . **provided that you** [Gentiles as a group] **continue in his kindness. Otherwise, YOU** [Gentiles as the preeminent group] **ALSO WILL BE CUT OFF. And if they** [national Israel] **do not persist in unbelief, THEY WILL BE GRAFTED IN, for God is ABLE to graft them in again."** (Romans 11:22b–23) (Emphases and explanations added.)

Nowhere is it stated or implied that **the wild olive branches** [Gentiles] and **the natural olive branches** [Israel] can both be in the place of preeminence at the same time, as the Dominionists' theory requires. On the contrary, the whole point of the allegory is to spell out how and why Israel lost their preeminence to the Gentiles, and how they will in the future be restored to their previous position.

As we have considered, this agrees with the whole tenor of prophetic Scripture and Israel's covenants. All prophecy that deals with the Messianic Kingdom portrays Israel as a restored believing Nation, preeminent in the Messiah's administration of His Millennial Kingdom on earth.

Conversely, all the prophecies that deal with the condition of the institutional Church just before the coming of Christ portray it as a time of evil and apostasy.[5] The believing remnant of the Church will be snatched out of a Christ-rejecting world to meet the LORD in the air.[6] Most of those who are left behind in the counterfeit Church will become part of the Man of Lawlessness's one-world religion and government.

Dominionists may be unwittingly helping to set up the kind of programs that will fit right in with the programs the Antichrist will establish. Any move toward uniting the world under one religion and one government can actually be used by the Antichrist.

It is imperative to remember that hope founded on *"positive falsehoods"* will turn out to be worse than *no hope at all*. And how terrifying it will be to find that in defiance of what the Prophets have plainly predicted, they will have helped to set up a one-world order that the Antichrist will take over.

God's Warning to Gentile Anti-Semitic Attitudes
(Romans 11:17–21)

These verses reveal that there were already strong anti-Jewish feelings in the large Gentile-dominated first-century Roman

Church. It was well known that the fanatical sect of Judaism known as the Pharisees had instigated a great persecution upon both the Jewish and Gentile believers.

Paul was especially referring to this sect of Jews when he wrote, **"For you, brothers, became imitators of God's churches in Judea, which are in Christ Jesus: You suffered from your own countrymen** [i.e., the Greeks of Thessalonika] **the same things those churches suffered from the Jews, who killed the Lord Jesus and the prophets and also drove us out. They displease God and are hostile to all men in their effort to keep us from speaking to the Gentiles so that they may be saved. In this way they always heap up their sins to the limit. The wrath of God has come upon them at last."** (1 Thessalonians 2:14–16)

In spite of this, Paul warns the Gentiles in this letter against developing an anti-Jewish attitude. The powerfully presented reasons in this allegory of the olive tree are: (1) that it is their covenants that secure our salvation; (2) that God still has a great purpose for the Nation of Israel in the future.

To those who say that God has cast off the Nation of Israel forever, that it has no more future in His plan, and that all her blessings have been irrevocably given to the Church, God answers this way, **"If some of the branches have been broken off, and you, though a wild olive shoot, have been grafted in among the others and now share in the nourishing sap from the olive root, DO NOT BOAST OVER THOSE BRANCHES."** (11:17) (Emphasis added.)

The phrase **"some of the branches"** refers to the mass of unbelieving Israelites. It brings out again what was asserted in the first ten verses of this chapter, that not *all* Israelites are rejected in this present age. But assuredly, most Israelites are unbelievers today, and these are the focus of this chapter.

This precise situation was predicted in the very terms of this allegory by Jeremiah: **"The LORD called you a thriving OLIVE TREE with fruit beautiful in form. But with the roar of a mighty storm he will set it on fire, and ITS BRANCHES WILL BE BROKEN."** (Jeremiah 11:16) As I have said so many times, nothing that has happened to Israel; her apostasy, her destruction as a nation, her worldwide dispersion, her great persecution, her physical return to statehood in the land of Israel, etc., has taken God by surprise. He predicted it all long ago. Yet in terms just as specific, God predicted that He would not forsake the people of

Abraham, Isaac, and Jacob, but would restore them as a *believing Nation* to all the things promised to their fathers.

The allegory in this verse describes a procedure that was completely contrary to nature. Frequently a farmer would graft a branch from a cultivated olive tree into a wild one. But every husbandmen knew that grafting a branch from a wild olive tree into a cultivated one would not work. It simply would not bear fruit. Yet the LORD reminds us that we Gentiles have been grafted in **"contrary to nature."** (11:24)

We now share in **"the nourishing sap from the olive ROOT."** This is a very sobering statement. This reveals that Gentile salvation continues to be secured through the covenants made with Israel's patriarchs, who continue to be the root of the olive tree. Paul recognized this precedent when he said at the beginning of the Epistle to the Romans, **"I am not ashamed of the gospel, because it is the power of God for the salvation of everyone who believes: FIRST TO THE JEW, then for the Gentile."** (1:16) (Emphasis added.)

In the light of this, we Gentiles are warned not to **"boast over those BRANCHES."** (11:18a) The important question is, Which branches? The branches that are still in the olive tree, or the ones that have been broken off? The context, particularly verse nineteen, reveals that it absolutely refers to the branches that have been broken off. In other words, we Gentiles are not to boast over the Jews who are at the present time under God's discipline.

Paul further warns, **"If you do, consider this: You do not support the ROOT, but the ROOT supports you."** (11:18b) The inescapable meaning here is that the Patriarchs and their covenants secure and support our (the Gentiles') eternal salvation. These broken branches are still special to God because they are the physical lineage of those Patriarchs. If you are sitting out on the end of a limb that is over a great precipice, it is stupid to curse the tree and saw off the limb on which you are sitting. Yet what the Dominionists are doing is even dumber, for they are condemning the very people on whose covenants our salvation from eternal damnation depends.

Paul anticipates that the Gentiles might seek to justify their attitude of superiority over the unbelieving Jews: **"You will say then, 'Branches were broken off so that I could be grafted in.'"** (11:19) Some Gentiles could reason that we are so special to God that He cast out the Israelites *in order to* graft us into their place.

Paul turns the tables on this kind of reasoning. He demonstrates that far from boasting about this situation, we should have a healthy fear. The Nation of Israel was rejected and destroyed because of persistent unbelief. We Gentiles stand precariously on the same ground of faith from which they fell.

Paul warns, **"Do not be arrogant, but be AFRAID. For if God did not spare the NATURAL BRANCHES, he will not spare you either."** (11:20b–21) (Emphasis added.) God has far less reason to spare us wild branches than He did the natural ones. We are exhorted to fear on the grounds that it is more difficult for wild branches to stay in the cultivated olive tree than for the natural branches to be grafted back in. The clear message is that it is easier for Gentiles to fall into unbelief than it was for the Israelites.

Arrogance Against Israel Is a Hallmark of Dominion Teaching

This exhortation should cause the Gentile-dominated Church to take a very careful look at the false teaching that is once again being spread through our ranks. The arrogance manifested by the Dominion preachers against Israel as a distinct national people is awesome.

A prime example of this is the book by Earl Paulk entitled *To Whom Is God Betrothed*. One of the main issues he raises is that most teachers of prophecy today exhort us to bless a nation that is godless and has rejected the Lord Jesus Christ. He charges that no thought is given to preaching the Gospel to them, but rather we insulate them from the truth by giving them a false sense of security in their unbelief.

The prophetic teachers I know certainly take every opportunity to share the Gospel with the Israelites. But once the Gospel has been made clear to a Jew, I don't believe it is necessary to break off fellowship with him because he doesn't accept it, or to push it on him in every conversation. However, the Dominionists, who proclaim that the Church is now Israel and that the descendants of Abraham, Isaac, and Jacob have no future hope as a distinct people, are finding a very wary eye cast their way. The Jews have heard this kind of rhetoric from the Church before. They remember vividly the anti-Semitism and persecutions it inevitably set in motion. They remember well the historic progression: The Church said "You have no right to live among us as Jews!" The secular governments followed with "You have no right to live among us!" The Nazis concluded with "You have no right to live!"

194

On the other hand, the Premillennialists have had the greatest burden for the Jews and the greatest success in evangelizing them. They have received a much greater open door to share the Gospel with the Jews than the Dominion teachers will ever have. The American Board of Missions to the Jews and The Biblical Research Society, headed by the great Hebrew scholar Dr. David L. Cooper, are just a couple of groups who have had great success as missionaries to the Jews. It was their Premillennial view of prophecy that gave them such compassion and patience with the Jews, for it was through these prophecies that they came to share God's great undying love for the Jews.

In writing *The Late Great Planet Earth*, I had the Jews constantly in mind. I prayerfully and deliberately sought to present my prophetic case in such a way that it would especially appeal to them. It has been published in more than fifty foreign editions and has been instrumental all around the world in bringing tens of thousands of Jews to faith in Jesus as their Messiah. I run into them everywhere. They continue to write me from virtually every part of the world. The first Prime Minister of Israel, David Ben Gurion, was reading it shortly before he died. Since everything in his room has been kept the way it was when he died, a copy of *The Late Great Planet Earth* remains on his desk. A friend of mine who is one of Israel's top military commanders passed out hundreds of copies of the Hebrew translation of *The Late Great Planet Earth* to the Israeli Defense Forces, even though he personally hasn't as yet believed in Jesus as the Messiah.

But you don't bring a Jew to believe in Jesus as Messiah by teaching that in effect Jews are imposters as a covenant people, without any hope or destiny as a Nation. Most Jews know something about the unconditional covenants made to their fathers, even if they don't presently believe them. When they hear the teaching that the Church is Israel, now and forever, they know from a general awareness of the Bible that this is a distortion of Scripture.

Dominionist Earl Paulk writes, "Many well-intentioned Church leaders raise money by taking excursions to Israel/Palestine. How many of them go to preach salvation to the Jews? How many speak to Israeli government leaders, telling them Jesus is the Messiah who has already come?"[7] My answer to that is, Many do! I certainly do. But you can't cram a message about Jesus down the throats of a people who have been persecuted for centuries by people professing to be doing it in Christ's name. It takes a demonstration of genuine love as well as the Gospel to overcome the effects of those so-called Christians in past history who believed that the Church was God's theocratic kingdom on earth, and in its name sought to either convert the Jews or eliminate them.

Paulk continues, "The tremendous error of waiting for the restoration of Israel as God's 'special people' is very evident. The Church is the restoration of Israel."[8] Premils are not waiting to give the Gospel to the Jew because of their belief in Israel's future national restoration, as Paulk charges in this context. But, while vigorously seeking to evangelize them today, the Premillennialist realizes that the majority will be saved by the Lord Jesus Christ's direct future intervention.

Because Israel failed under the Mosaic Covenant, which was a conditional covenant to begin with, the Dominionists teach that all of their covenants were forfeited. As we have considered, this ignores the fact that Israel's other four covenants are all unconditional and not dependent on the Mosaic covenant. That is why this allegory says that **"we do not support the root, but the root supports us."** (Romans 11:18) This statement affirms that the covenants are still in force, and that they are being kept in reserve for the descendants of the Patriarchs whom the LORD will bring to faith.

Gentiles Warned of Future Rejection by God

The LORD urges us Gentiles to weigh carefully His actions in history: **"Consider therefore the kindness and sternness of God: sternness to those who fell, but kindness to you, provided that you continue in his kindness. Otherwise, YOU ALSO WILL BE CUT OFF."** (11:22) This is a clear warning that we Gentiles can lose our place of preeminence in God's plan just as the Israelites did. God will one day remove us from our place of leadership in His plan just as he did Israel, especially since it was only God's mercy that allowed us into this exhalted position in the first place.

A Preview of Things to Come

"And if they [Israel as a nation] **do not persist in unbelief, they will be grafted in, for GOD IS ABLE TO GRAFT THEM IN AGAIN."** (11:23) This is the first solid hint in this passage of what God intends to do with the mass of unbelieving Israelites. Note carefully that the grafting in again of the unbelieving Israelites is linked to the removal of Gentiles in the previous verse.

Once again, it is imperative to remember that this allegory is not talking about the total removal of all Gentiles from the olive tree, nor is it merely talking about the ingrafting of a larger number of Jews. Jews are being saved today, and Gentiles were saved under the Old Covenant. The issue addressed here has totally to do with which *group* is God's preeminent vessel.

The main point of verses twenty-two and twenty-three is that if the majority in the Gentile-dominated Church fall into unbelief, then God is ready and able to save and restore the Nation of Israel back to her former place of preeminence and leadership. God would also have us remember that He has promised with an oath to do this very thing!

The Olive Tree Still Belongs to the Jew

The LORD explains why He is not only able to remove the Gentiles and to put Israel back into the place of leadership, but that it is by far the most natural thing for Him to do, **"After all, if you were cut out of an olive tree that is wild by nature, and contrary to nature were grafted into a cultivated olive tree, how much more readily will these NATURAL BRANCHES be grafted into THEIR OWN OLIVE TREE!"** (11:24) (Emphases added.)

The **natural branches** in this context refers to that mass of national Israel that is presently in unbelief. Yet God clearly reveals that the tree into which we Gentiles have been grafted contrary to nature is *still* the Jew's **own olive tree.** The simple meaning of this is that the covenants are *still* valid to the physical race of Israel. Their fulfillment only awaits that predicted time when God will bring them back to faith again. This is the very fact that the Holy Spirit brings out in the next paragraph.

Dr. James Stifler gives an excellent insight into this verse:

> Divested of the figurative language, Paul's thought is this: if God could wean some Gentiles from their idol-worship and their gross immorality and lead them to adopt the religion of another nation, can he not "much more" lead Israel to adopt their own ancestral worship when they are once brought to see what it is, and that it is their own, and that their ignorant works have been

perverting it? God's ability is in His unfailing love toward Israel.

What is gained in the figure lies in its suggestion. "Nature" seems to mean here the established course of things in the kingdom. Its course lay through Israel. Gentile salvation is contrary to "nature," and Jewish rejection is also contrary to "nature." The course of things, that is, nature, will in due time assert itself. Therefore let the Gentile fear; let the Jew hope. The wild branch may be broken off, the fallen one grafted in again.[9]

THE GREAT MYSTERY OF *ALL* ISRAEL'S FUTURE SALVATION (ROMANS 11:25–32)

Paul, still exhorting Gentile believers, warns us not to be ignorant of one of God's great mysteries. His reasoning is that knowledge of this *mystery* will keep us from becoming conceited in our attitude toward the national Israelites who have fallen because of unbelief. The Holy Spirit says:

> **I do not want you to be ignorant of this mystery, brothers, so that you may not be conceited: Israel has experienced a hardening in part UNTIL the full number of Gentiles has come in. And so ALL ISRAEL WILL BE SAVED, as it is written:**

> > **"The deliverer will come from Zion;**
> > **he will turn godlessness away from**
> > **Jacob."**
> > **"And this is my covenant with them**
> > **when I take away their sins."**

> > (Romans 11:25–27)

These verses spell out the Holy Spirit's summary application of the **olive tree** allegory.

The most important and obvious fact revealed in verse twenty-five is that Israel's partial hardening in this age is only for a *specific, limited time.*

Why is it that the Holy Spirit says an understanding of this fact will keep us Gentiles from becoming conceited? The humbling answer is this: If Israel's partial hardening is only for a limited time, then the Gentiles' days of preeminence in God's redemptive plan *are numbered.*

The Mystery Behind Israel's Restoration

The **mystery** concerns how national Israel's future salvation is contingent upon the coming in of **the full number of the Gentiles** *first.*

The Greek word for mystery, *musterion* (μυστηριον), does not mean a secret that is unknowable. In the New Testament, it means something heretofore not revealed, but now made understandable to those who have been born Spiritually and are taught by the Holy Spirit. The Holy Spirit Himself gives the term, **mystery,** this definition: **"Now to him who is able to establish you by my gospel and the proclamation of Jesus Christ, according to the revelation of the MYSTERY hidden for long ages past, but now revealed and made known through the prophetic writings by the command of the eternal God . . ."** (Romans 16:25–26)

Until, God's Key Prophetic Word

So many critical events in prophetic Scripture depend upon the simple temporal conjunction, **until.** The following are some important illustrations of the term **until** that are related to its prophetical usage in Romans 11:25.

The *Until* of Earthly Jerusalem's Future Restoration

A key statement in the Lord Jesus' great prophetic discourse on the Mount of Olives is this: **"They** [national Israel] **will fall by the sword and will be taken as prisoners to all the nations. Jerusalem will be trampled on by the Gentiles UNTIL the times of the Gentiles are fulfilled."** (Luke 21:24)

This was a prediction of Israel's national destruction, the desolation of Jerusalem, and Israel's dispersion throughout the world. This occurred in A.D. 70. The LORD did not originate this prophecy, but simply summarized something that was a theme in the Old Testament Prophets.

But Jesus predicted that the desolation of Jerusalem would last only for a specific period which He called **"the times of the Gentiles."** The "times of the Gentiles" is a technical prophetic phrase that describes the period of time during which the Gentile kingdoms have dominion over the earth, and particularly over God's land, God's city, and God's people.

The term **until** predicts the time of *termination* for Gentile dominion over the literal earthly city of Jerusalem. The Greek word from which **until** is translated is *achri* (αχρι). Gingrich and Danker show that when *achri* is used, as it is here, in its temporal conjuctive sense it means the termination point of existing conditions, resulting in a change to new conditions.[10]

In Luke 21:24, Jesus predicted that the end of the desolation of Jerusalem would be co-terminus with the end of Gentile world dominance. The end of Gentile domination will result in Jerusalem being returned to the Jews in accordance with many specific prophecies. In the rest of this context, Jesus clearly prophesies that Gentile world-rule will be destroyed by His personal return, and that He will then replace it with God's Kingdom.

The **times of the Gentiles** began under God's permissive will when the Neo-Babylonian Empire took the Davidic dynasty captive and destroyed the nation of Israel. The successive Gentile kingdoms that in God's view would have world dominance are all predicted in the book of Daniel, chapters two, seven, and eight. They are the Neo-Babylonian, Media-Persian, Greek-Macedonian, Roman Empire (phase one), and the revived Roman Empire (phase two in the form of a ten nation confederacy). This final form of the Roman Empire will rise to power at the time just prior to the Messiah's Second Coming. Daniel predicted that it would be the Messiah, the Stone cut out without human hands, who will suddenly destroy Gentile power, rule, and world dominance. At this time, God will establish a Theocratic Kingdom on earth, and replace Gentile dominance with the dominance of His chosen Nation, Israel.

In the context following Luke 21:24, the Second Coming is described as the event that will end **the times of the Gentiles**, and specifically their desecration of Jerusalem. (See Luke 21:25–28.) Another important prophecy that describes these same events is Zechariah chapters twelve through fourteen.

"Black Is White," If You Know How to Use Allegory

Typical of Dominion teachers, David Chilton tries to make Jesus' Olivet Discourse apply almost entirely to the destruction of Jerusalem in A.D. 70. But as we will consider in the next chapter, this is an impossible interpretation. *The Roman destruction of Jerusalem in* A.D. *70 did not establish Israel's promised Kingdom to the Church or anyone, but rather it marked an escalation of Jerusalem's desolation by the Gentiles.* According to numerous prophetic Scriptures, God's Kingdom cannot be established on earth until this Gentile domination of Jerusalem is terminated by the personal intervention of the Lord Jesus Himself.

This is such a clear theme of prophecy that it should be obvious to everyone who studies it. Gentile world-rule must be terminated by **the rock cut out of the mountain without human hands** before the God of Heaven will set up His Kingdom (see Daniel 2:44–45). This means that the Messiah, without the help of human agency, will destroy the Gentile world-rule at His Second Advent.

The Holy Spirit predicts in Revelation 11:2 that Gentiles will have dominion over the city of Jerusalem during the final three and a half years before the Messiah returns. (Once again, the Dominionists' interpretation of this verse is a direct contradiction. They say that this was the destruction of the Jewish Temple in A.D. 70. *Yet that did not end Gentile domination of Jerusalem, it established it!*)

In this same context, the Spirit predicts that Gentile domination will be terminated only by the cataclysmic intervention of the Lord Jesus during the time of the **Seventh Trumpet** judgments: **"The seventh angel sounded his trumpet, and there were loud voices in heaven, which said: 'The kingdom of this world has become the kingdom of our LORD and of his Christ, and he will reign for ever and ever.'"** (Revelation 11:15) The seventh trumpet judgment contains all of **the seven golden bowl** judgments. The Bowl judgments are clearly global in scope. They will completely destroy the earth's ecological system (see Revelation chapter sixteen).[11] Their effect will be so great that they would destroy all life apart from personal intervention of Jesus, the Messiah. (See Matthew 24:21,22)

After the Messiah's Advent, as Zechariah predicts, Jerusalem will become the center of world worship and government, the capital of the restored believing Nation of Israel, and the place of the Messiah's throne. (Zechariah 14:9–21)

The *Until* of Israel's National Repentance

When Jesus pronounced the beginning of the dreadful, predicted fifth stage of Divine discipline (Deuteronomy 28:59–68) upon the

Nation of Israel of His generation, He left them one ray of hope with the word *until:* **"For I tell you, you will not see me again UNTIL you say, 'Blessed is he who comes in the name of the LORD.'"** (Matthew 23:39) Many Dominionist teachers quote the condemnations of Israel from Matthew chapter twenty-three, but they conveniently leave out an interpretation of this last verse.

"Until" in the original Greek is the temporal conjunction, *heos* (ἑως). According to the leading Greek lexicon, it means, **". . . you will not see me again until** *the time when* **you say, 'Blessed is he who comes in the name of the LORD.'"**[12] That time and its circumstances were clearly predicted by the Prophet Zechariah. (Zechariah 12:10; 13:1 and 8–10)

The *Until* of Israel's National Conversion

Israel's partial hardening of heart is said to continue **"until the full number of Gentiles has come in."** (11:25 NIV) The original Greek literally says, **"until the FULLNESS of the Gentiles has come in,"** but the New International Version correctly interpreted the word **fullness** in the light of the context. There is a wide difference of opinion on just what this *"coming in of Gentile fullness"* means.

Paul frequently wrote about Gentiles being added to the body of Christ to make up a certain number of redeemed people. He saw this process continuing until its future prophetic time of completion. This idea of filling out the full number of saved Gentiles during this age definitely is what is meant by the statement, **". . . until the full number of Gentiles has come in."**

In this unique age, God is calling out of all nations a people who become His holy, spiritual nation. This idea is contained in the very meaning of the word *Church,* which literally means *"the called out ones."*

This process began with a great miracle on the Day of Pentecost when the Baptism of the Holy Spirit was first initiated (this will be more fully explained in chapter twelve). As it is written, **"For by one Spirit we were all baptized into one body, whether Jews or Greeks, whether slaves or free, and we were all made to drink of one Spirit. For the body is not one member, but many."** (1 Corinthians 12:13–14 NASB) As this age progresses, that Gentile-dominated number of saved people in the body of Christ is nearing completion. There will soon come a time when the last person will believe in Christ and be baptized by the Holy Spirit into union with Him. Then, just as the Church began with a

202

miracle, its earthly mission will end with a miracle. Christ will suddenly come for His own and take them to His Father's house. (John 14:1–4; 1 Thessalonians 4:15–18)

This is what Paul had in mind when he wrote, **"And now you know what is holding him** (the Man of Lawlessness) **back, so that he may be revealed at the proper time. For the secret power of lawlessness is already at work; but the one who now holds it back** [the Holy Spirit resident in the Church] **will continue to do so TILL he is taken out of the way. And then the LAWLESS ONE will be revealed, whom the Lord Jesus will overthrow with the breath of his mouth and destroy by the splendor of HIS COMING."** (2 Thessalonians 2:6–8) *You cannot remove the special ministries of the Holy Spirit until you remove the vessels in whom He now dwells to perform them.* Maranatha!

Second, *the salvation of all Israel* is said to take place immediately after the completion of **the full number of Gentiles. "AND SO all Israel will be saved."** The words "and so" are intended to correlate with the **"until"** of verse twenty-five, thereby acquiring a temporal force. The adverb translated **"so"** is *outos* (οὗτος) in the Greek. Gingrich and Danker, in the most authoritative lexicon we have on the Greek New Testament, write about the usage of *outos* in this verse, "what is so introduced follows immediately after."[13] They would translate this verse, ". . . **until the full number of Gentiles has come in. AND IMMEDIATELY AFTER THIS, all Israel will be saved."** (Emphasis added.)

Postmillennialists try to say that **"And so all Israel will be saved"** only means that the majority of ethnic Israelites will believe in Jesus as Messiah and become part of the Church. According to them, this will then result in the salvation of even greater numbers of Gentiles. They interpret this to be the meaning of **"the fullness of the Gentiles,"** and the blessings for the world after the ingathering of a remnant of Israelites. If that were the meaning, Romans chapters nine, ten, and eleven would make no sense at all. Israelites who believe during this age become part of the Church and *lose their national identity* (this does not mean they must lose cultural identity). But the whole point of these chapters is that national Israel has a future that is different from the present order of things. If this were not so, there would have been no need for such an elaborate explanation about their future.

The Dominionists' Dilemma

This passage clearly declares that the saving of the *full number* of Gentiles is completed *before* Israel's salvation can take place. Therefore their salvation *cannot be the cause* of greater Gentile blessings as the Dominionists teach. And Israel's salvation is not said to be *caused* by the completion of **the fullness of the Gentiles,** but rather by **the coming of the Deliverer from Zion.**

It is this coming of the Messiah that brings about the conversion of Israel as a Nation. Then the Kingdom promised to them follows. It is the establishment of this Kingdom that will bring the greatest blessing ever known to the world. This is **"the greater riches"** the Holy Spirit predicted in Romans 11:12, 16, and 8:18–24. Indeed, **"how much greater riches for the world will Israel's fullness bring!"**

Israel's salvation is linked by the Holy Spirit to **"the Deliverer who will come out of Zion and turn godlessness away from Jacob."** The first half of the above quotation is from Isaiah 59:20, which is in a context that clearly refers to the coming of the Messiah to rescue the Nation of Israel and to establish them in their promised Messianic Kingdom. National Israel's salvation is linked to the Messiah's personal coming by scores of prophecies.

The Messianic title, **Deliverer,** is a translation of the Hebrew word *goel,* which means **"Kinsman-Redeemer."** This concept is elaborately developed in the Old Testament, particularly in the Book of Ruth. It is used here to emphasize that the Messiah is coming to ransom His near-kinsmen who are hopelessly enslaved. No title could be more appropriate for the Messiah's Premillennial mission to restore His fallen kinsmen, the Israelites.

The Messiah **"will turn away ungodliness from Jacob."** The Holy Spirit uses the unregenerate name **Jacob** to describe the people. The LORD renamed Jacob **"Israel"** only after he had met Him face to face. In the same way the nation, which is now unregenerate, will become Israel when it meets the Messiah Jesus face to face at His coming. The verb **"turn away"** (αποστρεφω) means *to remove decisively* ungodliness from the people. This reflects what Ezekiel predicted for the nation at the time they are restored to their land by the Messiah's coming: **"I will give you a new heart and put a new spirit in you . . ."** (Ezekiel 36:26a) The verb is in the future tense and indicative mood, which emphasizes the certainty of its fulfillment.

In fact, Paul's quotes in Romans 11:26–27 are a montage of several prophecies from the Old Testament that all relate to the restoration of the Nation of Israel at the personal coming of the Messiah.

The statement, **"And this is MY COVENANT with them when I take away their sins,"** definitely summarizes and emphasizes the forgiveness promised to the Nation of Israel in the New Covenant. (Jeremiah 31:31–40) The institution of the New Covenant to Israel is promised to occur at a time when **"The city [Jerusalem] will never again be uprooted or demolished."** (Jeremiah 31:40) This correlates precisely with what Jesus predicted in Luke 21:24.

According to the Holy Spirit's interpretation of this Old Testament prophecy, the New Covenant is not complete until God **takes away** the Nation of Israel's sins. The verb *aphaireo* (ἀφαιρέω) is an intensive word which literally means *to thoroughly remove* sin. It is in the Greek aorist tense which emphasizes that this *removal of sin* will occur in a single event, not a process. Though two aspects of the New Covenant (a finished forgiveness and the giving of the Holy Spirit to all believers) are now in effect for the Church, the complete fulfillment can only occur when the Nation of Israel is suddenly converted at the advent of the Messiah.

A Nation Saved in a Day

"And so all Israel will be saved." This clause presents a real problem for the Dominionists. If, as they so confidently teach, the Church is *now and forever* the New Israel, then why does the Holy Spirit speak of a *future* salvation for Israel? This clause certainly cannot refer to the Church. It can only be referring to the unbelieving nation of Israel, not individual Israelites. As we saw in Romans chapter nine, only the physical descendants of Abraham, Isaac, and Jacob *who believe* in God's revealed means of forgiveness are *the true Israel*. Now that it is fully revealed that Jesus is the Messiah, Israel must believe in Him to be saved. Zechariah reveals just how that will take place for the nation:

> **"And I will pour out on the house of David and the inhabitants of Jerusalem a spirit of grace and supplication. They will look on ME, the one they have pierced, and they will mourn for HIM as one mourns for an only**

child, and grieve bitterly for HIM as one grieves for a firstborn son.

"ON THAT DAY a fountain will be opened to the house of David and the inhabitants of Jerusalem, to cleanse them from sin and impurity.

"In the whole land [of Israel]," declares the LORD, "two-thirds will be struck down and perish; yet one-third will be left in it. This third I will bring into the fire; I will refine them like silver and test them like gold. They will call on my name and I will answer them; I will say, 'They are my people,' and they will say, 'The LORD is our God.'" (Zechariah 12:10; 13:1; and 8–10)

This will nullify God's previous rejection of Israel when He said through Hosea, "Then the LORD said, 'Call him Lo Ammi [Hebrew=*not my people*], for you [Israel] are not my people, and I am not your God.'" (Hosea 1:9) The Dominionists cling to this verse but ignore the following ones.

Isaiah the Prophet foresaw the salvation of all surviving Israelites:

Shout for joy, O heavens; rejoice, O earth; burst into song, O mountains! For the LORD comforts his people and will have compassion on his afflicted ones.

This is what the Sovereign LORD says: "See, I will beckon to the GENTILES, I will lift up my banner to the peoples; they will BRING YOUR SONS [Israel's] in their arms and carry your daughters on their shoulders. Kings will be your foster fathers, and their queens your nursing mothers.

"They will bow down before you [the believing remnant of Israel] with their faces to the ground; they will lick the dust at your feet.

"Then you [Israel] will know that I [the Messiah] am the LORD; those who hope in ME will not be disappointed." (Isaiah 49:13, 22, 23)

"Who has ever heard of such a thing? Can a COUNTRY be born in a day or a NATION [Israel] be brought forth in a moment? Yet no sooner is Zion in labor than she gives birth to her children. [Remember, according to the Apostle Paul, *the Redeemer will come out of Zion* to bring salvation to ALL ISRAEL in Romans 11:26. This prophecy makes it clear that the saving of **all Israel** means the saving of the Nation.]

"Rejoice with Jerusalem and be glad for her, all you who love her; rejoice greatly with her, all you who mourn over her."

For this is what the LORD says: "I will extend peace to her like a river, and the wealth of nations [Gentiles] like a flooding stream; you will nurse and be carried on her arm and dandled on her knees. As a mother comforts her child, so will I comfort you; and you will be comforted over Jerusalem." (Isaiah 66:10, 12, 13)

In each one of these prophecies, Israel's distinct and exalted position after her spiritual rebirth is clearly promised. Zephaniah makes this very clear:

"On that day you will remove from this city those who rejoice in their pride. Never again will you be haughty on my holy hill. But I will leave within you the meek and humble, who trust in the name of the LORD.

"The REMNANT OF ISRAEL will do no wrong; they will speak no lies, nor will deceit be found in their mouths. They will eat and lie down and no one will make them afraid."

"Sing, O daughter of Zion; shout aloud, O Israel! Be glad and rejoice with all your heart, O Daughter of Jerusalem! The LORD HAS TAKEN AWAY YOUR PUNISHMENT, He has turned back your enemy. The LORD, the KING OF ISRAEL, is with you; never again will you fear any harm.

"At that time I will deal with all who oppressed you; I will rescue the lame and gather THOSE WHO HAVE BEEN SCATTERED. I will give them praise and honor in every land where they were put to shame. At that time I will gather you; at that time I will bring you home [to the land of Israel].

"I will give you honor and praise among all the peoples of the earth when I restore your fortunes before your very eyes," says the LORD. (Zephaniah 3:11–15, 19–20)

These verses clearly show that the LORD has promised to forgive and restore the nation of Israel from the worldwide dispersion which they have received as discipline for their sin. Unless one goes off into allegorical la-la land, these prophecies literally demand a National restoration of Israel as a distinct and unique believing Nation in the future Kingdom.

But alas, there are those who refuse to take straightforward statements of the Scripture at face value. David Chilton writes concerning Israel's future conversion:

> The Bible promises the restoration of Israel as a *people*, but not necessarily as a *State;* nothing requires that the two must go together. Even assuming, however, that there is still A State of Israel when the Jews are converted, Israel would simply be one Christian nation among many, with no special standing. The people of genetic Israel will be part of the covenantal tree of life, but there is no longer any religious significance belonging to Palestine.[14]

All I can say in response to Chilton is this: If the many solemn and clear promises of God to restore Israel as a unique Nation in her own ancient homeland do not make it a necessity, *then what would*?

Beloved Enemies

The Holy Spirit reveals a very profound truth behind the fall of Israel: **"From the standpoint of the gospel they are enemies for your sake . . ."** (Romans 11:28a NASB) The Gospel and the age of grace would not have come to us Gentiles unless Israel had fallen in unbelief. So in one sense, they were made enemies so that the Gospel could be spread throughout the Gentile world.

Yet from God's perspective the Scriptures say, **". . . but from the standpoint of God's choice they are beloved for the sake of the fathers."** (Romans 11:28b NASB) Some find this verse contradictory to John the Baptist's statement, **"And do not think to yourselves, 'We have Abraham as our father.' I tell you that out of these stones God can raise up children for Abraham."** (Matthew 3:9) But John was simply declaring that the Israelites could not be saved by physical descent *alone*. As we have seen, God has always taught that physical covenant descent was not enough. God has always required faith on the part of the ones with whom the covenant is made.

But the LORD has sworn that He Himself would always preserve a remnant of the physical people with whom the covenant was made so that there would always be a source out of which He could bring forth a believing Nation for the promised Messianic Kingdom. This is the meaning of, ". . . **but from the standpoint of God's choice** [election] **THEY are beloved for the sake of the fathers . . .**" God's choice (or literally His election) here cannot refer to the elect remnant that are now in the Church, but rather to the Nation of Israel which is presently in unbelief so that the blessings of the Gospel may be showered upon the Gentiles. However, this election of the Nation of Israel was forever secured by the unconditional convenants made with the fathers.

How Binding Are God's Promises?

It is in this context concerning the issue of God's keeping His covenants with the fallen elect Nation that the Holy Spirit makes this dogmatic declaration, ". . . **for the gifts and calling of God ARE IRREVOCABLE.**" (Romans 11:29 NASB) This verse throws the issue of Israel's national restoration back upon the very Character of God. God's attributes of *immutability, veracity,* and *omniscience* are all involved with this statement.

Immutability means that once God makes a sovereign unconditional promise it cannot be changed. This Divine attribute is the basis of the word **"irrevocable."**

Veracity means that God must always be true to Himself and His Word. God's Word is the basis of all reality and certainty in the universe.

Omniscience means that God has always known all things, both actual and possible. His election of an individual or a nation is based on this foreknowledge. Therefore this attribute assures us that the LORD was fully aware of Israel's future failures before He elected them and promised that they would always be a Nation in His Divine purpose.

"God's gifts" refer back to those listed by the Holy Spirit in Romans 3:2 and 9:4–5. As I commented on these passages in chapter six, this includes such things as being *intrusted with the very words of God,* being adopted nationally as God's sons, being given the Shekinah glory of God, the unconditional covenants, the ministry of God's law, the special national promises, the temple worship, and the honor of the Son of God being born of their race. These gifts are unique to Israel and are irrevocable.

The usual word for gift is *dora* (δωρα). But here the Spirit uses the word *charisma* (χαρισμα). This comes from the word for grace, *charis* (χάρις), and it emphasizes that Israel's **gifts** are given on the basis of grace and not human merit. Therefore these gifts cannot be forfeited for lack of merit.

"God's choice" of the Nation of Israel refers back to their original election for a unique God-ordained mission and destiny. These are emphatically said to be **"irrevocable."** Great emphasis is put upon the word **"irrevocable"** because it is placed at the beginning of the Greek sentence. In Greek syntax, that which is considered most important can be placed first in the sentence. The point cannot be stated more emphatically or clearly. God swears that He will not change His mind concerning all that He has promised and ordained for the Nation of Israel.

God's Consistent Mercy

The goal of the following verses is to demonstrate God's consistency in His treatment of both the Nation of Israel and the Gentiles. The Holy Spirit summarizes all of Romans chapter eleven when He says, **"Just as you who were at one time disobedient to God have now received mercy as a result of their disobedience, so they too have now become disobedient in order that they too may now receive mercy as a result of God's mercy to you. For God has bound all men over to disobedience so that he may have mercy on them all."** (Romans 11:30–32) The point is that God is absolutely fair and consistent in showing mercy to the disobedient Nation of Israel. If the Dominionists have a problem with that, then let them remember that God showed us Gentiles mercy even after we had pushed Him out of our memories and run off to worship demons. So if God was just in showing mercy to us Gentiles, He is most certainly just in showing mercy to a people with whom He has already sovereignly aligned Himself by several convenants.

The LORD has pronounced all men, Jews and Gentiles, disobedient, in order that all of God's gifts and callings may be freely given on the basis of His mercy and grace, and not on human merit.

So What's the Big Deal

Much has been written to bring out the certainty of Israel's future restoration as a distinct and special Nation in God's eternal plan. You may have questioned why this is so important: the heart of the controversy between the Dominionists and the Premillennialists is the issue of whether Israel and the Church are two distinct programs in God's scheme of history.

As was explained in chapter two, the most basic essentials of Dispensational theology are, first a consistent literal interpretation of the Scriptures, and second the fact that the Nation of Israel and the Church are two distinct and unique programs in God's dealing with mankind. Each one has its own special promises, purpose, and destiny.

I believe that the Scriptures we have examined clearly demonstrate that the Nation of Israel will once again be God's preeminent servant, and that this will happen much sooner than most people think.

CHAPTER TEN

Now Learn the Parable From the Fig Tree

For then there will be a great distress, unequaled from the beginning of the world until now—and never to be equaled again. If those days had not been cut short, no one would survive, but for the sake of the elect those days will be shortened. At that time if anyone says to you, "Look, here is the Christ!" or, "There he is!" do not believe it. For false Christs and false prophets will appear and perform great signs and miracles to deceive even the elect—if that were possible [and it is]. See, I have told you ahead of time.

Jesus, the Messiah
Matthew 24:21–25

THE PROPHETIC VIEW FROM THE MOUNT OF OLIVES

The most important prophecy Jesus gave during His lifetime on earth was given to His disciples on the Mount of Olives just after He had pronounced judgment on Israel's religious leaders for spiritually blinding the Nation. It is commonly called the Olivet Discourse. The Holy Spirit recorded it in Matthew 24 and 25, Mark 13, Luke 17:20–37, and Luke 21:5–36.

The Dominionists contend that the Olivet Discourse was fulfilled in the destruction of Jerusalem and the Nation of Israel in A.D. 70. This view hinges on the Dominionists' contention that there is no such thing as a double-reference interpretation of prophecy. But this poses a problem for them. As mentioned in chapter three, the Lord Jesus gave an obvious double-reference interpretation to Isaiah 61:1–2a in Luke 4:16–30 when He stopped reading in the middle of a sentence. He read up to the point where it stopped speaking of His First Coming and began speaking of His Second Coming.

Peter also used a double-reference prophecy when he explained the phenomenon of the Day of Pentecost (Acts 2:14–40). Even David Chilton admits that Peter's quote of Joel's prophecy had a double reference. Chilton interprets it to have been partially fulfilled on the Day of Pentecost and the rest fulfilled in the holocaust of A.D. 70.[1] Premils say the second part will be fulfilled at the time of the Second Advent. The double-reference principle, however, is the same—the only difference is a longer time gap.

David Chilton wrote concerning the Olivet Discourse:

> In Matthew 24 (and Mark 13 and Luke 21) Jesus spoke to His disciples about a "great tribulation" which would come upon Jerusalem. It has become fashionable over the past 100 years or so to teach that He was speaking about the end of the "Church Age" and the time of His Second Coming. But is this what He meant? We should note carefully that Jesus Himself gave the (approximate) date of the coming Tribulation, leaving no room for doubt after any careful examination of the Biblical text. He said:

> **Truly I say to you, this generation will not pass away until all these things take place** (Matthew 24:34).

> This means that *everything* Jesus spoke of in this passage, at least up to verse 34, *took place before the generation then living passed away.* . . . The conclusion, therefore—*before we even begin to investigate the passage as a whole*—is that the events prophesied in Matthew 24 took place within the lifetime of the generation which was then living.[2]

Thomas Ice rightly observed the fallacy of Chilton's conclusion when he wrote that Chilton imposes his conclusion on the passage before he even investigates the details of the context. The proper way to interpret any Scripture is to first investigate the passage as a whole and then to draw overall conclusions. But instead, Chilton picks out the word **generation,** gives it a meaning that is in agreement with his system, then superimposes that meaning on the whole passage in defiance of the clear meaning of the context.[3]

In order to arrive at such an interpretation, Chilton and his mentor on this view, James Jordon, *switched methods* of interpretation within the same context without any justification. For instance they interpret war, earthquakes, and famine literally. But when they come to the celestial phenomena in the same immediate context, they arbitrarily switch to blatant allegory. Yet these celestial disturbances produce a very literal and real terror in the hearts of mankind, according to Luke's account: **"There will be signs in the sun, moon and stars. On the earth, nations will be in anguish and perplexity at the roaring and tossing of the sea. Men will faint from terror, apprehensive of what is coming on the world, for the heavenly bodies will be shaken."** (Luke 21:25–28). This is not a picture of some allegorical incident that occurred during the destruction of Jerusalem in A.D. 70, as the Dominionists would have us believe. This is a picture of unprecedented upheavals in nature that cause men to be stricken with heart attacks from sheer terror.

It should not be overlooked that killer storms of the type described here are now considered by scientists to be an imminent certainty. This is due to the continued destruction of the ozone layer and the greenhouse effect that is raising the mean temperature of the earth and changing global weather patterns. Hurricanes with sustained winds in excess of two hundred miles per hour have recently been recorded for the first time in history.

Jesus Warns of Judgment on Israel

The stage was set for this prophecy in Matthew chapter twenty-three. The Lord Jesus gave a scathing pronouncement of Judgment upon the Nation of Israel and its religious leaders for their long history of unbelief. This was culminated by their rejection of Him as the Messiah. Jesus concluded by saying:

> **[36]Truly I say to you, all these things shall come upon this generation. [37]O Jerusalem, Jerusalem, who kills the prophets and stones those who are sent to her!**

How often I wanted to gather your children together, the way a hen gathers her chicks under her wings, and you were unwilling. [38]Behold, your house is being left to you desolate! [39]For I say to you, from now on you shall not see Me UNTIL you say, "Blessed is He who comes in the name of the LORD!" (Matthew 23:36–39 NASB)

Jesus predicted in this chapter that He would send His witnesses to that *generation* of Israelites, and that they would persecute and kill them. He warns them that this would result in a terrible judgment upon the Nation. He then laments over Jerusalem and its people, recounting how often He sought to bring them to repentance so that they could be under His protective care. Finally, He declared that **their house** (meaning their Nation with its Temple-worship system) **was being left to them desolate.**

At this point, in verse thirty-nine, the Lord Jesus gave a ray of hope for the future of the Nation which was conveniently left out of Chilton's discussion of this chapter. Jesus said that they would not see Him again *UNTIL* they said, **"Blessed is He who comes in the name of the LORD."** This indicated that the Nation *was not* rejected for all time without hope of restoration. Chilton asserts the standard Dominionist party line on this: "Ethnic Israel was excommunicated for its apostasy and will never again be God's Kingdom."[4]

After this, the disciples were pointing out to Jesus how beautiful the temple buildings were. He shocked them by predicting that they would all be totally destroyed. (Matthew 24:1, 2)

THREE COMPLEX QUESTIONS

This was the immediate cause for the following question: **"As Jesus was sitting on the Mount of Olives, the disciples came to him privately. 'Tell us,' they said, 'when will this happen, and what will be the sign of your coming and of the end of the age?'"** (Matthew 24:3)

The disciples asked three questions that were based on their limited understanding of prophecy. They did not comprehend that all of the three events were not directly connected. Dr. Stan Toussaint, a distinguished theologian at Dallas Theological Seminary, makes a helpful observation concerning these questions.

NOW LEARN THE PARABLE FROM THE FIG TREE

The key to understanding the discourse is found in this first sentence. The disciples thought that the destruction of Jerusalem with its great temple would usher in the end of the age. The Lord separates the two ideas and warns the disciples against being deceived by the destruction of Jerusalem and other such catastrophes. The razing of the temple and the presence of wars and rumors of wars do not necessarily signify the nearness of the end. Therefore the disciples are warned against the things which could lead them astray. . . .[5]

Their confusion about prophecy was revealed in a question they asked the LORD just before He ascended to heaven, **"LORD, are you at this time going to restore the kingdom to Israel?"** (Acts 1:6) The LORD's answer spoke volumes. He *did not* tell them that Israel would *never* have a Kingdom in the future. He simply told them that they could not know the *exact* times and dates of its establishment. During His post-resurrection ministry, the main course of Christ's instruction consisted **"of the things concerning the kingdom of God."** (Acts 1:3) Had the Kingdom been forever removed from national Israel, then Christ would certainly have told His disciples. Instead, their question is, *"When* will the kingdom be *restored* to Israel?" The disciples' use of the word *restore* clearly indicates a belief that the Messianic Kingdom would one day be established to Israel.

So we must look at the disciples' questions in the light of the fact that they only saw prophecy from the perspective of the Old Testament hope for a Messianic Kingdom for Israel, and also, the fact that they expected its establishment to be imminent.

In this light, then, they first asked, "When will the temple buildings be destroyed?" Second, "What would be the sign of His coming to set up the Kingdom to Israel?" Third, "What would be the sign that the age was ending, referring to the age that preceded the setting up of Israel's promised Theocratic Kingdom on earth?"

Luke Clarifies the Chronological Order

Under the Holy Spirit's inspiration, Matthew only chose to record Jesus' answer to the second and third questions. Luke is the one

217

who specifically recorded Jesus' answer to the first question. (Luke 21:12–24)

After Luke gave Jesus' predictions concerning the general *birth pains* that would herald His return, he gives the chronological order for the fulfillment of the first question: **"But BEFORE all of these things . . ."** (Luke 21:12a) In other words, *BEFORE all of the signs that would herald Christ's return, and BEFORE the end of the age could begin, the destruction of the temple and Jerusalem must first occur.*

The LORD concludes the answer to the disciples' first question by predicting, **"They will fall by the sword and will be taken as prisoners to all the nations. Jerusalem will be trampled on by the Gentiles UNTIL the times of the Gentiles are fulfilled."** (Luke 21:24) Of course this happened in A.D. 70 when the Romans destroyed the nation and scattered the survivors all over the world.

Jesus predicted that it would only be *AFTER the Israelites would be scattered through all the nations,* and *AFTER Jerusalem would be trampled by the Gentiles until the times of the Gentiles are fulfilled,* that the cosmic and ecological chaos would occur:

> **There will be signs in the sun, moon and stars. On the earth, nations will be in anguish and perplexity at the roaring and the tossing of the sea. Men will faint from terror, apprehensive of what is coming on the world** [οἰκουμένη=entire inhabited earth], **for the heavenly bodies will be shaken. AT THAT TIME they will see the Son of Man coming in a cloud with power and great glory. When these things begin to take place, stand up and lift up your heads, because your redemption is drawing near.** (Luke 21:25–28)

As previously mentioned, the celestial signs are directly connected with some sort of catastrophic changes in the earth's weather patterns that cause cataclysmic storms on the oceans of unprecedented magnitude. These disturbances will be so terrifying that *the inhabitants of the whole world will be seized with apprehension and heart-stopping fear.* This entire passage is written in such a way that it must be taken in a literal sense. Mankind's killer-fear is said to be directly caused by two very real phenomena—the tempestuous ocean storms and the catastrophic disturbance of the celestial bodies. Since mankind's terror is unmistakably literal, it follows that the causes are intended to be also.

It is at that time, directly connected with the above events, that *the whole inhabited earth* (which is the only possible meaning of the Greek word οικουμενη) **will see the Son of Man coming in a cloud with power and great glory.** This is a common idea that is included in many different prophecies of Christ's Second Advent. The Apostle John predicted, **"Look, HE is coming with the clouds, and EVERY EYE will see HIM, even those who pierced him; and ALL THE PEOPLES OF THE EARTH will mourn because of HIM. So shall it be! Amen."** (Revelation 1:7) Zechariah, speaking by the Spirit of the Messiah, predicted, **". . . They will look on ME, the one they have pierced, and they will mourn for HIM as one mourns for an only child. . . ."** (Zechariah 12:10) And again, he predicted, **"Then the LORD will go out and fight against those nations, as he fights in the day of battle. On that day his feet will stand on the Mount of Olives, east of Jerusalem. . . ."** (Zechariah 14:3–4a)

The Dominionists try to localize these events to apply only to the land of Israel at the time of the Roman holocaust of A.D. 70. This is a clear illustration of the way they twist the Scriptures and show an utter disregard for the context in order to find justification for their preconceived prophetic views.

"Coming" Is "Going" . . . If You Know How to Allegorize!

It is concerning these verses from Luke that Chilton makes one of his most audacious misinterpretations. He uses his allegorical alchemy to concoct the idea that the LORD's *COMING* on the clouds at His Second Advent, was actually fulfilled by His *GOING* to meet the Father on the occasion of His Ascension to heaven.[6]

There are several factors in the context that make this an impossible interpretation. The first factor has to do with the *time* of this **coming of the Son of Man.** It will be at a *time* when both the solar system and the ecology of the whole world are so disrupted that all men will be in a state of terror. Second, it must follow after the worldwide dispersion of the Israelites and **"the times of the Gentiles"** are completed. Chilton contends that this is all "poetical language."

> The fact is that when Jesus spoke to His disciples about the fall of Jerusalem, *He used prophetic vocabulary.* There was a "language" of prophecy, instantly recognizable to those familiar with the Old Testament. . . . As

219

Jesus foretold the complete end of the Old Covenant system—WHICH WAS, IN A SENSE, *THE END OF A WHOLE WORLD*—He spoke of it as any of the prophets would have, in the stirring language of covenantal judgment.[6] (Emphasis mine.)

To say that the ending of the Old Covenant system was in any sense *"the end of a whole world"* as presented in this passage is not only stretching allegory to limits of rationality, it is preposterous! Jesus predicted judgments that are of a scope far beyond the A.D. 70 holocaust.

His use of the word οἰκουμένη specifies that this judgment will affect the whole inhabited earth, not end a religious age. As terrible as it was, A.D. 70 was a picnic compared to the magnitude of catastrophe forecasted in this passage. Jesus predicted concerning these future judgments:

For then there will be great distress, unequaled from the beginning of the world until now—and never to be equaled again. If those days had not been cut short, no one would survive [literally, **no flesh would be saved**]. . . . (Matthew 24:21–22)

Note the terminology **"unequaled from the beginning of the world until now—and never to be equaled again."** Even the most creative use of allegory cannot make the Roman destruction of Jerusalem fit this description. This involves the beginning and ending of world history, not just the history of Israel. Note also that Jesus literally said in the original Greek **"no flesh would be saved"** (ἐσώθη παρα σαρξ, *esothe pasa sarx*) unless the catastrophic judgments are cut short. He is clearly talking about all flesh on earth, man as well as animals. And in context, it is only His return that prevents the annihilation of all life on earth.

What Liberals and Dominionists Have in Common

It is well to remember that liberal theologians have used this same type of so-called *"prophetic vocabulary"* and *"poetic hyperbole"* argument to explain away virtually all of the predictive passages of the Bible as well as the truth of the Gospel.

Chilton goes on to quote numerous Old Testament prophecies which were couched in the context of warning various ancient empires of future judgment.

One of the examples he uses is from Isaiah, chapter thirteen. It is introduced by Isaiah as an oracle against Babylon (13:1). In the midst of the prophecy of contemporary Babylon's doom, the scope is greatly expanded to include God's future judgment of *the whole world*. Note that this expanded section is introduced by a title that usually speaks of the Second Advent judgments, **"the day of the LORD is coming."** Isaiah wrote:

> **See, the day of the LORD is coming—a cruel day, with wrath and fierce anger—to make the land desolate and destroy the sinners within it.**
>
> **The stars of heaven and their constellations will not show their light. The rising sun will be darkened and the moon will not give its light.**
>
> **I will punish the WORLD [Hebrew = *tebel*] for its evil, the wicked for their sins. I will put an end to the arrogance of the haughty and will humble the pride of the ruthless.**
>
> **I will make man scarcer than pure gold, more rare than the gold of Ophir.**
>
> **Therefore I will make the heavens tremble; and the EARTH will shake from its place at the wrath of the LORD Almighty, in the day of his burning anger.** (Isaiah 13:9–13)

Note that this section of Isaiah's prophecy has a number of statements that are global in scope, and not confined just to the Middle East. First, he speaks of punishing **"the whole world."** **"World"** is the translation of the original Hebrew word *tebel* in contrast to the word *eretz*, which can simply mean land. But *tebel* means "the world," not just the local lands.

Second, Isaiah predicts that God will make **"man"** more scarce than the pure gold of Ophir. The Hebrew word for man, *enosh*, means **"mortal man"** or **"mankind."** So this is a prophecy about the whole human race, not just the limited war between Babylon and the Media-Persians. This prophecy speaks of the same conditions predicted by Jesus in Matthew 24–25 and the Apostle John in the Apocalypse.

Third, Isaiah predicts that there will not only be severe cosmic disturbances, but that the earth itself will be shaken from its place. This agrees with numerous predictions in the Book of Revelation concerning the judgments of the Second Advent.[7]

221

Dominionists contend that since these things didn't literally happen when the Medes destroyed Babylon, it established the rule that all passages like this must be taken allegorically. Chilton dogmatically asserts, "God did not intend anyone to place a literalist construction on these statements. *Poetically,* however, all these things *did* happen: as far as the wicked nations were concerned, 'the lights went out.'"[8] The Dominionists' methodology is to deny without proof the possibility of double-reference prophecy, and then to allegorize all passages that would establish double-reference prophecy. I have shown what great Biblical scholars down through history have acknowledged—that there are double-reference prophecies throughout the Bible. The Prophets often couched prophecies of momentous events far in the future within prophecies of contemporary events.

For instance, when the Holy Spirit inspired King David around 1000 B.C. to speak of his painful experiences, he suddenly without warning begins to speak of the sufferings of the Messiah: **"For dogs have surrounded me; a band of evildoers has encompassed me; They pierced my hands and my feet. I can count all my bones. They look, they stare at me; they divide my garments among them, and for my clothing they cast lots."** (Psalm 22:16–18) Although David did suffer, these sufferings clearly go beyond any that he experienced. The statement **". . . they pierced my hands and my feet"** is an amazing reference to the crucifixion more than seven hundred years before it was devised as a method of execution. The Holy Spirit Himself applies the prophecy concerning "the casting lots for his clothing" to the events at the foot of Jesus' cross (see Mark 15:24).

The established principle of double-reference prophecy is a much better explanation of this passage. It does not require absurd spiritualizing of events and phenomena that are clearly intended to be taken in a normal, literal sense. And it doesn't accuse the Holy Spirit of meaningless poetic exaggeration.

The "Collapsing-Universe" Gimmick

In spite of ample evidence to the contrary, the Dominionists refuse to recognize the oft occurring phenomenon of double-reference prophecy. Chilton dismisses the predictions of judgment that disrupt the solar system at the time of Christ's Second Coming as being simply *poetic hyperbole.* He claims that predictions of judgment involving the sun, moon, and stars are a kind of stock formula which he labels "collapsing-universe terminology." Then he proceeds to write off all predictions of celestial disturbance as "collapsing-universe terminology" and therefore "poetic symbol."

There is no justification for the Dominionist practice of constructing "technical formulas" from a few Old Testament passages, and then imposing them like straitjackets upon every other Old and New Testament passage that may have even a remote word or two in common with them. This is like playing word-association games or using the Freudian ink blot test: each person has a different interpretation of what he sees. Once we get away from the control of word meanings, grammar, syntax, and context, it's anybody's guess what a passage means. This type of exegesis will result in what has happened in the past where priest-craft was substituted for the common man reading the Bible for himself.

The Dominionist system has already required the "experts" to leap to the aid of their "untrained" disciples so that they would not use their "symbol system" to explain away the Second Advent entirely.

This same method of interpretation has been used by the liberals to explain away prophecy concerning future events. Liberal theologians claim that all prophecy was just poetic terminology to get the contemporaries to repent.

The "Abomination That Causes Desolation"

The Lord Jesus predicted the specific historical event that will set in motion the devastating world conditions that lead to His Second Advent: **"So when you see STANDING IN THE HOLY PLACE 'the abomination that causes desolation,' spoken of through the prophet Daniel—let the reader understand—then let those who are in Judea flee to the mountains."** (Matthew 24:15–16) It is imperative to determine what the special prophetic phrase **"the abomination that causes desolation"** means.

Daniel and Jesus are the only two who mention the specific technical phrase **"the abomination that causes desolation."** In Daniel 11:31 it is used to predict the desecration of the holy of holies of Israel's Temple in 168 B.C. by a Syrian ruler named Antiochus Epiphanes. (This event is recorded in First Maccabees, chapter one.) He sacrificed a pig on the altar and set up an idol to the pagan god Zeus Olympus in the holiest part of the Temple.

Since this incident had already been fulfilled in history, it defines what would otherwise be a very difficult prophetic term. From this historical event, we see that it means to profane Israel's Temple, and to set up a pagan idol for worship in its holy of holies.

Jesus Predicts an "Abomination of Desolation" Before His Return

The Lord Jesus' prophecy clearly referred to the second **Abomination *of* Desolation** that Daniel predicted, **"From the time that the daily sacrifice is abolished and the abomination that causes desolation is set up, there will be 1290 days. . . ."** (Daniel 12:11) This prediction is connected with the person Daniel foresaw in Daniel 9:27, **"And HE** [the coming Roman prince of 9:26, who is commonly called the Antichrist] **will make a firm covenant with the many for one week** [a Sabbatical year = seven years], **but in the middle of the week** [three and one half years] **HE will put a stop to sacrifice and grain offering; and on the wing of ABOMINATIONS will come ONE WHO MAKES DESOLATE, even until a complete destruction, one that is decreed, is poured out on the ONE WHO MAKES DESOLATE."** (Daniel 9:27 NASB)

The time factor in all three of the prophecies of the future **Abomination of Desolation** fit together perfectly. First, the Daniel chapter twelve reference is in a context of end of time events that include an unparalleled time of tribulation (which I will develop carefully in a moment), the rescue of the believing Nation of Israel by the archangel Michael, a resurrection, and the coming of the Messiah.[9]

Second, the Daniel chapter nine reference speaks of this same **Abomination of Desolation** and predicts that it will occur in the last half of the Sabbatical week of years allotted to Israel (9:24) that are yet to be fulfilled. The 1290 days of chapter twelve work out to be exactly three and a half Biblical years which are 360 days each. (The biblical year is the 360-day lunar year instead of the 365¼ solar year.) Both prophecies say that this will cause sacrifice and offerings to cease, exactly as occurred in the historical prototype of Antiochus Epiphanes.

Third, the Lord Jesus prophesies that this same future **Abomination of Desolation** will signal the start of the catastrophic world events that lead to His Second Advent. He warns the believers not to be deceived by those who say that Christ has secretly returned and they have missed it (Matthew 24:23–26). He then describes how His Second Advent will not be secret, but rather instantly visible to the whole world: **"For as the lightning comes from the east and flashes to the west, so will be the coming of the Son of Man."** (Matthew 24:27) Lightning is sudden, visible to all, and awesome in its power.

None of these things happened in A.D. 70. Dominionist symbol dispensers cannot reduce the magnitude of these world-shaking events down to a scale that fits into the writings of first-century chronicler Josephus. Their use of the writings of the venerable Josephus to explain Scripture clearly goes far beyond the realm of credibility.

The Lord Jesus also tied Daniel's prophecies together with other very important New Testament ones when He said that **the abomination that causes desolation will STAND IN THE HOLY PLACE.** The Apostle Paul predicted exactly what this will be when he spoke of the advent of Satan's masterpiece, **the Man of Lawlessness, "[who] opposes and exalts himself over everything that is called God or is worshiped, AND EVEN SETS HIMSELF UP IN GOD'S TEMPLE, proclaiming himself to be God."** (2 Thessalonians 2:4)

The Apostle John gives more insight on this same prophecy: **". . . He [the False Prophet] ordered them to set up an image in honor of the beast who was wounded by the sword and yet lived [the Man of Lawlessness]. He was given power to give breath to the image of the first beast, so that it could speak and cause all who refused to worship the image to be killed."** (Revelation 13:14b–15) And, **"The beast was given a mouth to utter proud words and blasphemies and to exercise his authority for forty-two months (3½ years)."** (Revelation 13:5)

Putting all of this together we get these facts: The Man of Lawlessness (or the coming prince from the Roman culture) will take his seat in the holy of holies of Israel's Temple which will be rebuilt. He will there declare himself to be God. He, with the help of his future contemporary, the Jewish False Prophet, will set up an idol of himself in the holy place. The False Prophet will cause the image to speak through the use of Satanic powers.

It is important to note at this point that the New International Version correctly translated the meaning of the subjective genitive case of the word "desolation." Many English Bibles translate the original Greek, *bdelugma te eremoseos* (βδελυγμα τη ερημωσεως), as the "abomination *of* desolation." But the two terms are linked together in the Greek because the noun of action, **"abomination,"** defines the cause of the **"desolation."** So the New International

Version correctly translates it, **"the abomination that causes desolation."** (Matthew 24:15)

Dominionists "Divide and Conquer"

I mention this technical data because in the Dominionists' interpretation of the "abomination of desolation," they split the two words and deal with them as separate unrelated terms. In this way they feel justified in twisting the technical prophetic term to mean "the desolation of Jerusalem" in, you guessed it, A.D. 70.[10] They do this by making a long list of verses in which "desolation" is used, and then, with a deft sleight-of-hand, slip it into Luke 21:20–22. Since the coming destruction of Jerusalem is called its "desolation," Dominionists see this as the fulfillment of the "abomination of desolation." However, there are a few problems with this ingenious interpretation. The LORD said that **the abomination that causes desolation** was something that would **stand in the holy place** of the Temple. So what does the destruction of Jerusalem have to do with that? Furthermore, He instructed the believers of that day to flee for protection to the mountains. Jerusalem was besieged for some two years before it was finally destroyed. So if its destruction, which occurred in the space of two days, was **the abomination that causes desolation,** it would have been too late to flee anywhere. No one was able to leave the city for two years prior to that.

Titus, the Roman commander, did not set up an idol in the Temple. His soldiers utterly destroyed it looking for the gold that fire had caused to melt down between the stones. None of the details of the prophecy fit into the Dominionist scheme.

Of What Time Did Jesus Prophesy?

I believe that there is at least one specific prediction Jesus made that makes it impossible for this prophecy to have been fulfilled in A.D. 70. Concerning the time of **the abomination that causes desolation,** Jesus warned, **"For then there will be great distress, unequaled from the beginning of the world until now—and never to be equaled again. If those days had not been cut short, no one would survive, but for the sake of the elect those days will be shortened."** (Matthew 24:21–22) This prophecy is couched in the same exact terminology Daniel used concerning the time of the abomination that causes desolation: **"At that time Michael, the**

226

great prince who protects your people [Israel], **will arise. There will be a time of distress such as has not happened from the beginning of nations until then. But at that time your people— everyone whose name is found written in the book—will be delivered."** (Daniel 12:1)

Both of these passages predict that it will be a time of catastrophe of such magnitude that nothing in history either before or afterward will compare with it. It should be remembered that Scripture is to govern how we look at history, not vice versa. Nevertheless, anyone familiar with history recognizes that there have been many calamities greater than A.D. 70, both for the world in general and for the Israelites in particular.

Taking the Dominionists' authority, Josephus, at his word, there were about one and a quarter million Jews slaughtered in the destruction of Jerusalem by the Romans. There were some six million Jews systematically murdered by the Nazis. Was that not worse?

World War One and Two were enormously worse than A.D. 70. More than fifty million people were killed in World War Two alone. The misery and horror to which Jews were subjected in Auschwitz, Dachau, Bergen-Belsen, etc., were much greater than the Jerusalem holocaust.

But aside from that, Daniel prophesies that when **the abomination that causes desolation** is set up, Israel's time of DELIVERANCE will be near, *not her destruction.* And a resurrection of MANY (not all, as in the last judgment) occurs at that same time. (Daniel 12:2)

Letting Scripture Interpret Scripture

I agree with the Dominionists' statement that we should let the Scripture interpret Scripture. But this does not give us license to ignore the context of a passage at hand. Each passage must first be analyzed on its own merits. Then other passages can be brought in to further illuminate them. Daniel 12 and the Olivet Discourse in Matthew 24 are valid illustrations of this principle. Why? Because each context independently has particulars that are parallel to one another. The following are some of those parallel factors common to both:

(1) Both predict the greatest time of distress ever known in human history. There cannot be "two greatests," so they must be referring to the same event.

(2) They are both linked to the abomination that causes desolation.

(3) This ties both prophecies to the Temple and Jerusalem.

(4) Both promise *the deliverance* of Israel. (See especially Luke 21:24–28.)

(5) There are no factors in either passage that are in conflict with each other. On the other hand, Chilton's scenario attempts to merge Old Testament passages that are taken from a context of Israel's deliverance with the Olivet Discourse, which he interprets to be their final judgment.

"This Generation"

The Dominionists' system of prophecy stands or falls with whether the Olivet Discourse was fulfilled in A.D. 70. The Dominionists interpret Jesus' prophecy, **"This generation will certainly not pass away until all these things have happened,"** to mean the lifetime of the people that were then living. The meaning of a word is always determined by its usage in context.

After the Lord Jesus had given many signs of His coming and the end of the age, he applied their significance. Beginning with verse thirty-two, He first gives us a clue to help us understand when the general time of His coming is near. In this regard, He commands us to learn the following parable:

> **Now learn the parable from the fig tree: when its branch has already become tender, and puts forth its leaves, you know that summer is near; even so you too, WHEN you see ALL THESE THINGS, RECOGNIZE that He is near, right at the door. Truly I say to you, this GENERATION will not pass away until ALL THESE THINGS are fulfilled.** (Matthew 24:32–34 NASB)

We are commanded by Jesus to learn the parable of the fig tree. The parable's one basic point is *how to tell when the general time of summer is near*. So the main lesson for us to learn is how to tell a general time.

Many evangelicals have traditionally interpreted the term *he genea* (η γενεα) as *this race,* referring to the Israelite race. However, the best Greek lexicons list this as a third possible meaning. The determining factor is how it is used in *context*. The context is controlled by the parable which is unmistakably speaking of how to know a general *time*. The normal and most often used meaning of the term γενεα is to denote the life span of the average person in a given era. In this sense, it fits perfectly with the idea of a general time demanded by the parable.

The LORD makes a direct application of the parable by saying **"even so . . . when you see *all these things*. . . "** *"All these things"* in context must refer to *all* the prophetic signs that He has just given. Just as the first leaves on the fig tree herald that summer is near, so when the prophetic signs *all* begin to come together in concert within one generation, we are to recognize (this is a command) that Christ is at the door, *ready to return.*

Jesus then gives His main point: **"Truly I say to you, *this generation* will not pass away until *all these things* are fulfilled."** *In context*, the LORD must be referring to *the generation* who would see the predicted signs *all* coming together. This is *the generation* that He declares will see all of the predicted signs fulfilled. Our current generation is the only generation in history to have witnessed *all* these predicted signs come together in concert.

"This generation" could not have referred to the people who were living in Jesus' day, because they *did not* see all of the predicted signs come together. Furthermore, Israel had not yet been scattered into all the nations, as Luke's prediction requires (Luke 21:24). The restoration of the dispersed Israelites as a Nation while still in unbelief constitutes one of the central initial signs in the prophetic scenario (see Ezekiel 36–39).

So Jesus commands us to **recognize** the *general* time of His Coming, but warns that no one will know the *exact* time: **"But of that day and hour no one knows, not even the angels of heaven, nor the Son, but the father alone."** (Matthew 24:36 NASB)

Chilton's shallow interpretation of Matthew 24:32–34 was not based on the context nor examination of the passage, but rather on the presuppositions demanded by his prophetic system. This was clearly revealed in Chilton's own statement, "The CONCLUSION, therefore—BEFORE WE EVEN BEGIN TO INVESTIGATE the passage as a whole—is that the events prophesied in Matthew 24 took place within the lifetime of the generation which was then living."[11] (Emphases mine.)

We find it impossible to fit the enormous events of the LORD's prophecy into the localized events of Jerusalem's destruction in A.D. 70.

How Noah's Day Illustrates the Olivet Discourse

The Lord Jesus uses an historical illustration to further apply His predictions in Matthew 24:1–31: **"For the coming of the Son of Man will be JUST LIKE the days of Noah. For as in those days which were before the flood they were eating and drinking, they were marrying and giving in marriage, until the day that Noah entered the ark, and THEY DID NOT UNDERSTAND UNTIL the flood came and took them all away; so shall the coming of the Son of Man be."** (Matthew 24:37–39 NASB) (Emphases mine.)

David Chilton says, "Just as God had destroyed the 'world' of that day by the Flood, so would He destroy the 'world' of first-century Israel by fire in the fall of Jerusalem."[12]

If the Dominionists say that the Noah illustration refers only to the A.D. 70 holocaust, then to be consistent they have to say that the flood of Noah's day was local and not universal.

Jesus taught specifically that His coming would be *just like* the days of Noah. Jesus carefully chose Noah's day to illustrate His coming because it is the only other event in history that was worldwide in scope, cataclysmic/interventionist in nature, and a judgment of all mankind.

That Jesus used the Noah's-day illustration in the above sense is clearly brought out by His interpretation, **". . . and they did not understand until the flood came and TOOK THEM ALL AWAY."** (24:39) **"ALL"** referred to all of mankind with the exception of eight people.

Reconstructionist James Jordan teaches that Jesus' prophecy does refer to the Second Coming from Matthew 24:36–51. There is a major problem with this kind of pick-and-choose interpretation. Jordan gives no adequate reason for slashing the context right in the middle of a consecutive and homogeneous message. **"But of that day and hour no one knows"** is obviously part of Jesus' teaching concerning how to recognize the general time of His coming. (24:36) As Thomas Ice correctly surmises:

> How can Jordan, after taking the references to "coming" in verses 1–35 as referring to Christ's coming in judgment in A.D. 70, then turn around and say that starting at verse 36 through the end of the chapter, it refers to the second coming? Either he is wrong about the first 35 verses, and they *do* refer to the second coming, or

he should take verse 36 and following as referring to the A.D. 70 destruction. If he were to take the whole of the Olivet Discourse, as Chilton does the whole book of Revelation, then he is left with the problem of where does the Bible actually teach the second coming. What he should really do is become consistent and take the whole passage [Matthew 24:1–51] to refer to a future event—the second coming of Christ.[13]

Jordan, Chilton, and the Dominionists are guilty of, to say the least, "sloppy scholarship" in their interpretation of Matthew 24.

Scholars from both Dominionist and Premillennial viewpoints hold that whatever approach one uses to interpret the Olivet Discourse, whether as future prophecy or past history, to be consistent one must use the same method with the Book of Revelation. This being the case, since Chilton denies that the Second Coming is taught in Revelation (see my next chapter) then it would have to be denied in the Olivet Discourse. This would seem to follow, unless he resorts to a schizophrenic type of allegorical interpretation.

Peter Warns Against "Mocking" the Imminence of Christ's Coming

Peter knew when he wrote his second epistle that he had a very short time to live. As with any person who knows that his death is imminent, Peter selected and taught the things he considered to be most important. He said that he wanted us Christians to be constantly reminded of these things after his "departure." Then Peter proceeded to focus his whole final letter upon the certainty and importance of the prophetic Word concerning Jesus Christ's Second Coming.

In the second chapter, Peter warned of false teachers **who will secretly introduce destructive heresies** as the age moves toward its close and the LORD's Return draws near.

In the third chapter, Peter predicts that there would be false teachers from within the Church (for who else would understand or care about the time of Christ's coming) who would deny that the Lord Jesus' coming is something that is imminent or important: **"Know this first of all, that in the last days mockers will come with their mocking, following after their own lust, and saying, 'Where is the promise of His coming? For ever since the** fathers fell asleep, all continues just as it was from the beginning of creation.' For when they maintain this, it escapes their notice that by the word of God the heavens existed long ago and the earth was formed out of water and by water, through which the world at that time was destroyed, being flooded with water." (2 Peter 3:3–6 NASB)

The Dominionist teachers certainly *do* deny the imminence of the LORD's coming thus and minimize its relevance as an encouragement to moral living. Chilton demonstrates this type of attitude as he explains away the literalness of the one thousand years predicted for the Messianic Kingdom in Revelation chapter twenty: "The God of the covenant told His people that He would bless them to the thousandth generation of their descendants [Deuteronomy 7:9]. That promise was made (in round figures) about 3,400 years ago. If we figure the Biblical generation at about 40 years, a thousand generations is *forty thousand years*. We've got 36,600 years to go before this promise is fulfilled!"[14]

In *Days of Vengeance,* Chilton quoted Milton Terry, who had an even lengthier view as to, "How long the King of kings will continue His battle against evil and defer the last decisive blow, when Satan shall be 'loosed for a little time,' no man can even approximately judge. IT MAY REQUIRE A MILLION YEARS."[15] (Emphasis mine.)

How is that for expecting the LORD's soon return! This kind of teaching has made the Dominionists "so earthly-minded that they are no heavenly good." Though I would agree with some of their political views, unfortunately they often seem to be more interested in political takeover than evangelizing and discipling people for a spiritual kingdom. In some ways they are coming dangerously close to fulfilling Peter's prediction.

So What!

There are a few important observations to draw from this chapter.

If the prophecies of the Olivet Discourse are future, which any consistent analysis of the passage establishes, then the Book of Revelation is also, since all agree that both are speaking of the same events.

If they are future, then such world-affecting factors as the Tribulation, the Antichrist, the great end-time apostasy within the Church, the any-moment possibility of Christ's return, are also valid. These monumental events all greatly affect how we plan our lives and shape our strategy for the Church's mission.

There are over a hundred verses in the New Testament that refer to the coming of Christ and exhort hope and holy living on that basis. Let us close this chapter by meditating on just a few of those.

> **Therefore, prepare your minds for action; be self-controlled; SET YOUR HOPE FULLY on the grace to be given you WHEN JESUS CHRIST IS REVEALED. (1 Peter 1:13)**

> **For the grace of God that brings salvation has appeared to all men. It teaches us to say "No" to ungodliness and worldly passions, and to live self-controlled, upright and godly lives in this present age, WHILE WE WAIT FOR THE BLESSED HOPE—THE GLORIOUS APPEARING of our great God and Savior, Jesus Christ . . . (Titus 2:11–13)**

> **Dear friends, now we are children of God, and what we will be has not yet been made known. But we know that WHEN HE APPEARS, we shall be like him, for we shall see him as he is. Everyone WHO HAS THIS HOPE IN HIM PURIFIES HIMSELF, just as he is pure. (1 John 3:2–3)**

The Dominionists either play down verses like these, or say they were fulfilled in A.D. 70. They call people who believe them "pessimillennialists." But as for me, I find more motivation in looking for what the Bible emphasizes as our hope, than in their programs. I can't see how the prospect of struggling endless centuries to do what God promises that only Christ can and will do is a more "optimistic" view. If that makes you "pessimistic," then the problem is in your focus, not in God's Word.

CHAPTER ELEVEN

The Great
Dominionist Dating Game

The Book of Revelation is *not* about the Second Coming of Christ. It is about the destruction of Israel and Christ's victory over His enemies (i.e., Israel) in the establishment of the New Covenant Temple. In fact, as we shall see, the word *coming* as used in the Book of Revelation *NEVER REFERS TO THE SECOND COMING*. Revelation **PROPHESIES** the judgment of God on apostate Israel. . . . (Emphases mine.)

> David Chilton
> *Days of Vengeance* (p.43)

I warn everyone who hears the words of the PROPHECY of this book: If anyone adds anything to them, God will add to him the plagues described in this book. And if anyone takes words away from the book of PROPHECY, God will take away from him his share in the tree of life and in the holy city, which are described in this book.

> Jesus Christ
> Revelation 22:18–19

The whole Dominionist movement wreaks havoc with the Book of Revelation. In order to establish their view of prophecy, they must make virtually all of the prophecies of the Book of Revelation apply to Israel's holocaust in A.D. 70.

As we saw in the last chapter, the Dominionists do not believe that the Olivet Discourse teaches about the Second Coming of Christ. So it isn't surprising that they claim the Book of Revelation doesn't either.

David Chilton's commentary on Revelation has set forth *the official position* of the Dominionist movement. Gary North confirmed this by his extravagant boasts concerning *Days of Vengeance:* "This book is a landmark effort, the finest commentary on Revelation in the history of the Church. It has set the standard . . ."[1] And again, North writes, "From this time on, there will be only three kinds of commentaries on the Book of Revelation: Those that try to extend Chilton's; Those that try to refute Chilton's; Those that pretend there isn't Chilton."[2]

That Chilton's book is considered the representative model of the Reconstruction/Dominion interpretative method is revealed by another statement of North: "Chilton's *Days of Vengeance* can and should serve as the representative model of what *the 'new, improved' Christian Reconstruction movement is really all about: the fusion of covenant and symbol*. This is the distinctive theological insight of what people have called **Tyler theology**."[3] (Emphases added.) These are enormous claims for any book to live up to.

THE EXTERNAL EVIDENCE

Holy Smoke!

Based on their own testimony, the whole Dominion view of prophecy stands or falls with one main issue: When was the Book of Revelation written? This is true for the following reason. Since David Chilton's book, *Days of Vengeance*, represents the official view of Dominionist eschatology, and since the validity of *Days of Vengeance* depends upon a pre–A.D. 70 writing date for Revelation, their case stands or falls with that issue.

Even a fellow Postmillennialist agrees with this. Kenneth L. Gentry, who not only holds the same basic view as Chilton, but lavished praise upon his book, nevertheless made this observation in his review of *Days of Vengeance*: "If it could be demonstrated that Revelation were written 25 years after the Fall of Jerusalem, *Chilton's entire labor would go up in smoke*."[4] (Emphasis mine.)

As a matter of fact, if it can be shown that Revelation was written even one day after A.D. 70, it would destroy not only

Chilton's book, but the whole Dominionist system of prophecy. It would also force Dominionists to admit that *the Olivet Discourse is prophetic to our future as well,* since they deal with exactly the same subjects.

Gentry made another revealing admission in his review: "Chilton only gives four superficially argued pages in defense of what is perhaps the most crucial matter for consistent preterism: the pre–A.D. 70 date for the composition of Revelation."[5]

I agree with historian Thomas D. Ice's analysis of this issue.

> It must be pointed out, that if Revelation was written before A.D. 70, then Chilton's view may be correct. But if the Apocalypse was penned before A.D. 70, it would not by itself rule out the futurist and premillennial view (i.e., Revelation is still prophetic of the future). The futurist view could still be correct if it was written when Chilton says it was, since the date is not determinant to the validity of its view. However, if Revelation was written *even one day after the fall of Jerusalem,* then it ceases to be a *prophecy* concerning the destruction of Jerusalem.[6]

Let's consider what Kenneth L. Gentry has termed his "four superficially argued pages" that defend the whole foundation that supports their enormous superstructure of philosophically argued theology. The following are Chilton's arguments for the early dating of the Book of Revelation.

The "John's Poor Memory" Argument

Days of Vengeance declares, "St. John's intimate acquaintance with the minute details of Temple worship suggests that 'the Book of Revelation and the Fourth Gospel must have been written before the Temple services had actually ceased.'"[7] This argument does not take into consideration the doctrine of the Inspiration of Scripture. This doctrine teaches that the Holy Spirit supernaturally brought to remembrance and revealed the data the inspired writers used to compose the books of Scripture. He then supernaturally guided them in exactly how to write the message. The Lord Jesus had promised that this would occur: **"I have much more to say to you, more than you can now bear. But when he, the Spirit of truth, comes, HE WILL GUIDE YOU INTO ALL TRUTH. He will not speak on his own; he will speak only what**

237

he hears, and HE WILL TELL YOU WHAT IS YET TO COME."
(John 16:12–13)

In the second place, the Apostle John clearly testifies that he recorded only the things that the Lord Jesus Christ and His angel revealed to him in a supernatural vision. This fact is greatly emphasized by the frequent repetition of the command to John to write what **he saw and heard.** (See Revelation 1:1, 2, 11, 19; 4:1; 5:1, etc.) John solemnly testified that he wrote the whole Book of Revelation in strict accordance with what he *actually saw* and *heard:* **"I, John, am the one who heard and saw these things. And when I had heard and seen them I fell down to worship at the feet of the angel who had been showing them to me."** (Revelation 22:8) So shouldn't we expect the information concerning the Temple to be both minute in detail and extremely accurate, since the revealing angel had not only seen the earthly Temple, but the Heavenly One after which it was patterned?

Even if John's familiarity with the Temple were required to write the Book of Revelation, it would not be necessary for the Temple to still be standing, since persons are capable of remembering things of the past in great detail, especially if the Holy Spirit gives them Divine inspiration.

I am surprised that Chilton would use this line of argument since it is regularly used to explain away the inerrancy of the New Testament by the liberal theologians; and he does believe in the inerrancy of the Scriptures.

The "Questionable Accuracy of the Apostolic Fathers" Argument

Chilton boldly calls into question the consistent witness of the earliest Church Fathers in his frantic search for support of his pre–A.D. 70 composition of Revelation. Ice makes an amusing observation about Chilton's about-face from his normal use of church history:

> This by itself is most interesting, since it is Chilton and the whole Christian Reconstruction Movement which so often appeal to *"the voice of the mother church"* as support for their views.[8] Chilton often boasts of his view on certain issues as being "the position of the historic, orthodox Church on the question . . ."[9] In fact, Chilton uses a witness from church tradition to suggest that the Apostle John "was a priest, and wore the sacerdotal

plate." This was a "tradition of Eusebius" (a Church Historian of the fourth century).[10][11]

I agree that Church tradition should be weighed carefully, especially in issues which involve the dating of the New Testament books. But the Reconstructionists have reversed the normal priority. They use Church history most in trying to establish their interpretations of the Bible, and least in seeking to establish the date of when the books of the Bible were written.

Why Not Listen to "Mother"?

David Chilton is obviously torn between two loves here. He loves to use Church tradition as his source of authority for certain interpretations. But his beloved "voice of mother Church" betrays him in this instance, because it consistently witnesses against his need to establish an early date for the writing of Revelation. In view of his decision in this case not to listen to "the voice of mother Church," we must conclude that one should only listen to "mother" if she agrees with one's eschatology! . . .

The primary source for early Church tradition on the date of Revelation is the Apostle John's spiritual grandson, Irenaeus (A.D. 120–202). The great Apostolic Father, Polycarp (A.D. 70–155), who was discipled by John himself, personally discipled Irenaeus. His full quote on the origin of the Book of Revelation, which is seldom ever given, is as follows:

> We will not, however, incur the risk of pronouncing positively as to the name of *Antichrist*; for if it were necessary that his name should be distinctly revealed in this present time, it would have been announced by *him who beheld the apocalyptic vision*. For that was seen not a very long time since, *but almost in our day, towards the end of DOMITIAN's reign.* (Emphases mine.)[12]

In view of this straightforward and clear statement, Chilton's and other Dominionists' response was surprising. Chilton writes, "There is considerable room for doubt about his precise meaning (he may have meant that the Apostle John himself 'was seen' by others). The language of St. Irenaeus is somewhat ambiguous."[13] It is hard to reconcile Chilton's usual high regard for and extensive use of Church tradition with this statement. The Dominionists have taken statements that were not nearly so clear, and by far less dependable witnesses, as their authority for some major, "unique" interpretations.

Anyone who examines Irenaeus' statement fairly, without a system to protect, will conclude that there is not "considerable room for doubt about his precise meaning" at all. The ambiguity is not in the precision of the statement, but in Chilton's biased perception. There is not even a slight "mist" around Irenaeus' statement, but there is a dense self-induced fog over the Dominionists' understanding of it.

This is a classic example of how the Dominionists deal with both Scripture and history when it doesn't fit their theological system. Let's examine how Chilton uses the same "smoke and mirrors" approach within his interpretation of the passage above by Irenaeus, one of the most reliable and scholarly of the ancient Apostolic Fathers, as he does in his interpretation of the Bible.

His first tactic is to question whether Irenaeus' statement, *"that was seen not a very long time since,"* refers to *"the apocalyptic vision"* or to John himself. The impersonal pronoun, *"that,"* is in the neuter gender, therefore *"him,"* which is in the masculine gender (and refers to the Apostle John) *cannot* be its antecedent. The simple rule of Greek grammar is that a relative pronoun must agree in gender with the word, phrase, or clause to which it refers. So *"that"* can only refer to *John's apocalyptic vision of the Revelation, not to John*.

The whole point of the statement is that the Apostle John had received the Revelation vision only a short time before Irenaeus wrote. So reasoning from the fact that they were within one generation of that event, Irenaeus concludes that if it were God's Will for the Church of that era to know the specific name of **the Antichrist**, then certainly *the one who received the original vision* would have subsequently revealed it to them, *since they were living in such close proximity to John's era*. (Incidentally, isn't it interesting that both Polycarp and Irenaeus believed strongly in the coming of *a personal Antichrist*, and indicate that their belief came from the Apostle John! And remember, the Dominionists deny that there will be a personal Antichrist.)

In establishing *when* John was exiled and received the apocalyptic vision, Irenaeus used the standard method of historical dating of that time—he dated it by the reign of the contemporary Caesar. In this case it was **Caesar Domitian**, and it occurred near the end of his reign.

Clear Corroboration From Church's First Historian

Eusebius (A.D. 265–339) corroborates these facts and fills in some important historical details:

> After **Domitian** had reigned fifteen years, **Nerva** succeeded. The sentences of Domitian were annulled, and the Roman Senate decreed the return of those who had been unjustly banished and the restoration of their property. Those who committed the story of those times to writing relate it. *AT THAT TIME, too, the story of the ancient Christians relates that the Apostle John, after his banishment to the island, took up his abode in Ephesus.*
>
> After **Nerva** reigned a little more than a year (A.D. 96–98) he was succeeded by **Trajan** (Reigned A.D. 98–117) . . . At this time that very disciple whom Jesus loved, John, at once Apostle and Evangelist, still remained alive in Asia and administered the churches there, *for after the death of **Domitian**, he had returned from his banishment on the island.* And that he remained alive until this time may fully be confirmed by two witnesses, and these ought to be trustworthy for they represent the orthodoxy of the church, no less persons than **Irenaeus** and **Clement of Alexandria**.
>
> The former of these (Irenaeus) writes in one place in the second of his books *Against the Heresies*, as follows: "And all the presbyters who had been associated in Asia with John, the disciple of the Lord, bear witness to his tradition, for he remained with them until the times of **Trajan**." And in the third book of the same work he makes the same statement as follows: "Now the church at Ephesus was founded by Paul, but John stayed there until the times of Trajan, and it is a true witness of the tradition of the Apostles." Clement indicates the same time. . . .[14] (Emphases mine.)

Even commentators who agree with an early date for the Revelation conclude that Irenaeus was referring to the Book of Revelation and not to John in the above quote. History and Greek scholar J. A. Hort, for instance, is one.[15]

Eusebius, who is known as the first Church historian, certainly understood Irenaeus to be referring to the book and not to John. Eusebius observed, ". . . it would have been declared by him who saw the Revelation. For it has not been long since it was seen, but almost in our own generation, about the end of **Domitian's** reign."[16] Eusebius then commented on this quote, "These are what he (i.e., Irenaeus) states respecting the Revelation."[17] Certainly Eusebius and almost all other scholars down through Church history have had no difficulty in interpreting what Irenaeus meant.

Church historian Philip Schaff (1819–1893), who holds to the early date of Revelation and is an Amillennialist, nevertheless accepted as genuine both the testimony of Irenaeus and the many other Church Fathers who agreed with him.

> The traditional date of composition at the end of Domitian's reign (95 or 96) rests on the *clear and weighty testimony* of Irenaeus, is confirmed by Eusebius and Jerome, and has still its learned defenders.[18] (Emphasis mine.)

This demonstrates that even those who espouse an early date for Revelation usually use other grounds to argue their case rather than malign the accuracy of the early Church tradition.

The Qualifications of Irenaeus

Irenaeus was from Asia Minor, the region of the Apostle John's last ministry. He was discipled in the area around Ephesus where the Apostle John spent his last years. As I have mentioned, the great Polycarp, trained by the Apostle John himself, was Irenaeus' spiritual mentor. So there was only one generation between Irenaeus and John. Therefore the quality of his evidence is as strong and reliable as any we have for any book of the New Testament.

The very fact that the earliest Apostolic and Church Fathers accepted Irenaeus' testimony, and that none disputed it, in itself reveals the high regard and degree of confidence they had in both Irenaeus and his source of information. Certainly, since they were so close to the time and facts, they would have had access to evidence that would either confirm or disprove Irenaeus' witness. For someone today to claim that they have better information than those trusted Christian leaders who were closest to the facts, is to arrogantly assume some sort of "spiritual omniscience." I would urge the Dominionists to listen to "mother" as they so often claim to do in other cases.

Irenaeus' Scholarship Recently Confirmed

Irenaeus is noted for his careful scholarship and defense of the Faith. His refutation of the Gnostic heresy was so thorough that their writings virtually vanished. In his argument against the Gnostics, he first carefully defined their position and then refuted it. As a matter of fact, until the middle of this century, the only clear statement of their doctrines available was found in the writings of Irenaeus.

The Encyclopaedia Britannica (which certainly no man could accuse of a Premillennial bias) has this to say about Irenaeus' reliability as a scholar:

> In reconstructing Gnostic doctrines, therefore, modern scholars relied to a great extent on the writings of Irenaeus, who summarized the Gnostic views before attacking them. After the discovery of the Gnostic library near Naj' Hammādī (in Egypt) in the 1940s, respect for Irenaeus increased: he was proved to have been extremely precise in his report of the doctrines he rejected.[19]

In the light of his fair and scholarly treatment of the Gnostic doctrines which he believed to be heresy, it is ludicrous to reason that Irenaeus would be *less* careful and accurate with facts about the Book of Revelation *which he held to be the Word of God*.

The "Voice of Mother" Cries Out

The overwhelming consensus of the early Church Fathers testifies that Revelation was not only written after the fall of Jerusalem, *but that the Church Fathers looked for events predicted by the Apocalypse to happen future to their own times*. Among the many who believed these things were **Clement and Origen of Alexandria** (both of whom were enemies of Premillennialism), **Victorinus**, and **Eusebius** (who, as an avid admirer of Origen, was also no friend of Premillennialism). Since this was such an important part of the beliefs of the early Church, Philip Schaff lists the more important

Church Fathers and what they believed about prophecy, beginning with a definition of Chiliasm.

>The most striking point in the eschatology of the ante-Nicene age (A.D. 100–325) IS THE PROMINENT CHILIASM, OR MILLENNARIANISM, that is the belief of a visible reign of Christ in glory on earth with the risen saints for a thousand years, before the general resurrection and judgment . . .
>
>In connection with this the general expectation prevailed that the return of the LORD was near, though uncertain and unascertainable as to its day and hour, so that believers may be always ready for it. . . .
>
>**PAPIAS** OF HIERAPOLIS, a pious but credulous contemporary of Polycarp, entertained quaint and extravagant notions of the happiness of the millennial reign, for which he appealed to apostolic tradition. . . .
>
>**JUSTIN MARTYR** represents the transition from the Jewish Christian to the Gentile Christian chiliasm. He speaks repeatedly of the second parousia (advent) of Christ in the clouds of heaven, surrounded by the holy angels. It will be preceded by the near manifestation of the man of sin (2 Thessalonians 2:3–12) who speaks blasphemies against the most high God, and will rule three and a half years. He is preceded by heresies and false prophets. Christ will then raise the patriarchs, prophets, and pious Jews, establish the millennium, restore Jerusalem, and reign there in the midst of these saints; after which the second and general resurrection and judgment of the world will take place. *He regarded this expectation of the earthly perfection of Christ's kingdom as the key-stone of pure doctrine.* . . . [According to Schaff, Justin appealed to the Apocalypse for most of his eschatology.]
>
>**Irenaeus,** *on the strength of tradition from St. John and his disciples,* taught that after the destruction of the Roman empire, and the brief raging of Antichrist (lasting three and a half years or 1260 days), Christ will visibly appear, will bind Satan, will reign at the rebuilt city of Jerusalem with the little band of faithful confessors and the host of risen martyrs over the nations of the earth, and will celebrate the millennial sabbath of preparation

for the eternal glory of heaven; then, after a temporary liberation of Satan, follows the final victory, the general resurrection, the judgment of the world, and the consummation in the new heavens and the new earth. (Ad. Her. V.23–26)

TERTULLIAN, was an enthusiastic Chiliast, and pointed not only to the Apocalypse, but also to the predictions of the Montanist prophets. But the Montanists . . . ran into fanatical excesses, which brought chiliasm into discredit, and resulted in its condemnation by several synods in Asia Minor.

After Tertullian, *and independently of Montanism*, chiliasm was taught by **COMMODIAN** towards the close of the third century, **LACTANTIUS**, and **VICTORINUS** of Petau, at the beginning of the fourth. Its last distinguished advocates in the East were **METHODIUS** (martyred in A.D. 311), the opponent of Origen, and **APOLLINARIS** of Laodicea in Syria.[20]

This History Is the Best We've Got

We don't have any more reliable Church tradition than this. But David Chilton uses a typical debater's tactic to cast doubt on the reliability of the source. There is no legitimate reason to doubt the veracity of the source. This is why Chilton resorts to the weak statement, ". . . he [Irenaeus] *may* have meant that the Apostle John himself 'was seen by others.'" Chilton is using the same tactics as the liberal theologians when he says, "there is considerable room for doubt about the precise meaning [of Irenaeus' witness]." If we have "considerable room for doubt" about something as clear and authenticated as this, then *let's forget Church history altogether*, because most of it is far less documented.

Chilton concludes his argument *against* the consistent witness of early Church tradition by making a totally unfounded, unsupported, and speculative statement: "Certainly, there are other early writers whose statements indicate that St. John wrote the Revelation much earlier, under Nero's persecution."[21] But then he doesn't give us even one of these phantom "other early writers" to support his confident boast. In all honesty, he should have said, "*One would hope that* there are other early writers, etc. . . ."

Hope does seem to spring eternal in the hearts of those who keep trying to find support for a tenuous presupposition. In some ways it reminds me of the valiant evolutionists, who in hope against hope keep searching for the transitional evolutionary link from the invertebrate to a vertebrate. They "know" that they will find it some day because their presuppositions demand it. Whenever they are cornered with questions about facts, they just add a few more million years to the equation and, shazaam! All is solved. That kind of reasoning sounds vaguely familiar when I tune in the Dominionists. They say that it may take tens of thousands of years, but the Church will perfect herself and establish the Kingdom of God on earth. Then Jesus will finally be able to return to the earth.

Theodor Zahn, a widely respected scholar on the formation of the New Testament, accurately summed up the significance of the early Church's witness concerning the date of the Book of Revelation.

> The correctness of the date [A.D. 96] is also confirmed by all those traditions which refer the exile of John upon Patmos to his extreme old age, or which describe Revelation as the latest, or one of the latest, writings in the N.T. On the other hand, all the differing views as to the date of the composition of Revelation to be found in the literature of the Church are so late and so manifestly confused, that *they do not deserve the name of tradition.*[22] (Emphasis mine.)

Former Dominionist Thomas Ice concludes, "The strength of external evidence in favor of the later date is seen to be so strong that even opponents of the late date are forced to admit it."[23] He further writes:

> The testimony of this external evidence is so strong that even Hort, an advocate for a Neronian date, concluded, "If external evidence alone could decide, there would be a clear preponderance for [Emperor] **Domitian.**" On the principle that a strong tradition must be allowed to stand unless internal evidence makes it impossible, which is certainly not true in this case, the Domitianic dating must have the decision in its favor.[24]

The Neronian Illusion

If the Apostle John were exiled to Patmos and wrote the Book of Revelation during the reign of Nero (A.D. 54–68), as Chilton and the Dominionists contend, we would expect to see at least some trace of an early tradition to this effect. But there isn't any. On the contrary, there is a strong unopposed tradition in the earliest times that associates John's exile to Patmos with the Domitian persecution.

Chilton "confidently" presents his explanation as to why so many Apostolic and Church Fathers were in error concerning Domitian's persecution and the time of John's exile: "A good deal of the *modern presumption* in favor of a Domitianic date is based on the belief that a great, sustained period of persecution and slaughter of Christians was carried on under his rule."[25] Then, *with a good deal of modern presumption,* he says, "This belief, as cherished as it is, *does not seem* to be based on any hard evidence at all."[26] (Emphases mine.) The question that must be raised here is, Why did the earliest, most trusted witnesses all believe in the Domitian date? Could it just be possible that they had available to them witnesses and sources in the second and third century that are not available to us in the twentieth?

But then in a later sentence, Chilton makes this revealing admission as he argues for what a "good old boy" Domitian was: "It is true that he did temporarily banish some Christians; but these were eventually recalled."[27] Unless I am missing something in the translation here, this is exactly what Premillennialists teach. This statement supports *my* case, for *this is exactly what happened to John.* After all, *John wasn't executed.* He was banished to the Island of Patmos, and then later released to minister again in Ephesus and Asia Minor. If John had suffered under Nero's persecution, he would have been executed as Paul and Peter were.

The "Who Was the Meanest" Contest

Here are a few contrasts of the Nero versus Domitian persecution.

Nero's persecution was more local. There is no hard evidence that his persecution ever got as far as Asia Minor.

Domitian's persecution, on the other hand, did extend through most of the Empire.

Nero slaughtered Christians, including the Apostle Paul.

Nero's madness was primarily motivated by the need for scapegoats to cover his burning of Rome. Nero's was a short but furious, fanatical, and brutal persecution. Once again, the Christians apprehended were mercilessly and brutally executed, not exiled. According to tradition, some were even dowsed with oil, impaled on poles, and set fire to light Nero's garden parties.

Domitian's persecution had a more defined purpose. He primarily exiled Christians for refusing to worship Caesar. On this point, J. Peter Lange reports, "It is a well-known fact that banishment for the sake of the Christian faith was a form of imperial violent justice, of whose exercise under Nero nothing is known; it is employed, however, by Domitian in company with other regular measures."[28]

So there is no need for believers in the later date for Revelation to argue for "a great, sustained period of persecution and slaughter of Christians" under Domitian. *Banishment will do just fine!*

Another factor that argues against the Nero date is this: Even though John was exiled to Patmos under a persecution, he predicts that another more severe one was yet to come. (Revelation 2:10) A Christian named **Antipas** (which means in Greek, "against everybody") had already been a martyr in Pergamum of Asia Minor. These factors do not fit the history of Nero's era. However, they do fit the general history of Domitian's era.

Scholar Leon Morris surmises, "All that we can say from the evidence of persecution is that it accords with all that we know of Domitian that there should have been such persecution, and that there is no other period in the first century which fits nearly as well."[29]

Neither Chilton nor any of the Dominionists establish a historical case for the pre-A.D. 70 writing of Revelation. Instead, they merely seek to cast doubt upon the clear and consistent, historically accepted witness to a Domitian date by the early Church. That's no way to treat "mother," boys.

THE INTERNAL EVIDENCE

David Chilton attempts to prove an early date for Revelation by three arguments from within the book itself.

His first argument is, "The Book of Revelation is primarily a prophecy of the destruction of Jerusalem by the Romans. This fact alone places St. John's authorship somewhere before September of A.D. 70."[30] He then promises to demonstrate this fact through-out the rest of the commentary.

We are treated in this section to some classic, pristine cases of circular reasoning. He assumes his conclusion, then proves his conclusion with an assumption. This is blatant circular reasoning that proves nothing.

Dominionists offer no hard historical evidence whatsoever for the early date of Revelation, since the entire basis of their case is the assumption that it was written to describe the A.D. 70 destruction of Jerusalem. Thomas Ice raises some discomforting questions for Chilton concerning his argument.

> If this were such a clear "fact," then why did none of the early church writings reflect Chilton's views in their interpretation of Revelation?
>
> If the A.D. 70 destruction of Jerusalem fulfilled so much of biblical prophecy, then why is this not reflected in the views of the early church?
>
> Why is it that all of the early fathers, when referring to Revelation and Matthew 24, see these as future events? They all wrote well after A.D. 70.
>
> Did even those who knew the writer of Revelation, the Apostle John, not pick up on such an important understanding?
>
> If the early date were true, then the early Church would have had a twenty-five-year head start to establish this view and would have made it more difficult for the later date to have arisen.[31]

Nero, Nero, Everywhere . . . But Where Is the Evidence?

For his second "internal evidence" Chilton argues, "as we shall see, St. John speaks of Nero Caesar as still on the throne—and Nero died in June 68."[32] I've really looked through Revelation, and I ain't found old Nero yet. He seems to be just as elusive as he ever was.

Ice's comments on this point are not any more comforting for Chilton than his earlier comments on Chilton's first point.

> Chilton argues that "St. John speaks of Nero Caesar as still on the throne—and Nero died in June 68."[33] If Chilton could show that Nero is the ruler[34] spoken of in

Revelation, then he would have a major victory for his view. But he cannot. He plugs Nero into certain passages without demonstrating from those passages that it has to be Nero. Then he turns around and argues that it proves his point.

He concludes his argument by claiming, "more important than any of this, however, we have *a priori* teaching from Scripture itself that all special revelation ended by A.D. 70."[35] Even someone only casually familiar with the Bible should be wondering where he finds this *a priori* teaching from Scripture. The fact is, this statement is based upon *his a priori* theological commitment that the book of Revelation is about the destruction of Jerusalem.[36]

Chilton attempts to prove that the New Testament books had to have all been written prior to A.D. 70. He does this by reducing the great prophecies of Daniel 9:24–27 into something that doesn't even remotely resemble the meaning of the original words, grammar, syntax, and context—not to mention what he does to parallel passages. When he finishes subjectively mixing his symbols with some more "allegorical wizardry," he comes out with his own special mythology. Concluding with a grand "give or take fifty years approach," he extorts from Daniel 9 "the proof" that the New Testament was finished prior to A.D. 70. Once again, Chilton asks the reader to draw enormous concrete conclusions from highly subjective, "mushy" suppositions.

There are some great works on Daniel 9:24–27, which is one of the Bible's most profound prophetic passages, by such renowned scholars as Sir Robert Anderson,[37] Dr. Harold Hoehner,[38] Alva J. McClain,[39] Dr. Paul D. Feinberg,[40] etc. These men refute such subjective, sloppy interpretation with solid exegesis. Their works do not require the reader to accept things that are simply not in the text.

The most competent scholars overwhelmingly agree that part of Daniel's prophecy is yet future. The most important witness is Jesus Himself. He interpreted the **"abomination that causes desolation"** predicted in Daniel 9:27 as a key sign that His Second Coming would be imminent. (Review my comment on Matthew 24:15 in chapter ten.) Needless to say, I'll take the Lord Jesus' interpretation over the Dominionists' any day.

The Seven Churches and the Domitian Date

A major argument for the Domitian date of John's exile to Patmos comes from the internal evidence of the conditions in the seven churches which are described in Revelation chapters two and three.

First, according to Polycarp (A.D. 70–156), who in addition to being a disciple of the Apostle John was also a bishop of **Smyrna,** the **church at Smyrna** was not founded until *after the martyrdom of the Apostle Paul.* New Testament scholar Theodore Zahn concludes that from the witness and dates of the life of Polycarp we may conclude the church of Smyrna could not have been born any earlier than A.D. 68–70.[41] The "voice of mother church tradition" indicates that the Smyrnan church was founded by the Apostle John and others of the apostolic circle. There is no way for the Smyrnan church to have reached such a degree of development that the Apostle John would have chosen it as a representative church above the hundreds of other churches that existed before A.D. 70. The church of Smyrna probably did not even exist in A.D. 68 when Chilton insists that the Revelation was written. And even if it did, it would not fit the situation described. All these factors fit in perfectly, however, with the Domitian persecution dates.

Κυριος Καισαρ!

ΚΥΡΙΟΣ ΚΑΙΣΑΡ! (KURIOS KAISAR!) Caesar is Lord! This oath is what the Domitian persecution was all about. This created an impossible situation for the Christians. For Christians must recognize Jesus alone as LORD and God. Therefore the most basic Christian confession was ΚΥΡΙΟΣ ΙΗΣΟΥΣ (KURIOS IESOUS!), **"Jesus is LORD!"** This was so essential that the apostle Paul declared it to be the chief evidence that a person was a true believer: **". . . and no one can say, 'Jesus is LORD,' except by the Holy Spirit."** (1 Corinthians 12:3)

The kind of emperor-worship revealed in Revelation was not found under Nero, yet it was not only present but enforced under Domitian. This is a second reason why the internal witness of Revelation does not fit into the Nero scenario. Christians in the Book of Revelation were forced to choose between Christ or Caesar as Lord. This was not the case under Nero who slaughtered Christians as convenient "scapegoats" to cover his own crime of burning Rome in A.D. 64. Nero burned Rome down to make room for the construction of his "Golden House" which later covered a great part of the center of Imperial Rome. Since Christians were already disliked and regarded with suspicion, he found them ideal victims to blame. Yet the resulting persecution, though vicious, was mainly confined to the regions near Rome and it had nothing to do with swearing allegiance to Nero as Lord.

As previously stated in connection with another point, Domitian's persecution extended throughout the empire because he demanded worship of himself and punished Christians for worshipping Christ as the only God. Domitian did not mind his subjects worshipping other gods as long as they also worshiped him as god. But he considered it treason to confess that Christ alone was LORD. The circumstances of Revelation fit this situation and not Nero's.

Ephesus From Paul's and John's View

Third, Paul's last letter, Second Timothy, was written from Rome during his second imprisonment just shortly before he was executed by Nero in A.D. 66. Since Timothy was in Ephesus, the conditions described in this letter apply primarily to the local Asian churches which were under the jurisdiction of the Ephesian church. These include the same churches addressed in Revelation. Leon Morris observes that it would have taken far more than from A.D. 66 to 68 for the churches to have degenerated from the conditions reflected in Second Timothy to the complacency revealed in Revelation.[42]

Fourth, and related to the above point, the kinds of false doctrines and heresies revealed in John's seven letters to the seven churches would have required considerably more time to develop than allowed by the A.D. 68 date. In Paul's Second Timothy letter to that same general area, he primarily dealt with the legalism introduced from within the Church by the Judaizers. This reflects the great influence Jews had in earlier times. But John deals with problems that developed *after* the churches became dominated by Gentiles. They brought in licentiousness or "loose living," Greek philosophy, and the mystery cults. John deals with these sorts of things. Once again, this would have taken more time to develop than allowed by the Nero date. M. J. Brunk rightly summarizes this factor.

When we read the messages to the churches in the Apocalypse, we are in a different atmosphere. Not the narrowness of Judaism, but the wild immorality and worldliness of heathenism, is now striving to gain the upper hand; and the Christian has to overcome, not Judaism but the world in its widest sense.[43]

Fifth, another argument against the early dating of Revelation arises from this statement, **"I, John, Your brother and fellow partaker in the tribulation . . ."** (Revelation 1:9 NASB) If the Apostle John had written this in A.D. 68, it would not have fit in with Nero's persecution, since it was local and both he and the churches addressed were in Asia. However, this does agree with the details of the Domitian persecution. Once again, no matter how intense Nero's persecution was, it was not extensive enough to explain John's statement.

Sixth, the destruction of Laodicea by an earthquake in the early A.D. 60s militates against an early date for Revelation. Though the city was very wealthy and paid for its own rebuilding instead of taking the usual aid given by Rome in such cases, there simply would not have been enough time to have rebuilt the whole city by A.D. 68. Even with today's modern equipment and methods, it would take much longer than five or so years to rebuild such a city. I have seen its ruins. It must have been magnificent in its day. Once again the Domitian date would have allowed ample time for this wealthy city of Asia Minor to have rebuilt itself and to develop the self-sufficient complacency reflected in Revelation 2:14–22.

Reducing Worldwide Catastrophe to Fit Little Israel

Certainly the most difficult claim for Chilton and the Dominionists to defend is that virtually all of the prophecies in the Revelation were fulfilled in the A.D. 70 destruction of Jerusalem and the State of Israel.

One of the techniques Chilton uses to localize, reduce, and focus all those enormous judgments of Revelation to fall upon the Israel of A.D. 70 is to translate all twelve occurrences of the Greek words *tes ges* (της γης) to mean *"the land"* instead of their normal meaning, **"the earth"** or "the world." Having made this unsupported pronouncement, he then declares that "the land" always refers to the land of Israel. Chilton gives no supporting evidence for doing this from either a lexicon or the context. He just declares it to be so in order to fit his assumptions. The meaning of a word is determined by its usage in context. Although της γης can mean "the land" in certain contexts, it is rare. In the Book of Revelation it most often means the whole planet. Even a quick reading of the Book of Revelation will reveal to the unbiased inquirer that **"the earth"** is most often used in a global sense.

Do You Smell Smoke?

David Chilton and the Dominionists "have bet their whole farm" on the early date of the Revelation. Their enormous claims concerning prophecy, on which their whole system depends, must have a pre–A.D. 70 date for the Revelation to support them.

The external evidence for the A.D. 95–96 date for the Revelation rests upon the clearest and best sort of witness that we have from ancient Church history. We don't have any better evidence for the dating of any other book of the New Testament. Yet remember, the Premillennial position could still be true even if the Revelation were written before A.D. 70.

Chilton's interpretation of the internal evidence to support his claims of a pre–A.D. 70 date for the Revelation was all based on the prior assumption that the prophecies contained therein all referred to the A.D. 70 destruction of Jerusalem. He used classic "circular reasoning" in his interpretations.

To say the very least, we need a much stronger case than has been presented in order to disagree with the prophetic views of those early Apostolic Fathers who were discipled and taught by the very one who had seen the apocalyptic vision. Certainly they would have been aware of an early date if it were true.

The Dominionist's interpretation of prophecy is out of step with Christian scholarship in the most important era of Church history. The first majority view was Premillennialism. Then from the fourth century through the eighteenth century, Amillennialism prevailed. The distinctive doctrines of Postmillennialism can not be documented earlier than the sixteenth century. As a doctrine, it made its strongest showing in the nineteenth century. But beginning in the early eighteenth century, at the same time of the resurgence of literal interpretation, Premillennialism had a rebirth. By the late nineteenth century, Premillennialism had become the majority view of the evangelical Church.

The Dominionists have often tried to claim that they have the witness of Church history on their side. They have certainly not proven that to be true in this case.

But Premillennialists feel very comfortable standing with such believers in a literal thousand year reign of Christ on earth as Barnabas, Polycarp, Irenaeus, Papias of Hierapolis, Tertullian, Justin Martyr, Ignatius of Antioch, Lactantius, Methodius, etc. Most of these spiritual giants were martyred for their faith. Most lived in the first and second centuries and had direct lines of training that were either first or second generation from the Apostles. And yes . . . Premillennialists believe they have the witness of the Apostle John and his Book of Revelation with them too.

CHAPTER TWELVE

Quo Vadis, Church?

Now his Kingdom *is* of this world. Now His Followers *do* fight for His honor . . . His Kingdom is *now* visible in this world through His People.

Gary North[1]

My kingdom *is not* of this world. If it were, my servants would fight to prevent my arrest by the Jews. But Now my kingdom is from another place.

Jesus, the Messiah[2]

If the Church has not taken over Israel's covenants, as we Premillennialists contend, then there are many questions that must be clearly understood: What is the Church? Did the Church exist in the Old Testament? When did the Church begin? Has the Church become spiritual Israel—if so, in what sense? What is the Church's primary mission in the world? What is the Church's ultimate goal? What is the Church's hope and destiny?

These are all crucial questions in resolving the controversy between the Dominionists and Premillennialists. Could you answer these questions clearly from the Scriptures? I find that few Christians can accurately answer most of these questions. And even fewer could give answers with chapter and verse. Yet great confusion could be dispelled with an accurate understanding of these issues.

It is impossible for the Church to reach its goal if Christians don't know what that goal is—or worse, if they are striving toward the wrong goal. It is impossible for the Church to complete her mission if most of her members don't clearly understand what that mission is. In fact, it is impossible for the Church to really be effective if Christians don't even know what the Church truly is.

If churches continue to embrace the wrong hopes and pursue the wrong mission currently being taught by the Dominionists, there will not only be eventual disappointment, but devastating disillusionment. Christians will be ill prepared to face the frightful events that are rapidly coming together into the prophetic pattern that precedes the Second Coming of the Messiah. What lies close ahead is going to take a clear understanding of where present world events are headed coupled with a personal combat faith.

The Dominionist movement is guilty of sowing some of their most serious confusion in this vital area of Christian doctrine. Gary North's frequent use of the term "pessimillennialists," which was coined by South African Reconstructionist Francis Nigal Lee, may sound cute to some, but the reasoning behind this term betrays a gross lack of understanding of the Church's nature, mission, goal, and hope.

WHAT IS THE CHURCH?

The Church Is a Mystery

In defining what the Church is, it is most helpful to keep in mind that the Holy Spirit often speaks of the Church as a **"mystery."** As we considered in chapter nine, the term **"mystery"** is used in the New Testament to mean something that was formerly covered up and unknowable, but is now made known by the Holy Spirit through the Scriptures to those who are born spiritually.

The Apostle Paul used this term as he explained his extraordinary understanding concerning what the Church truly is:

> . . . **that by revelation there was made known to me the mystery, as I wrote before in brief. And by referring to this, when you read you can understand my insight into** *the mystery of Christ,* **which in other generations was not made known to the sons of men, as it has now been revealed to His holy apostles and prophets by the Spirit; to be specific,** *that the Gentiles are fellow heirs and fellow members of the body, and fellow partak-*

ers of the promise in Christ Jesus through the gospel . . .

To me, the very least of all saints, this grace was given, to preach to the Gentiles the unfathomable riches of Christ, and to bring to light what is the administration of *the mystery which for ages has been hidden in God,* **who created all things. . . .** (Ephesians 3:3–6, 8, 9 NASB) (Italics added for emphasis.)

These verses clearly define the meaning of the term **"mystery"** as it is used in the New Testament. It is something *previously hidden in God and not made known in other generations and ages, but now revealed to the New Testament Apostles and Prophets by the Holy Spirit.*

Paul explains *why* the Church was a mystery before its birth. If the Church had been understood in the Old Testament ages, then Jesus, the Messiah, could not have given a bona fide offer of the Kingdom to Israel, since the Israelites would have known that their failure was already anticipated and sealed. The Church was God's secret, preplanned alternate program to be instituted *after* the Israelites had rejected the Lord Jesus as the Messiah (see also Romans 16:25–26).

This passage makes it clear that the Church of Jesus Christ as revealed in the New Testament *is new and unique,* and *was not understood* in the Old Testament ages.

That which makes the Church new and unique is the fact that both Jews and Gentiles have been placed as equal heirs of the promises concerning salvation and the Holy Spirit during this age through *union with Christ.* This personal union with Christ is the essence of what the Church is in her most foundational sense.

The Most Important Phrase in the New Testament

There is one key statement that explains how we Gentiles now share in promises and privileges that formerly were exclusively granted to the Israelites and proselytes. It is the phrase **"in Christ Jesus."** Understanding this phrase is at the heart of understanding what the Church really is.

The importance the Holy Spirit attaches to the simple phrase, **"in Christ,"** is brought out by the fact that *it is repeated in one form or another more than 160 times in the New Testament Epistles* (particularly Paul's). It would take a whole book just to fully explain what this wonderful phrase means for the Christian. All that we have been given by God comes as a direct result of the eternal relationship indicated by this phrase. Let's consider this crucial phrase **"in Christ."**

The Church Is the Body of Christ

The Apostle Paul gave an exact definition of what the one true Church is to the believers at Colosse:

> **Now I rejoice in what was suffered for you, and I fill up in my flesh what is still lacking in regard to Christ's afflictions, for the sake of HIS BODY, WHICH IS THE CHURCH.** (Colossians 1:24) (Emphasis added.)

The one true Church is **the body of Christ**. This is a mystery that is so deep and profound that it can only be understood by those who have had it revealed to them from the Word of God by the Holy Spirit. There is a relationship revealed in the BODY OF CHRIST that is such a heavenly reality that most Christians stumble over it and do not grasp its full meaning. The Scriptures reveal this relationship in these blessed terms: **"we are members of His body, of His flesh, and of His bone."** (Ephesians 5:30 KJV)

How We Become Part of Christ's Body

The Apostle Paul further defines the meaning of the true church:

> **For even as the body is one and yet has many members, and all the members of the body, though they are many, are one body, so also is Christ. For by one Spirit we were all baptized into ONE BODY, whether Jews or Greeks, whether slaves or free, and we were all made to drink of one Spirit. For the body is not one member, but many.** (1 Corinthians 12:12–14 NASB)

The main problem with most of us Christians is that we view this Scripture as merely an illustration of the Church. We think, "Oh yes, the body is a wonderful illustration of how interrelated and dependent the members of the Church are." But the Holy Spirit is presenting something much more profound than that.

Note that *every believer* is a member of the **one body** which is said to be **Christ** Himself. And remember, **the Church** is **His body.**

Each believer enters into the body in the same way, by an instantaneous act of **the Spirit**. This is brought out by the verb **"were baptized"** (ἐβαπτισθημεν from βαπτιζω). It is in the aorist tense in the original Greek, which means an act at a point of time. It is in the passive voice which emphasizes that the believer *simply receives* the baptism by the Spirit. It is the Holy Spirit's sovereign work of grace.

Therefore, since **ALL** believers are declared to be in the Body of Christ, and since no one can be a Christian without being in the Body of Christ, this *baptism by the Spirit* must occur to each believer at the moment of salvation. We must also conclude that the *baptism by the Spirit* is God's only means of forming the one true Church.

WHEN DID THE CHURCH BEGIN?

The Lord Jesus was the first one to ever mention **His Church**, when He predicted it in response to Peter's first public confession that **You are the Messiah, "the Son of the Living God."**

> **And Jesus answered and said to him, "Blessed are you, Simon Barjona, because flesh and blood did not reveal this to you, but My Father who is in heaven.**
>
> **"And I also say to you that you are Peter** [petros, πετρος] **and upon this rock** [petra, πετρα] **I will build MY CHURCH; and the gates of hades shall not overpower it."** (Matthew 16:17–18 NASB)

It is necessary to clear up one important technical point before dealing with the main idea of this verse. The LORD predicted that **His Church** would be built, not upon Peter, but upon Peter's confession of faith in Him. This is clear in the Greek, because the gender of **"Peter"** is masculine and the gender of **"rock"** is neuter. From the standpoint of grammar, it is impossible for **Peter** to be the antecedent of **rock**, since it is not in the same gender.

My main point in this verse is that the Lord Jesus used the future tense to announce **"I *will build* My Church."** This in itself demonstrated that the Church was yet future.

But the most important factor in determining *when* the Church began involves establishing when the Baptism of the Spirit, which is the only means of forming the Church, started.

261

John the Baptizer Predicted the Baptism With the Spirit

John the Baptist spoke of three different kinds of baptism in one glorious message.

> **As for me, I baptize you with water for** [because of] **repentance, but He who is coming after me is mightier than I, and I am not fit to remove His sandals; He will baptize you with the Holy Spirit and fire. And His winnowing fork is in His hand, and He will thoroughly clear His threshing floor; and He will gather His wheat into the barn, but He will burn up the chaff with unquenchable fire.** (Matthew 3:11–12 NASB)

The baptism of John was administered with water in response to a person who changed his mind (repented) so that he saw his need for salvation and believed in the coming Messiah as his Savior and Lord.

John predicted that just as the Messiah is greater in His person than he, so His baptism is greater than his. He predicted that the Messiah would not just baptize with water, but with the **Holy Spirit** and **fire.**

It is all important to note that the Greek verb βαπτιζω (baptizo), "to baptize," is used in a very special sense in the New Testament. It is not translated, but rather transliterated letter for letter from the original. *Baptizo* literally means *"to dip an object into something."* But it is most often used in a metaphorical sense.

For instance we speak of a soldier's first experience in battle as his "baptism of fire." The idea is that the soldier is so immersed or identified with battle that he is not the same as he was before. This is at the heart of *baptizo's* meaning in the New Testament, i.e., *to be so identified with something that a change is produced.*

When someone is baptized with the Holy Spirit, he is so identified with Him that he is not the same person as he was before. The one baptized is changed in his standing before God through union with Christ, and in his nature and destiny through the new birth. The believer is so immersed into the Holy Spirit that the Spirit takes up permanent residence in the new convert through His indwelling ministry.

But as we have considered, the most important aspect of the baptism of the Holy Spirit is that He baptizes us into an eternal union with Christ. This union is so real that God the Father sees us as having been put to death with Christ, buried with Him and raised into His resurrection life (Romans 6:1–14). Believing these facts is the basis of living the Christian life.

The Baptism of Fire Will Usher in the Millennial Kingdom

In the Lord Jesus' First Coming, He initiated the baptism with the Holy Spirit for all who believe in Him, which began the Church age. But in His Second Coming, He will baptize all the living who have rejected Him **with fire,** which ushers in the Millennial Kingdom. Jesus illustrated the baptism with fire in Matthew 3:12. In Jesus' day farmers in Israel piled harvested wheat into stacks to dry. Then on a windy day they built a fire downwind from the pile. With a great wide shovel-like fork (winnowing fork), they pitched the wheat into the air. Since dried chaff was lighter, it was blown into the fire. The heavier wheat fell back to the ground. After a short time, all that would be left was the wheat.

The baptism of fire perfectly illustrates the judgment Christ will execute upon the survivors of the Great Tribulation immediately after He returns to the earth (Matthew 25:31–51). It is no accident that John the Baptist, who proclaimed the Kingdom of heaven, which would ultimately be postponed, also announced Christ's future judgment that will inaugurate that very Kingdom.

John the Baptist was the first to predict the baptism with the Holy Spirit. It was considered so important that all four of the Gospels record it (Matthew 3:11–12; Mark 1:8; Luke 3:16–17; John 1:33).

Just before the Lord Jesus ascended to the Father, He said to His disciples, **"Do not leave Jerusalem, but wait for the gift my Father promised, which you have heard me speak about. For John baptized with water, but in a few days you will be baptized with the Holy Spirit."** (Acts 1:5–6)

Then on the Day of Pentecost (which was a Jewish feast that was exactly fifty days after the feast of Passover), the Holy Spirit was first given in His unique New Testament ministries. The advent of the Holy Spirit was visibly manifestated by the spiritual gift of speaking in a language never learned before (Acts 2). Some time later, Peter preached under Divine compulsion to a group of Gentiles and the same outward evidence occurred with them when they believed in the Lord Jesus. When Peter was called upon to explain to the elders of the Jerusalem Church why he had gone to Gentiles, he gave this account:

> **As I began to speak,** *the Holy Spirit came on them as he had come on us at the beginning.* **Then I remembered what the Lord had said, "John baptized with water,** *but you will be baptized with the Holy Spirit." So if God gave them the same gift as he gave us,* **who believed in the Lord Jesus Christ, who was I to think that I could oppose God!** (Acts 11:15–17) (Emphases mine.)

Peter clearly identifies the Day of Pentecost as the beginning of the Holy Spirit's baptizing ministry, as promised and predicted by John the Baptist and the Lord Jesus.

The Church's Birthday

So the Day of Pentecost, A.D. 33, was the Church's birthday. It first came into being when the Holy Spirit took 120 Jews, who had already believed and were waiting for the fulfillment of Christ's promise, and baptized them into union with Christ. This was the beginning of the formation of the greatest reality in all the universe, **the Body of Christ.**

I must note that a transition had to take place in the beginning of the Church's tenor on earth. Since the Jews were the covenant people of the past age, God gave the new ministries of the Holy Spirit to them first. Afterward, these ministries were given to the Samaritans, who were part Israelite (Acts 8:14–17). Then the new ministries were inaugurated to the Gentiles (Acts 10:44–48). After this transition, the norm has been that the Holy Spirit and all his New Covenant ministries are given to every believer at the moment of salvation. The Scriptures make clear the norm for today, ". . . if anyone does not have the Spirit of Christ, he does not belong to Christ." (Romans 8:9b) So it is impossible in this age to be a Christian and not have the Holy Spirit.

DID THE CHURCH EXIST IN THE OLD TESTAMENT?

As we have seen, the Church *could not have existed* in the Old Testament for three reasons: (1) the Church was unknowable in that era; (2) the baptism by the Holy Spirit had not yet been given; and (3) the Church, which is composed of both Jews and Gentiles on an equal footing, could not have been created *until the racial barriers, which were an inextricable part of the Law of Moses, were removed in Christ.* Paul summarizes this point:

> **For he himself is our peace, who has made the two one and has destroyed the barrier, the dividing wall of hostility, by abolishing IN HIS FLESH the law with its commandments and regulations. His purpose was to create IN HIMSELF ONE NEW MAN out of the two, thus making peace, and in this ONE BODY to reconcile both of them to God through the cross, by which he put to death their hostility.** (Ephesians 2:14–16) (Emphases added.)

If the Law of Moses were still in force today, there could be no Church, since racial segregation of Israelites from the Gentiles was an essential part of that covenant. This reveals another major flaw in the Reconstructionist doctrine of Theonomy (which, as you may recall, teaches that virtually all of the Law of Moses is still in effect today). Some try to say that only part of it is still applicable, but as we saw in chapter seven, the law is a unit that cannot be divided. You either put yourself under the whole law, or not at all.[3]

Paul explained in Ephesians chapter three the source of his knowledge concerning the new truths about the Church and why he had more insight on the subject than any of the other Apostles. The mystery of how both Jew and Gentile are now united in the body of Christ, sharing the same promises and inheritance, was revealed to Paul directly by the Holy Spirit. Paul considered the fact that *the Church is the body of Christ* to be at the center of his teaching.

IS THE CHURCH NOW ISRAEL?

This question has been raised from many points of view in this book. But now, in the light of the discussion of Israel's covenants and the force of the argument of Romans chapter eleven, some conclusions can accurately be drawn.

There is no question that the Christian today is a spiritual seed of Abraham. The Holy Spirit said through Paul:

> **Understand, then, that those who believe are children of Abraham. . . . You are all sons of God through**

faith in Christ Jesus, for all of you who were baptized into Christ have clothed yourselves with Christ [the baptism of the Holy Spirit]. **There is neither Jew nor Greek, slave nor free, male nor female, for you are all one in Christ Jesus. If you belong to Christ, then you are Abraham's seed, and heirs according to the promise.** (Galatians 3:7, 26–29)

Because of our union with Christ in this age, we share in Christ's lineage from Abraham and in His inheritance rights of the promises. This is part of the enormous blessings that are ours through being **"bone of Christ's bone and flesh of His flesh."** (Ephesians 5:30 KJV)

But this does not in any way abbrogate nor annul the covenants made with the physical seed of Abraham, Isaac, and Jacob who will yet believe in the future and be grafted back into "their own olive tree." We Gentiles, as "wild olive branches," have been grafted into Israel's cultivated olive tree. But we should always remember that we are supported by their tree and their root only through our union with Christ.

Does Spiritual Circumcision Eliminate the Jew?

In another crucial passage, the Apostle Paul said, **"A man is not a Jew if he is only one outwardly, nor is circumcision merely outward and physical. No, a man is a Jew if he is one inwardly; and circumcision is circumcision of the heart, by the Spirit, not by the written code. Such a man's praise is not from men, but from God."** (Romans 2:28–29)

However, it is clear that Paul did not mean by this that the physical Jew was eliminated and had no further purpose in God's plan. He immediately clarified this by saying, **"What advantage, then, is there in being a Jew, or what value is there in circumcision? MUCH IN EVERY WAY! . . ."** (Romans 3:1–2) Paul's point is that no ethnic Israelite has ever been a true Jew by mere outer ritual. In all ages men have had to come to God by faith. Rituals are only valid if they are the result of an inner spiritual reality through faith. But Paul's statements in no way annul the unconditional covenants made with the future believing Nation of Israel.

The Two Jerusalems

Some Dominionists attempt to use the Apostle Paul's allegory in Galatians 4:21–31 to somehow prove that the Church has now taken over Israel's covenants on a permanent basis. A careful reading of the allegory in the light of the purpose of the book of Galatians reveals clearly that Paul's point was to show the contrast between the present ethnic Israel, who is today blindly clinging to the annulled conditional Mosaic Law Covenant, and the Church, which is by grace through faith relying on the New Covenant.

One factor in the allegory that is mostly overlooked is the fact that it says, **"the Jerusalem from above is our** [the Church's] **mother"** (Galatians 4:26). This points to the obvious fact that the Church's Kingdom is not on this earth. The Christian is looking forward to **the New Jerusalem** which is his destiny at the return of Christ. Our destiny is heavenly, not earthly.

But this does not mean, as Dominionists have argued, that the earthly Jerusalem will not be the center of the Millennial Kingdom. The Messiah will yet fulfill the prophecy of Zechariah: **"And in that day His feet will stand on the Mount of Olives, which is in front of Jerusalem";** and again, **"Then it will come about that any who are left of all the nations that went against Jerusalem will go up from year to year to worship the King, the LORD of hosts. . . ."** (Zechariah 14:4, 16)

Who Is the Israel of God?

Here is another passage that is frequently used by the Dominionists to prove that national Israel has been forever replaced by the Church: **"For neither is circumcision anything, nor uncircumcision, but a new creation. And those who will walk by this rule, peace and mercy be upon them, and upon the Israel of God."** (Galatians 6:15–16)

There are three possible interpretations of this passage that have been advanced by reputable Bible expositors. The first is that **"the Israel of God"** is the Church. The second is that **"the Israel of God"** refers to the Jewish believers in the Church of Paul's day. The third is that **"the Israel of God"** refers to that body of ethnic Israel who will be saved at the Messiah's Second Coming.

If **"Israel"** refers to the Church, as the Dominionists contend, then it would be the only case out of more than sixty-five occurrences in the New Testament in which it means something other than *ethnic Israel*. In fact, there is not one other instance in all the Bible wherein the name "Israel" is used to describe the Church or any group other than the ethnic descendants of Abraham through Jacob.

In spite of the fact that the terms *Israel* and *the Church* are used side by side in the book of Acts, they are always carefully distinguished as separate and distinct entities. Therefore the consistent usage of the two terms argues formidably against the novel view that Paul is teaching that *the Church* is *the Israel of God*.

The first view also requires a novel and unusual interpretation of the Greek conjunction και (kai) (i.e., *"even* the Israel of God") to support this interpretation. Greek scholar and theologian Dr. S. Lewis Johnson, Jr., in his brilliant analysis of this passage, said concerning the first view:

> Coming to the problem, the first interpretation referred to above, that in which the term **"the Israel of God"** is referred to the believing church involves taking *kai* in an explicative sense and the rendering of it as *even* (as the NIV DOES). There are compelling objections to this view. In the first place, this usage in the light of *kai* in all phases of the literature is proportionately very infrequent, as both G. B. Winer and Ellicott acknowlege. Ellicott contends that it is doubtful that Paul ever uses *kai* in "so marked an explicative sense." There is not anything in recent grammatical study and research that indicates otherwise.
>
> Finally, if it were Paul's intention to identify the **"them"** of the text as **"the Israel of God,"** then why not simply eliminate the *kai* after "mercy?" The result would be far more to the point, if Paul were identifying the **"them,"** that is, the church, with the term **"Israel."** The verse would be rendered then, **"and as many as shall walk by this rule, peace be upon them and mercy, upon the Israel of God."** A case could be solidly made for the apposition of **"the Israel of God"** with **"them,"** and the rendering of the NIV could stand. Paul, however, did not eliminate the *kai*.
>
> These things make it highly unlikely that the first interpretation is to be preferred grammatically. Because both of the other suggested interpretations are not cumbered with these grammatical and syntactical difficulties, they are more likely views.[4]

I believe along with many Greek scholars that Paul's unusual use of the Greek word *kai* was used to set apart the specific group **"the Israel of God"** from the Church, represented in the verse by the term **"them,"** not to identify them as synonymous terms. I therefore interpret the verse from the original Greek as follows:

> **And to those who will order their lives by this rule, peace be upon them, and (καῖ) mercy also (καῖ) be upon the Israel of God.** (Galatians 6:16 HL)

This interpretation brings out Paul's unusual double usage of the Greek word *kai*. The punctuation follows the syntax of the Greek, which sets the last clause apart as something distinct.

After weighing all the evidence, I believe that the title **"the Israel of God"** refers to that believing remnant of ethnic Israelites who will be saved when the Messiah returns in His Second Advent. This agrees with Paul's most definitive teaching about the status of Israel in Romans chapters nine, ten, and eleven.

But just for the sake of argument, even if this passage did mean that the Church is the spiritual Israel of God in this age, it would in no way mean that ethnic Israel could not be restored to the national preeminence promised them in the unconditional covenants.

The New Testament consistently presents the Church and Israel as two distinct and separate works of God with two distinct but parallel purposes and destinies.

WHAT IS THE CHURCH'S PURPOSE AND MISSION?

This is perhaps the most urgent question to arise out of the controversy between the Premillennialists and the Dominionists. If they are right and we are wrong, then at least there is time for history to bear out our error and for us to correct it. But if we are right and they are wrong, there is a desperate situation developing in which there is little time to correct the error. The last days of the Church on earth may be largely wasted seeking to accomplish a task that only the LORD Himself can and will do directly.

On a question as important as the Church's purpose and mission, it is especially important not to be deceived by the theoretical, subjective reasoning of men. This issue must be decided on the basis of an objective exegesis of the Bible text.

The Present World-System Is Under Satan's Control

The Bible presents the picture that Christians are aliens in enemy territory while in the world. Satan, though defeated at the cross, has been granted temporary provisional powers during this age. This is clearly revealed by the following Scriptures.

Satan is called **"the god of this age"** who is able to blind the minds of the unbeliever during this present era to the Gospel and to the Divine nature and glories of Christ. (2 Corinthians 4:3–4) The term "age" (αιων, *aion*, in the original) is used in the sense of the specific segment of time the Church is on the earth. This situation is presented as a general principle with which the Church must reckon during its tenure on earth. Whereas the Scripture predicts that the Messiah will rule the earth with a rod of iron during the Kingdom age, Satan is "the god of this present age."

The unbelieving **"rulers of this age"** are presented as demonically blinded to God's wisdom by the **"wisdom of this age."** (1 Corinthians 2:6–8)

The Lord Jesus called Satan **"the prince of this world."** (John 14:30) The Holy Spirit also warns that **"the whole world is under the control of [or lies in the power of[5]] the Evil One."** (1 John 5:19) The title **"prince"** is from the Greek word αρχων (*archon*), which literally means **"ruler or lord."[6]** The term **"world"** is κοσμος (*kosmos*), which literally means a well-organized system. The use of the term **"whole"** before **"world-system"** emphasizes the universal extent of Satan's present control over it.

Satan's control over the thought patterns within the world-system is further revealed by the Apostle Paul: **". . . in which you used to live when you followed the ways of this world and of the ruler of the kingdom of the air, the spirit who is now at work in those who are disobedient."** (Ephesians 2:2) The original Greek text is so full of meaning here that it is difficult to bring out in a translation. It literally says that we used to live "according to *the age of this world-system*." This refers to the contemporary *"in thing"* that most influences and captivates the thinking of each generation within the world-system. The next clause strengthens this idea, **"according to ruler [Satan] of the authority of the atmosphere."** I translated **"air"** in its figurative sense, since this passage is not concerned with the air we breath, but with the atmosphere of thoughts that shape men's actions.

To sum up what the Bible teaches on this subject, the world-system is organized under Satan's rulership and energized by his power. It is totally organized against God's viewpoint, reality, and life. Part of the world-system contains culture, beauty, and even nobility, but at its core, it is organized to blind mankind to the Gospel about Jesus Christ and the truth of God's Word.

The "Crown Before the Cross" Mentality

Many Dominionists may believe that the above teaching about Satan is a negative confession and defeatest thinking. But it is in fact what the Bible teaches. We can't beat an enemy if we grossly misjudge his strengths and weaknesses. Nor can he be defeated if we misunderstand the areas in which God has sent us to fight him. If we seek to fight the Devil in areas that the Word of God reveals only the Lord Jesus Himself can directly conquer him, we are doomed to defeat.

What Is the Course of This Age?

The Holy Spirit reveals that one of the main purposes for Christ's atonement is **"to rescue us from this present evil age."** (Galatians 1:4) The LORD did not send us to conquer this present evil age, but to rescue people out of it. Our mission is to rescue as many as possible out of this evil age through our witness. Then we are to take those who believe and disciple them for God's spiritual kingdom, which at present is not of the world.

The characteristic of this present age is the development of **"the mystery of lawlessness,"** which will climax with the unveiling of Satan's masterpiece, the Antichrist. (See 2 Thessalonians 2:1–7.) At that time in history the Scriptures reveal, **"And then the lawless one will be revealed, whom the Lord Jesus will overthrow with the breath of his mouth and destroy by the splendor of his coming."** (2 Thessalonians 2:8) These words reveal a direct catastrophic intervention of the Lord Jesus into history in the clearest possible terms.

This and scores of other prophetic Scriptures all unanimously reveal that God has sovereignly permitted evil to grow parallel with the spread of the Gospel in this age. The **"tares"** are being allowed to grow alongside the **"wheat"** until **"the harvest,"** which is the Second Advent of Christ.

If the Dominionists raise the objection, "Why would God

271

allow Satan to tempt and persecute the Church?" we could raise the same kind of question concerning Jesus: "Why did God permit Satan to tempt and persecute the Lord Jesus when He was upon the earth?" Indeed, why didn't the Lord Jesus organize a revolution along with Barabas and overthrow the Roman government instead of submitting to their brutality and murder?

If we were to use the same kind of logic the Dominionists use to arrive at their idea of the Church's purpose, we would find ourselves thinking Jesus Himself was "a wimp." After all, He submitted to the crucifixion.

If an intelligent person is granted his premise, he can come up with many reasons as to why the Church should take over the world. This appeals to the fleshly mind and "tickles the ears" of those who are operating according to the thought patterns of the world-system. The situation is much the same as when the Lord Jesus announced to the disciples that He was going to Jerusalem **"to suffer many things at the hands of the elders, chief priests and teachers of the law, and that he must be killed and on the third day be raised to life."** Peter didn't like that idea. It didn't fit in with his plans to sit on a throne as co-ruler with the Lord Jesus over the promised Kingdom. So **"Peter took him aside and began to rebuke him. 'Never, Lord!' He said. 'This shall never happen to you!'"** Jesus' response was startling: **"Jesus turned and said to Peter, 'Out of my sight, Satan! You are a stumbling block to me; you do not have in mind the things of God, but the things of men.'"** (Matthew 16:21–23) Peter wanted a crown before a cross. This is the main error of the modern-day Dominionists.

No matter how appealing the idea of the Church taking over the world and establishing the Kingdom of God is, it is not what the Bible teaches. The only way that we can establish what the purpose of the Church is for this age is by carefully seeking out what the Bible says.

The Great Commission and Dominion

When pressed for New Testament Scriptures to support their view of the Church's purpose, the Dominionists appeal to Matthew 28:18–20. Matthew's version of the Great Commission is viewed by the Dominionists as simply an extension and New Covenant update of the Creation Mandate God gave to Adam in the so-called Edenic Covenant wherein man was commanded to take dominion over the earth and all the living creatures in it.

This idea shapes and controls the Dominionists' thinking. Although they see evangelism as part of the Great Commission, their main focus and goal is to Christianize the world's culture and political systems, and to take dominion over them. This is not even what God had in mind in the Eden Mandate, but it certainly is not what the Great Commission teaches.

Below is a typical Dominionist interpretation of the Great Commission expressed by George Grant:

> Personal redemption is not the do-all and end-all of the Great Commission. Thus, our evangelism must include sociology as well as salvation; it must include reform and redemption, culture and conversion, a new social order as well as a new birth, a revolution as well as a regeneration. Any other kind of evangelism is shortsighted and woefully impotent. Any other kind of evangelism fails to live up to the high call of the Great Commission.[7]

Other Dominionists like Gary North and David Chilton have echoed and written similar opinions.

But did the Lord Jesus really have in mind the Christianizing of the world's sociology and culture? Did He mean for us to promote revolution in order to bring in a new social order? I believe the most radical, revolutionary thing anyone can do is to bring a sinner from spiritual death to spiritual life. Everything else pales by contrast.

Let us analyze the several Great Commission passages and determine whether they indeed do teach what the Dominionists say they do. The Lord Jesus considered the Great Commission so important that He included it in all four Gospels and the Book of Acts. It is obviously very important since it focuses upon the Church's mission on earth during this age.

Mark's View of the Commission

Mark's account of the Great Commission is the closest to Matthew's wording. (For the record, Mark wrote down Peter's account of the life of Christ.) Mark wrote, **"He [Jesus] said to them, 'Go into all the world and preach the good news to all creation. Whoever believes and is baptized will be saved, but whoever does not believe will be condemned.'"** (Mark 16:15–16) There can be no confusion as to the meaning of this account. The entire focus of the command is to proclaim the Gospel to all the world. The salvation of men's souls is the specific central goal.

The LORD also reveals that some will not believe the message. Nowhere are we led to expect that a majority of mankind will believe the Gospel in this age. The Lord Jesus Himself did not convert the majority of those who heard Him. The reason certainly wasn't a flaw in the message He preached, nor in the power with which He presented it. The variable was in the hearts of those who heard. Since we have the Holy Spirit to empower us just as He did, we can expect the same kind of success in evangelism. But though the Church will win a greater total number of mankind than Jesus did, it will not win a greater percentage of those who hear.

Luke's Account of the Commission

Luke's account gives a similar emphasis, with the important exception that he specifies what the content of the Great Commission message is: **"He [Jesus] told them, 'This is what is written: The Christ** [Messiah] **will suffer and rise from the dead on the third day, and repentance and forgiveness of sins will be preached in his name to all nations, beginning at Jerusalem. You are witnesses of these things.'"** (Luke 24:46–48) This account is clearly a command to evangelize all the nations with the salvation message. (For the student of theology, it is totally soteriological in content.)

The Witness of the Book of Acts

Luke gives additional instructions in his statement of the Great Commission in the Book of Acts. The disciples were confused as to what their future purpose was. They still were confused about the timing of the establishment of the promised Kingdom to Israel. So after Jesus told them that it was not for them to know the time when Israel's Kingdom would be established, He revealed the purpose for this present age: **"But you will receive power when the Holy Spirit comes on you; and you will be my witnesses in Jerusalem, and in all Judea and Samaria, and to the ends of the earth."** (Acts 1:8)

Luke's two accounts clearly stress the worldwide proclamation of the following message: (1) to believe in the death and resurrection of the Lord Jesus Christ; (2) and to repent for the forgiveness of sins in His name.

The supreme example as to how we should understand and implement the Great Commission is set forth in the Book of Acts. The message the Apostles preached always followed the pattern the LORD gave in Luke's account of the Great Commission. Their message focused on the need for faith in Christ's atonement for the forgiveness of sins.

Thomas Ice accurately applies the teaching of Acts to the Dominionist error:

> Throughout Acts, the proclamation is always the soteriological gospel. Never are the apostles and evangelists involved in the Christianization of their culture. This does not mean that a by-product of the gospel was not some degree of Christianization of their culture, but this was never advocated as the goal in Acts. The Christian missionaries certainly had many opportunities to speak like modern Reconstructionists if this had been included in their divine agenda. Certainly the pagan Roman Empire was in as much need of Christianization, and probably more so, than is America and the rest of the world today. If the early church was called to be involved in the Christianization of the culture it would certainly have been recorded.[8]

There is absolutely nothing, stated or implied, to support the Dominionist interpretation of the Great Commission in either Mark, Luke, or Acts. The purpose of the decision demanded is forgiveness of sin and a spiritual new birth, not the reformation of society and political revolution. In fact, if such a command had been given, the Christians would have been slaughtered in mass as political subversives.

The promised ministry of the Holy Spirit which was prominent in both of Luke's accounts is also evident in John's account of the Great Commission: **"Again Jesus said, 'Peace be with you! As the Father has sent me, I am sending you.' And with that he breathed on them and said, 'Receive the Holy Spirit. If you forgive anyone his sins, they are forgiven; if you do not forgive them, they are not forgiven.'"** (John 20:21–23) Jesus had always taught that forgiveness of sin was the result of belief in the Gospel. This is a parallel passage with the others. If a person believed, they were to confirm to him that his sins were forgiven. If a person did not believe, they were to warn him that his sins were not forgiven. The Holy Spirit was expressly given for the purpose of empowering the disciples to effectively preach this salvation message, and to give them boldness to do so in the face of opposition and danger.

Matthew's Account of the Great Commission

Matthew's account is similar to the other accounts, with the exception that he stresses making disciples out of those who believe, and bringing them into the obedience of Christ's teachings: **"Then Jesus came to them and said, 'All authority in heaven and on earth has been given to me. Therefore go and make disciples of all the nations, baptizing them in the name of Father and of the Son and of the Holy Spirit, and teaching them to obey everything I have commanded you. And surely I will be with you always, to the very end of the age.'"** (Matthew 28:18–20)

Thomas Ice again accurately explains the Dominionists' view of these verses:

> Reconstructionists often point to three factors which they believe carry the day for their "Dominion Commission." First is the word "disciples" (Matthew 28:19). Gary North gives us insight into what the Reconstructionist means by discipleship:
>
>> Step by step, person by person, nation by nation, Christians are to disciple the nations. *This means that they are to bring men under the discipline of the legal terms of God's covenant. . . .* How can we disciple the earth if we are not involved in running it?[9]
>
> According to North, a disciple is more than a mature believer in Christ; he is also a social and political activist.[10] (Emphasis mine.)

The term "disciple" and its verbal form "to disciple" do not have the meaning that Dominionists try to superimpose upon them. The terms are translated from the Greek noun μαθητης (*mathetes*) and the verb μαθητευω (*matheteuo*). The noun simply means "a learner" or "pupil." The verb means "to learn."

The term is most often used as a synonym for "a Christian," as demonstrated by this verse in Acts: **"So for a whole year Barnabas and Saul met with the church and taught great numbers of people. The disciples were first called Christians at Antioch."** (Acts 11:26b)

The Lord Jesus interpreted the term this way: **"To the Jews who had believed him, Jesus said, 'If you hold to my teaching, you are really my disciples. Then you will know the truth and the truth will set you free.'"** (John 8:31–32) Jesus went on to explain that He Himself was the Truth they would come to know, and that this knowledge would set them free from their sins. So He gave the term "disciple" a definite salvation (soteriological) focus.

The Way of Jesus or Barabas?

The Dominionists seek to make Matthew's account of the Great Commission not only out of harmony with the parallel accounts, but with the rest of the New Testament. They interpret the command **"make disciples of all the nations"** to mean the Christianizing of society and culture, and the systematic taking over of all the governments of the world.

There is a very important reason, in addition to those listed above, why this interpretation is unsupportable from the Bible. The original Greek text of Matthew 28:19 will not permit this interpretation. The genitive construction means "a part out of a whole." The term **"nations"** is the same Greek word (εθνη) I dealt with in chapter four. In this context it is best understood in its most frequently used sense, **"the Gentiles."** Making a disciple in the Biblical sense is an individual thing. A disciple is one who believes the Gospel, is born spiritually, and continues to grow in the faith.

It is impossible to make a disciple out of a whole nation because no whole nation will ever believe the gospel *en masse* in this age. There never has been and there never will be a totally Christian nation *until* the Lord Jesus Christ personally reigns upon this earth. When He returns, He will remove all unbelievers through the judgment of the Gentiles predicted in Matthew 25:31–46.

This interpretation fits perfectly with the Apostle James' exposition of Amos 9:11–12 at the first Church council, which dealt with the same issue, **"When they** (Paul and Barnabas) **finished, James spoke up: 'Brothers, listen to me. Simon has described to us how God at first showed his concern by taking from the Gentiles a people for himself.'"** (Acts 15:13–14) In this context, the same word for **Gentiles** is used as in Matthew 28:19. This passage definitely means to save a group of Gentiles from among the masses for God's Kingdom. James goes on to show that God's prophetic program is to first save a group of Gentiles, and then afterward to return and restore the fallen dynasty of David.

The Dominionists also seek to find justification for their views in Jesus' command "to teach the disciples to obey all that He has commanded." But once again, the disagreement is not over whether the disciples should be brought into obedience to the whole New Testament message, but over what that message is.

What we are to *obey* is modeled for us in the examples of the life of Christ and the Apostles. They did not call for political revolution, organize a political party, or plot the systematic takeover of society. Instead they spent their energy saving souls and transforming the lives of those converts into citizens of God's spiritual kingdom.

Transformed people should have an influence on the society in which they live. We should use every freedom we have to elect officials who will support an agenda that is compatible with Christian concerns. This is especially true in regard to the educational system to which our children will be subjected. But the Bible does not give us the goal or the hope of taking over this present world-system and establishing a Theocratic Kingdom on earth. That will come, but only when the Messiah, the Lord Jesus, personally returns to remove all unbelievers, bind Satan, remove the curse from nature, and reign over the earth. There is a time of victory and perfect environment coming within history for the earth. But we must not confuse God's time and God's agent for effecting this monumental change. The *time* is not now, it is the soon coming Millennium. The *agent* who will establish the Millennial Kingdom is not the Church, but the Lord Jesus Christ.

WHAT IS THE CHURCH'S HOPE AND DESTINY?

God's Plan for Discipleship

The LORD did not leave us without a guide as to what we should teach our disciples. All the Epistles focus on the issues for teaching and training in the faith. But the following passage from Titus summarizes the main points.

> **For the grace of God that brings salvation has appeared to all men. It teaches us to say "No" to ungodliness and worldly passions, and to live self-controlled, upright and godly lives in this present age, WHILE WE WAIT FOR THE BLESSED HOPE—THE GLORIOUS APPEARING OF OUR GREAT GOD AND SAVIOR, JESUS CHIRST, who gave himself to redeem us from all wickedness and to purify for himself a people that are his very own, eager to do what is good.**
> **These, then, are the things you should teach. Encourage and rebuke with all authority. Do not let anyone despise you.** (Titus 2:11–15)

The Apostle Paul carefully lists the most essential things that we are to teach disciples to obey through the power of the Holy Spirit. As we saw previously, Christ died for us in order to rescue us from **this present evil age.** These verses also show what our *focus, motivation,* and *hope* should be **in this present age.** We are to live with the constant expectation of the any-moment appearing of our LORD to this earth. The Dominionists ridicule this idea of living in anticipation of the LORD's return. They haven't begun to grasp the many clear Scriptures that teach about this as one of the prime motivation factors for living a godly life in this age.

Render to Caesar the Things That Are Caesar's

The New Testament doesn't give one exhortation for the Church to make an organized effort to infiltrate governments and seek to take them over in the sense taught by the Dominionists—in short term or long term. This does not mean that Christians shouldn't run for government positions, but it does mean that the Church is not to focus on those programs as its major purpose.

It isn't as if the Scripture has nothing to say about this issue. Our civil duties are given in two passages in the New Testament.

> **Submit yourselves for the LORD's sake to every authority instituted among men: whether to the king, as the supreme authority, or to governors, who are sent by**

him to punish those who do wrong and to commend those who do right. For it is God's will that by doing good you should silence the ignorant talk of foolish men. Live as free men, but do not use your freedom as a cover-up for evil; live as servants of God. (1 Peter 2:13–17)

I urge, then, first of all, that requests, prayers, intercession and thanksgiving be made for everyone— for kings and all those in authority, that we may live peaceful and quiet lives in all godliness and holiness. This is good, and pleases God our Savior, who wants all men to be saved and to come to a knowledge of the truth. (1 Timothy 2:1–4)

These verses teach only a few simple principles as far as the believer's relationship to government. First, we are to submit to those who are in authority as long as there is no direct violation of conscience before God. Second, we are to pray for all in authority, that we may live in peace and follow our faith. Third, we should live above reproach as far as the civil laws are concerned. Fourth, all of this should be done for the purpose of bringing as many to a saving knowledge of Christ as possible.

Why does God give only these simple principles? Because only Christ can transform this present evil age into the new world promised in the Millennial Kingdom—a world in which the knowledge of God will cover the earth as the sand covers the seashore. In the meantime, we are to do everything possible to spread the Gospel.

The Lord Jesus gave what should be our attitude toward worldly kingdoms during this age when Pontius Pilate asked Him if He was a King: **"My Kingdom is not of this world. If it were, my servants would fight to prevent my arrest by the Jews. *But now my kingdom is from another place.*"** (John 18:36) (Emphasis mine.) The LORD made it clear that His Kingdom is from another place for the present. It is not of this world but it is in heaven during this age. Christ's Kingdom on earth exists only in the spiritual realm today.

Citizens of Eternity

Though we should be good citizens of the countries in which we live and utilize every liberty that is available to promote good and just government, we should always remember where our most important allegiance and citizenship is.

> **But our citizenship is in heaven. And we eagerly await a Savior from there, the Lord Jesus Christ, who, by the power that enables him to bring everything under his control, will transform our lowly bodies so that they will be like his glorious body.** (Philippians 3:20–21)

Our hope and destiny are to be focused in the return of Christ to take us to the place where our true citizenship is. We are commanded to be eagerly awaiting His return and the transformation of our present bodies of humility into ones like His.

The destiny of the Church was given by the Lord Jesus as He began to prepare the disciples for His departure:

> **"Do not let your hearts be troubled. Trust in God; trust also in me. In my Father's house are many rooms; if it were not so, I would have told you. I am going to prepare a place for you. And if I go and prepare a place for you, I will come back and take you to be with me that you also may be where I am."** (John 14:1–3)

This is the hope and promise of destiny for the Church. It was born and continues to be formed by the miracle of the baptism by the Holy Spirit. The day will soon come when the Church will leave these earthly scenes as miraculously as it came into being. The Church's destiny was never promised to be here on the earth during this present age. Instead, Jesus promised that He is preparing a place for us where He is now—in heaven. He has promised to come and take us to be with Him where He is.

This promise cannot refer to His Second Advent because He will at that time return to the earth and remain. This has to refer to the event that has been called the Rapture. In this glorious event, the Lord Jesus will suddenly and secretly come for all of us who believe in Him, and in an instant, snatch us up to meet Him in the clouds. In that glorious moment, those alive at that time will be transformed from mortal to immortal without experiencing physical death. We will then return to His Father's house to await the end of the period of great judgment on the earth called the

Tribulation. (See 1 Corinthians 15:51–53 and 1 Thessalonians 4:13–18)

The Amazing Thing

It is amazing to me that at just the time virtually all of the predicted signs of Christ's return are forming on the horizon, that a movement like the Dominionists should arise and deny it all. Although I guess I really shouldn't be surprised, because such false teaching was predicted.

In looking back over the nineteen years since *The Late Great Planet Earth* was written, virtually all the things that were anticipated in the book have emerged and fit into the prophetic scenario. The only major prophetic sign that is not yet visible is the appearance of the Antichrist and the False Prophet. But I do not believe they can be manifested until the Church has been snatched out in the Rapture. With the European Economic Community's announcement that they will unify politically by 1992, the predicted revival of the old Roman Empire in the form of a Ten Nation Confederacy appears to be a possibility in the very near future. Once that is established, the Antichrist of Rome must appear and lead the Confederacy to establish a world government. It is because of factors like these that I believe the Rapture cannot be far off.

This is a time when every Christian should be so thankful to God that He has revealed the future course of history to us. We are rapidly entering the most fearful period in human history. Only those who know and believe the prophetic Scriptures in a plain literal sense will be able to have the inner strength, peace, and stability in the days ahead to seize the opportunities to evangelize. They are the only ones also who will not be deceived by Satan's ultimate conterfeit, the Antichrist. He will bring in a plan for world political and religious unification which will result in a pseudo-peace that will deceive many of the elect. And he will do this with the accompaniment of **"signs, wonders and false prophecies."** (Matthew 24:11, 24)

Let's Avoid the Road to Holocaust

Those who know and understand the prophetic era in which we live must also strive to prevent the Church from creating the kind of philosophical atmosphere that can lead to another period of anti-Semitism. Let the true Christian *never again* give a theological framework from which unscrupulous men can promote another holocaust for the children of Israel. Anti-Semitic organizations are already arising at an alarming rate.

As we seek to please the LORD in this present age, let us remember what the Scriptures hold up as the greatest motivating hope:

> **See how great a love the Father has bestowed upon us, that we should be called children of God; and such we are. For this reason the world does not know us, because it did not know Him. Beloved, now we are children of God, and it has not appeared as yet what we shall be. We know that, when He appears, we shall be like Him, because we shall see Him just as He is. And everyone who has this hope fixed on Him purifies himself, just as He is pure. (1 John 3:1–3 NASB)**

> **Maranatha!**

ENDNOTES

Chapter One

[1] Adolph Hitler, *Mein Kampf,* translated by Ralph Manheim (Boston: Houghton Mifflin Co., 1971), p. 65

[2] Robert E. Conot, *Justice At Nuremberg,* p. 242

[3] *Encyclopedia Judaica* (Jerusalem: Keter Publishing House, Ltd., 1973 ed.) Vol. 8, p. 852

[4] Hal Lindsey, *There's A New World Coming* (New York: Bantam Books, 1973). See chapter 12 for more details.

[5] Hal Lindsey, *The Promise* (Eugene, OR: Harvest House Publishers, 1982). This book documents many of the prophecies that were fulfilled in Christ's First Advent.

[6] Barry R. Leventhal, *Theological Perspectives of the Holocaust* (Th.D. dissertation, Dallas Theological Seminary, 1982), p.4

[7] Raul Hilberg, *The Destruction of the European Jews* (New York: Harper Colophon Books, 1961), pp. 1– 4

[8] William L. Shirer, *The Rise and Fall of the Third Reich: A History of Nazi Germany* (New York: Simon and Schuster, 1960), pp. 134–35 and 326–28

[9] Hilberg, op. cit., pp. 1–4

[10] A. H. Newman, *A Manual of Church History* (2 Volumes) (Philadelphia: The American Baptist Publication Society, 1957), Vol. 1, p. 286

[11] *Encyclopedia Judaica,* Vol. 5, p. 507

[12] J. L. Neve, *A History of Christian Thought* (2 Volumes) (Philadelphia: The Muhlenberg Press, 1946), Vol. 1,p. 43

[13] H. H. Ben-Sasson, *A History of the Jewish People* (Cambridge, MA: Harvard University Press, 1976), pp. 349–50

[14] *Encyclopedia Judaica,* Vol. 8, p. 655

[15] Nathan Ausubel, *Pictorial History of the Jewish People* (New York: Crown Publishers, Inc., 1979), p. 92

[16]*Encyclopedia Judaica,* Vol. 5, p. 1139

[17]Ibid., Vol. 4, p. 1121. Paraphrased from article.

[18]Ibid., Vol. 4, p. 1120

[19]Ibid., Vol. 5, p. 1127

[20]*The Christian Defense League Report,* Issue 64, May 1984, p. 10 (P.O. Box 449, Arabie, LA 70032)

[21]*Encyclopedia Judaica,* Vol. 8, pp. 1040–43

[22]Ibid., Vol. 4, p. 1063–5

[23]Ibid., Vol. 8, p. 676

[24]David A. Rausch, *A Legacy of Hate,* p. 29

[25]*Encyclopedia Judaica,* Vol. 8, p. 693

[26]Taped sermon given by David Chilton at Reformation Covenant Church, Beaverton, OR, August, 1987.

Chapter Two

[1]H. Wayne House and Thomas Ice, *Dominion Theology: Blessing or Curse?* (Portland, OR: Multnomah Press, 1988)

[2]Floyd E. Hamilton, s.v. "Premillennialism" in the *Zondervan Pictorial Encyclopedia of the Bible,* Editor Merricll C. Tenney (Grand Rapids: Zondervan Publishing House, 1975), Vol. 4, pp. 845–6

[3]Norman Shepherd, s.v. "Postmillennialism," ibid., Vol.4, p.822

[4]David Chilton, *Letter to Thomas D. Ice, Dec. 17, 1986,* p.4

[5]House and Ice, op. cit., pp.15–16

[6]House and Ice, ibid., p. 21

[7]Gary North, *Unholy Spirits: Occultism and New Age Humanism* (Fort Worth, TX: Dominion Press, 1986), pp. 392–3

[8]David Chilton, *Letter to Thomas D. Ice, Dec. 17, 1986,* p. 2

[9]David Chilton, *Paradise Restored: An Eschatology of Dominion* (Tyler, TX: Reconstruction Press, 1988), p. 5

[10]Gary North, "Publisher's Preface" in David Chilton, *Days of Ven-*

geance: An Exposition of the Book of Revelation (Fort Worth, TX: Dominion Press, 1987) pp. xxix

[11]Ibid., p. xxix

[12]Chilton, *Paradise Restored*, pp. 224–5

Chapter Three

[1]David Chilton, *Days of Vengeance* (Fort Worth, TX: Dominion Press, 1987), p. xxiii

[2]Hal Lindsey, *There's a New World Coming* (New York: Bantam Books, 1973). See chapter 9.

[3]F. W. Farrar, quoted by J. Dwight Pentecost, *Things to Come* (Findlay, OH: Dunham Publishing Co., 1958), p. 22

[4]Philip Schaff, *Ante-Nicene Christianity:* A.D. *100–325*, Vol. 2 of *A History of the Christian Church* (Grand Rapids, MI: Wm. B. Eerdmans Publishing Co., 1958), p. 521

[5]Pentecost, op. cit., p. 23

[6] F. W. Farrar, quoted by Pentecost, Ibid., p. 23

[7]Tape #4 of series by David Chilton at Reformation Covenant Church, August 8, 1987

[8]William Tyndale, quoted by Pentecost, op. cit., p. 27

[9]Martin Luther, quoted by Pentecost, Ibid., p. 27

[10]Sir Isaac Newton, quoted by Nathaniel West, D.D., *The Thousand Years in Both Testaments* (New York: Fleming H. Revel, 1880), p. 462

[11]Bishop Richard Hooker, quoted by Nathaniel West, Ibid.

[12]David L. Cooper, *The God of Israel* (Los Angeles: Biblical Research Society, 1945), front page

[13]David Chilton, *Paradise Restored* (Tyler, TX: Dominion Press, 1986), pp.100–101

[14]Ibid., p. 117

[15]Ibid., pp. 100–101

[16]H. Wayne House and Thomas Ice, *Dominion Theology: Blessing or Curse?* (Portland, OR: Multnomah Press, 1988), p. 202

[17]J.N.D. Kelly, *Early Christian Doctrines* (San Francisco: Harper & Row, 1978), p. 465

[18]Ibid., pp. 467, 469

[19]R. G. Clouse, s.v. "Millennium, View of the," *Evangelical Dictionary of Theology*, p. 716

[20]Henry Melville Gwatkin, *Selections from Early Christian Writers* (reprinted by Westwood, NJ: Fleming H. Revell Co., 1958), p. xiii

[21]Ibid., p. 43

[22]Kelly, *Early Christian Doctrines*, p. 469

[23]*The Oxford Dictionary of the Christian Church*, Edited by F. L. Cross, s.v. "Gaius," p. 535

[24]op. cit., House and Ice, p. 204

[25]H. Hoekstra, quoted by Harry Bultema, *Maranatha! A Study of Unfulfilled Prophecy* (Grand Rapids, MI: Kregel Publications, 1985) p. 29

[26]David Chilton, *Days of Vengeance*, p. 494

[27]Gary North, *Unholy Spirits: Occultism and New Age Humanism* (Fort Worth, TX: Dominion Press, 1986), p. 381

Chapter Four

[1]Dr. John Walvoord, quoted by J. Dwight Pentecost, *Things to Come* (Findlay OH: Dunham Publishing Co., 1958), pp. 75–76

[2]C. F. Keil and F. Delitzsch, *Commentary of the Old Testament* (10 Volumes) (Grand Rapids, MI: Wm. B. Eerdmans Publishing Co., reprinted 1983), Vol. 1, p. 214

[3]David Chilton, *Paradise Restored* (Tyler, TX: Reconstruction Press, 1985), p. 131

[4]Ibid., p. 82

[5]David Levi, quoted by Nathaniel West, *The Thousand Years in Both Testaments* (New York: Fleming H. Revel, 1880), p. 462

[6]Isaac DaCosta, quoted by Nathaniel West, Ibid.

ENDNOTES

Chapter Five

[1]*Webster's Third International Dictionary, Three Volumes* (Chicago: Encyclopædia Britannica, Inc., 1981), Vol. 2, p. 1096

[2]J. Dwight Pentecost, *Things to Come* (Findlay, OH: Dunham Publishing Co., 1958), pp. 100–101

[3]George N. H. Peters, *The Theocratic Kingdom* (3 volumes) (Grand Rapids, MI: Kregel Publications, reprinted 1978) Vol. 1, cover statement

[4]Ibid., Vol. 1, pp. 315–316

[5]Ibid., Vol. 1, pp. 351

[6]Charles C. Ryrie, *The Basis of the Premillennial Faith* (New York: Loizeaux Brothers, 1953), pp. 112–114

[7]Pentecost, op. cit., pp. 117–118

Chapter Six

[1]Robert B. Thieme, Jr., *Anti-Semitism* (Houston, TX: R. B. Thieme, Jr. Bible Ministries, 5139 W. Alabama, Houston, TX 77056, 1974), pp. 126–130

[2]Ibid., pp. 126–128

[3]Ibid., pp. 71–72

[4]Ibid., pp. 128–129

[5]*A Greek-English Lexicon of the New Testament and Other Early Christian Literature,* Second Edition of Walter Bauer revised and augmented by F. W. Gingrich and Fredrick Danker (Chicago: Chicago University Press, 1979), p. 214

Chapter Seven

[1]Greg Bahnsen, *Theonomy in Christian Ethics,* as quoted in *Christianity Today*

[2]John Rousas Rushdoony, *The Foundations of Social Order* (Phillipsburg, NJ: Presbyterian and Reformed Publishing Co., 1968), p. 127

[3]John Rousas Rushdoony, *The Biblical Philosophy of History* (Phillipsburg, NJ: Presbyterian and Reformed Publishing Co., 1969), p. 142

[4]John Rousas Rushdoony, *The Institutes of Biblical Law* (Phillipsburg, NJ: Presbyterian and Reformed Publishing Co., 1973), p. 75

[5]John Rousas Rushdoony, *Politics of Guilt and Pity* (Tyler, TX: Thoburn Press, 1970), p. 11

[6]Gary North, *Liberating Planet Earth* (Fort Worth, TX: Dominion Press, 1987), pp. 43–44

Chapter Eight

[1]Everett T. Harrison, *The Expositor's Bible Commentary In Twelve Volumes*, Vol. 10, Commentary on Romans, p. 116

[2]F. Godet, *Commentary on the Epistle to the Romans* (Grand Rapids, MI: Zondervan Publishing House, 1956), p. 391

[3]Kenneth S. Wuest, *Romans in the Greek New Testament for the English Reader* (Grand Rapids, MI: Wm. B. Eerdmans Publishing Company, 1956), pp. 185–186

[4]Ibid., p. 187

[5]A Calvinist believes that once a person has believed in Christ's atonement and been born spiritually, he cannot be subsequently lost, since his salvation depends upon the finished work of Christ on the cross, not on human merit.

[6]Arminians believe that it is possible for a saved person to undo the finished work of Christ by his sin and become lost again.

[7]James M. Stifler, D.D., *The Epistle to the Romans* (Chicago: Moody Press, 1960), p. 186

[8]John Murray, *The Epistle to the Romans* (Grand Rapids, MI: Wm. B. Eerdmans Publishing Co., 1984), p. 78

[9]Ibid., pp. 78–79

[10]David Baron, *Types, Psalms, and Prophecies* (Jerusalem: Yanetz Ltd., [1906] 1978), pp. 345–49

Chapter Nine

[1]David Chilton, *Paradise Restored* (Tyler, TX: Reconstruction Press, 1985), pp. 224, 226

[2]F. Everett Harrison, "Commentary on Romans" in the *Expositor's Bible Commentary*, Vol. 10, p. 122

[3]John Murray, *The Epistle to the Romans*, p. 85

[4]Kenneth Wuest, *Romans in the Greek New Testament for the English Reader*, p. 195

[5]See the following passages that describe the "last times" and "last days" of the Church: 2 Timothy 3:1–4:5; 2 Peter 1:12–3:9; Jude; 2 Thessalonians 2:9–12.

[6]Hal Lindsey, *The Rapture* (New York: Bantam Books, 1983). This gives a detailed coverage of the subject.

[7]Earl Paulk, *To Whom Is God Betrothed* (Atlanta, GA: Dimension Publishers, 1985), p. 7

[8]Ibid., p. 18

[9]James Stifler, *The Epistle to the Romans: A Commentary, Logical and Historical* (Chicago: Moody Press, 1960), p. 194

[10]F. W. Gingrich and Fredrick Danker, *A Greek-English Lexicon of the New Testament and other Early Christian Literature* (Chicago: Chicago University Press, 1979), p. 128

[11]Hal Lindsey, *There's A New World Coming* (New York: Bantam Books, 1973), chapter 16

[12]Gingrich and Danker, op. cit., p. 334, section 1d

[13]Ibid., p. 598, section 2(1)

[14]David Chilton, op. cit., p. 130, point #7

Chapter Ten

[1]David Chilton, *Paradise Restored* (Tyler, TX: Reconstruction Press, 1985), p. 117

[2]Ibid.

[3]H. Wayne House and Thomas D. Ice, *Dominion Theology: Blessing or Curse?* (Portland, OR: Multanomah Press, 1988), chapter 13, pp. 285–302

[4]Chilton, op. cit., p. 224

[5]Stanley Toussaint, *Behold The King: A Study of Matthew* (Portland OR: Multanomah Press, 1980), p. 270

[6]Chilton, op. cit., p. 98

[7]Hal Lindsey, *The Rapture* (New York: Bantam Books, 1983), chapter 9

[8]Chilton, op. cit., p. 99

[9]Hal Lindsey, op. cit., chapter 9

[10]David Chilton, *Days Of Vengeance* (Fort Worth, TX: Dominion Press, 1987), p. 531 (especially footnote)

[11]Chilton, *Great Tribulation* (Fort Worth, TX: Dominion Press, 1987), p. 4

[12]Chilton, *Days Of Vengeance*, p. 540

[13]Op. cit., House and Ice, p. 298

[14]Chilton, *Paradise Restored*, p. 221

[15]Chilton, *Days Of Vengeance*, p. 507

Chapter Eleven

[1]Gary North, "Publisher's Preface" in David Chilton, *Days Of Vengeance* (Fort Worth, TX: Dominion Press, 1987), p. xxiv

[2]Ibid., p. xxxiii

[3]Gary North, *Christian Reconstruction*, Vol. 12, No. 2, March/April 1988

[4]Kenneth L. Gentry, *"The Days Of Vengeance:* A Review Article," *The Council Chalcedon*, Vol. 11, No. 4, p. 11

[5]Ibid., p. 10

[6]From the rough draft to H. Wayne House and Thomas D. Ice, *Dominion Theology: Blessing or Curse?* (Portland, OR: Multanomah Press, 1988), p. 250

[7]Alfred Edersheim, *The Temple: Its Ministry and Services as They Were at the Time of Christ* (Grand Rapids, MI: Wm. B. Eerdmans Publishing Co., 1980), p. 141

[8]David Chilton, op. cit., p. 3

[9]Ray Sutton, quoted by House and Ice, op. cit., p. 251

[10]Chilton, op. cit., p. 493

[11]Ibid., p. 2, fn.#5

[12]H. Wayne House and Thomas Ice, *Dominion Theology*, p. 251

[13]Irenaeus, *Against Heresies*, v. xxx. 3

[14]*The Ecclesiatical History of Eusebius Pamphilus*, translated by Isaac Boyle (Grand Rapids, MI: Baker Book House, 1977), p. 188

[15]Henry B. Swete, *Commentary on Revelation* (1911; reprint, Grand Rapids, MI: Kregel Publications, 1977), p. cvi

[16]Boyle, op. cit., p. 188

[17]Ibid.

[18]Philip Schaff, *History of the Christian Church* (Grand Rapids, MI: Wm. B. Eerdmans Publishing Co., 1910), Vol. 1, p. 834

[19]*Encyclopædia Britannica* (Chicago: Encyclopædia Britannica Inc., 1982), Vol. 9, p. 889

[20]Philip Schaff, ibid., Vol. 2, pp. 614–618

[21]Chilton, *Days Of Vengeance*, p. 4

[22]Theodore Zahn, *Introduction to the New Testament* (Minneapolis: Klock and Klock Christian Publishers, 1909), Vol. 3, pp. 183–184

[23]House and Ice, op. cit., p. 254

[24]Donald Guthrie, *New Testament Introduction* (Downers Grove, IL: Inter Varsity Press, 1970), p. 957

[25]Chilton, op. cit., p. 4

[26]Ibid.

[27]Ibid.

[28]J. Peter Lange, *The Revelation of John*, Vol. 12 of *Lange's Commen-*

tary on the Holy Scripture (Grand Rapids, MI: Zondervan Publishing House, 1960), p. 59

[29]Leon Morris, *Revelation* (Grand Rapids, MI: Wm. B. Eerdmans Publishing Co., 1972), pp. 36–37

[30]Chilton, op. cit., p. 4

[31]House and Ice, op. cit., pp. 258–9

[32]Chilton, op. cit., p. 4

[33]Ibid., see pp. 329, 344–45, 350–51, 583

[34]Ibid., p. 4

[35]Ibid.

[36]House and Ice, op. cit., p. 259

[37]Sir Robert Anderson, *The Coming Prince* (Grand Rapids: Zondervan Publishing House, reprinted 1975)

[38]Dr. Harold W. Hoehner, *Chronological Aspects of the Life of Christ* (Grand Rapids: Zondervan Publishing House, 1977)

[39]Alva J. McClain, *Daniel's Prophecy of the Seventy Weeks* (Grand Rapids: Zondervan Publishing House, 1940)

[40]Dr. Paul D. Feinberg, *An Exegetical and Theological Study of Daniel 9:24–27 in Tradition and Testament: Essays in Honor of Charles Lee Feinberg*, Edited by John S. Feinberg and Paul D. Feinberg (Chicago: Moody Press, 1981), pp. 189–220

[41]Theodore Zahn, op. cit., Vol. 3, pp. 412–413, 422

[42]Leon Morris, *Revelation*, pp. 36–37

[43]M. J. Brunk, *The Date, Authorship and Interpretation of the Apocalypse* (Th.D. dissertation, Dallas Theological Seminary, 1933), pp. 19–20

Chapter Twelve

[1]Gary North, *75 Bible Questions Your Instructors Pray You Won't Ask* (Tyler, TX: Spurgeon Press, 1984), p. 170

[2]John 18:36

[3]Hal Lindsey, *Satan Is Alive and Well on Planet Earth* (Grand Rapids, MI: Zondervan Publishing Co., 1972). See chapter 11.

[4]S. L. Johnson, Jr., "Paul and 'The Israel of God': An Exegetical and Eschatological Case-Study," Edited by Stanley D. Toussaint and Charles H. Dyer, *Essays in Honor of J. Dwight Pentecost* (Chicago: Moody Press, 1986), p. 188

[5]New American Standard Bible, 1 John 5:19

[6]*A Greek-English Lexicon of the New Testament and Other Early Christian Literature*, Second Edition of Walter Bauer revised and augmented by F. W. Danker (Chicago: Chicago University Press, 1979), p. 113

[7]George Grant, *Bringing in the Sheaves* (Atlanta: American Vision Press, 1985), p. 70

[8]H. Wayne House and Thomas Ice, *Dominion Theology: Blessing or Curse?* (Portland, OR: Multnomah Press, 1988), p. 152

[9]Gary North, *Liberating Planet Earth* (Fort Worth: Dominion Press, 1987), p. 9

[10]House and Ice, op. cit., p. 153

All Bible quotations are from the New International Version (NIV) unless otherwise noted.
The New American Standard Version = NASB
The New King James Version = NKJV
The King James Version = KJV
Personal translations from the original Greek New Testament = HL

ABOUT THE AUTHOR

HAL LINDSEY, named *the bestselling author of the decade* by the New York Times, was born in Houston, Texas. His first book, *The Late Great Planet Earth,*published in 1970, became the bestselling non-fiction book of the decade, selling more than 18 million copies worldwide. He is one of the few authors to have three books on the New York Times bestseller list at the same time.

Mr. Lindsey was educated at the University of Houston. After serving in the U.S. Coast Guard during the Korean War, Mr. Lindsey graduated from Dallas Theological Seminary where he majored in the New Testament and early Greek literature. After completing seminary, Mr. Lindsey served for eight years on the staff of Campus Crusade for Christ, speaking to tens of thousands of students on major university campuses throughout the United States.

Mr. Lindsey currently has an extensive ministry. He is senior pastor of the Palos Verdes Community Church, has a weekly radio talk show heard in over 200 cities, and a regular television show on Trinity Broadcasting Network.

Hal Lindsey has an extensive collection of messages on tape. He has taught many books of the Bible in verse by verse series, as well as prophetic lectures on current world events and issues.For information and catalog regarding audiotaped messages and "Countdown," a monthly news journal, please write:

Hal Lindsey
P.O. Box 4000
Palos Verdes, CA 90274